The Campus History Series

Gardner-Webb University

Barry E. Hambright and U.L. "Rusty" Patterson

The Campus History Series

Gardner-Webb University

Barry E. Hambright and U.L. "Rusty" Patterson

ARCADIA PUBLISHING

ISBN 0-7385-1797-6

Published by Arcadia Publishing
Charleston, South Carolina

Printed in the United States of America

Library of Congress Catalog Card Number: 2005924398

For all general information, please contact Arcadia Publishing:
Telephone 843-853-2070
Fax 843-853-0044
E-mail sales@arcadiapublishing.com
For customer service and orders:
Toll-Free 1-888-313-2665

Visit us on the Internet at www.arcadiapublishing.com

Contents

Acknowledgments 6

Introduction 7

1. Boiling Springs High School
The High School Era: 1907 to 1928 9

2. Boiling Springs Junior College
The Junior College before World War II 31

3. Gardner-Webb College
The Phil Elliott Era of the Junior College: 1943 to 1961 43

4. Gardner-Webb College
The Transition to Senior College Status: 1961 to 1985 71

5. Gardner-Webb University
The Emergence of the University: 1986 to 2005 101

ACKNOWLEDGMENTS

The authors wish to thank those who have helped to make this publication possible. President Dr. Frank Campbell; Vice President for University Relations and Development Ralph "Scoot" Dixon; and Noel T. Manning, director of university and media relations for Gardner-Webb, have been most helpful in producing this work. A special thank-you goes to Margaret Christopher, media assistant at Gardner-Webb, for all of her assistance organizing and reproducing material in the university's archives.

Lansford Jolley's *Dreaming, Daring, Doing* and Doris Banner's *Gardner-Webb Faculty Emeriti* have been valuable resources in identifying names, dates, events, and timelines. Thank-you to retired university archivist Cothenia Jolley and her husband, Lansford, for taking the time to record the school's history.

Thank-you to Sonny Huggins for sharing his grandfather's archives. It was a privilege to have access to Prof. J.D. Huggins's original high-school and college catalogs as resource materials. We appreciate Dobbin Lattimore allowing us to reproduce the Boiling Springs High School diploma of his grandfather, D.D. Lattimore. And lastly, thank-you to John Roberts (current GWU trustee and director of public relations at GWC from 1954 to 1960) for the interview he shared with the authors. John literally brought decades of photos to life with his stories of the Gardner-Webb of yesteryear.

A reasonable effort has been made to gather accurate information about each image within the timeline provided by the publisher. All of these people have helped make this publication possible. None of them are responsible for the errors, which are the authors' alone.

INTRODUCTION

Gardner-Webb University (GWU) is celebrating its centennial in 2005. The 100 years cover the time in 1905 when a group of Baptists voted to build a high school in Boiling Springs until the school, as a university, begins its second century. Two histories have been written about Gardner-Webb. Francis B. Dedmond's *Lengthened Shadows* celebrated the first 50 years, and Lansford Jolley's *Dreaming, Daring, Doing* covered the school from 1905 until the 1990s. These are excellent works, and we are not trying to duplicate either. We are interested in a visual history.

In keeping with the nature of the Arcadia series, we have created a visual work that will allow Gardner-Webb alumni and friends to remember "the good old days." Our emphasis is on the people who have attended the high school, the junior college, the senior college, or the university. Faculty, staff, and administrators are also featured. We have tried to feature people interacting with others, and thus pictures of single individuals are limited. We actually feel a need to apologize to the hundreds who are not pictured. Being included may have depended on being present when someone had a camera. The Gardner-Webb archives have hundreds of old photos, but often the pictures are not identified by time or persons. We usually chose to use identifiable shots, which gave the advantage to those whose group was identified on the picture, or to those who were well known, or even to those who still live in the senior author's mind—he first arrived on campus in September 1959. In that freshman year, his professors included Francis B. Dedmond and Lansford Jolley.

The pictures will show early days that are remembered by almost no one. Behind the people you will see buildings and the campus in general—the evolving places where memories occur. Lifestyles and dress styles evolve as the visual record moves from the past to the present.

We should point out the historical background against which we see the visual story. In 1905, the Kings Mountain and Sandy Run Baptist Associations voted to open a high school. The school opened in the fall of 1907 and functioned as a boarding high school for 21 years. In 1928, the school added a two-year college program. The next decade was probably the most difficult in the school's history. Surviving the Great Depression was possible only because of great dedication and great sacrifice. A number of local pastors led the school for little or no pay, and dedicated laymen in the community contributed anything possible to help the school survive.

By the time of World War II, Boiling Springs Junior College emerged without a high school but with hope for the future. In the early 1940s, two key events occurred. First, the school was named Gardner-Webb College in honor of former North Carolina governor O. Max Gardner and his wife, Fay Webb Gardner. The Gardners took a personal and financial interest in the college. In 1943, the line of dedicated Baptist ministers who had led the school on a part-time basis ended with the hiring of Western Carolina English professor Philip L. Elliott, who was to lead the college for a record 18 years.

During the years from 1943 to 1961, Dr. Elliott oversaw the building of H.A.P.Y., Stroupe, and Decker dormitories. Also added were the Dover Library (now Craig Hall), O. Max Gardner Memorial, and Bost Gymnasium. The first half of the Webb Administration Building was opened in 1960, just before Dr. Elliot announced his retirement. In April 1961, Dr. Elliott died in his office in Webb, two months before his projected retirement. Dr. Elliott left a respected two-year college that was a member of the family of seven colleges affiliated with the Baptist State Convention of North Carolina.

When Dr. E. Eugene Poston assumed the presidency upon Dr. Elliott's death in 1961, he saw a new educational world on the horizon. The age of the state community college was at hand. Therefore, Dr. Poston announced a "Decade of Advance" that would bring Gardner-Webb to senior college status. During the 1960s, a nursing program began, the college grew to well over 1,000 students, and senior college status became a reality in the fall of 1969. The physical development continued with the addition of a new John R. Dover Library, the Withrow Science Building, the Charles I. Dover Campus Center, and five new dormitories. The college also acquired the property of the Boiling Springs Baptist Church on Main Street.

In 1976, Dr. Craven E. Williams began his 10 years as president. The senior college was a maturing institution. Under Dr. Williams's leadership the college added a four-year nursing program, an adult evening program known as Greater Opportunities for Adult Learners (GOAL), and the first graduate programs. The major campus addition was the Lutz-Yelton Convocation Center.

When Dr. M. Christopher White came to Gardner-Webb in 1986, the college was ready to move to the next level. Dr. White's 16 years of leadership saw the institution successfully conclude a financial campaign that raised over $30 million. The college moved to university status in the 1990s. Progress during these years included the hiring of university-level faculty, the expansion of the graduate programs, the opening of the M. Christopher White School of Divinity, a move from NAIA athletics to NCAA Division II and then to NCAA Division I, and an enrollment of over 3,500 students in all programs.

As Gardner-Webb entered the new century, Dr. White resigned in 2002 and Dr. Frank Campbell came to lead the university on an interim basis, which became a two-and-a-half-year task. Dr. Campbell has established himself as a respected leader among faculty and students. He has prepared the university for a new president who will lead the institution into its second century with continued promise of dreaming, daring, and doing.

One

Boiling Springs High School

The High School Era: 1907 to 1928

Over 100 years ago, Baptists in the Cleveland County area determined there was a need to establish a high school "where the young could have the best possible educational advantages under distinctive Christian influence." In 1905, the Kings Mountain and Sandy Run Baptist Associations voted to form a high school at Boiling Springs, North Carolina. The boarding high school opened in 1907. The Boiling Springs High School catalog of 1910 noted that the town of Boiling Springs was selected "for its beauty, for the general thrift of its people, and for the high morale and religious tone of its citizenship."

For nearly 30 years, Boiling Springs High School served the citizens of Cleveland and surrounding counties in North and South Carolina. In 1928, a two-year college program was added as Boiling Springs Junior College. The high school was phased out after the Great Depression years. The following images depict life in the initial years of the school.

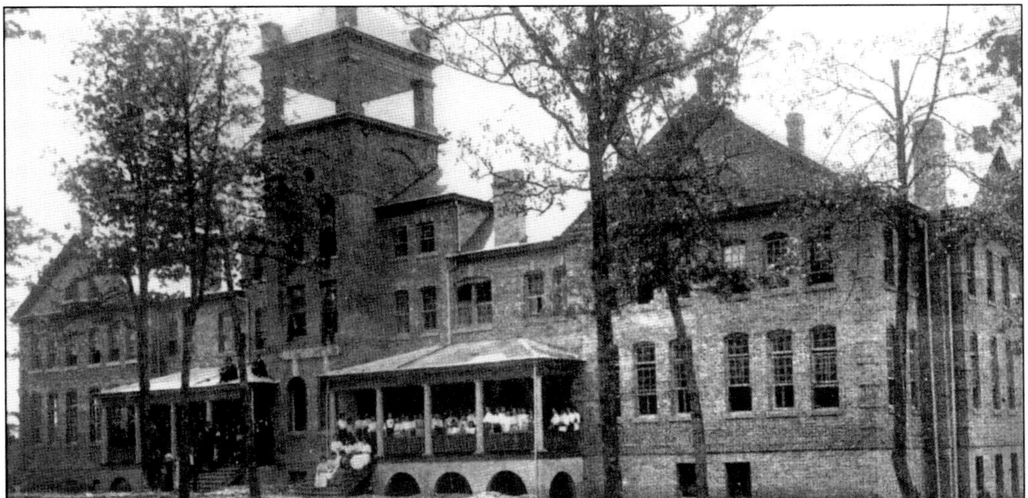

The Main Building was at the center of the campus and the center of student activities. When the town of Boiling Springs was formed, the bell tower on Main marked the center of the town, with the town limits extending a radius of one mile from the center point.

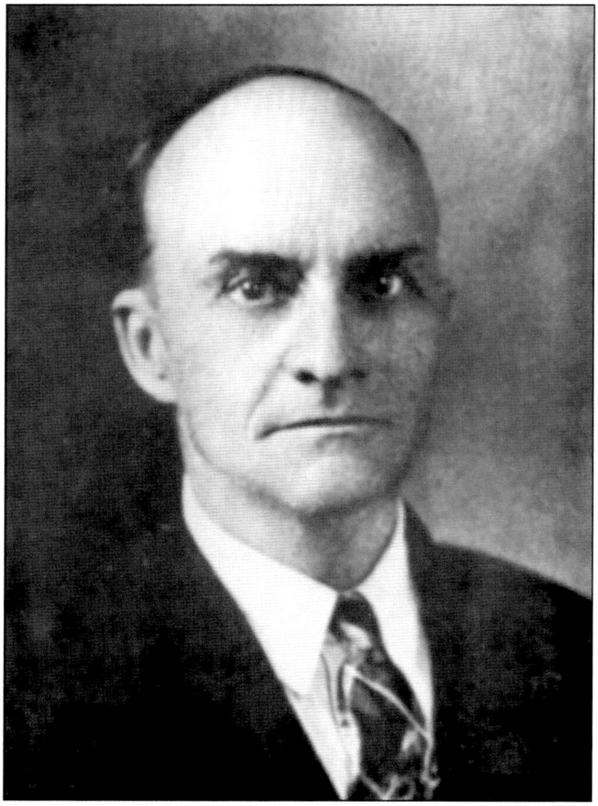

James Dwyre Huggins Sr. served as principal from 1907 to 1908, assistant principal from 1908 to 1910, co-principal from 1910 to 1914, and again as principal from 1914 to 1928. Additionally, Professor Huggins taught Bible, elocution, and commercial (business) studies.

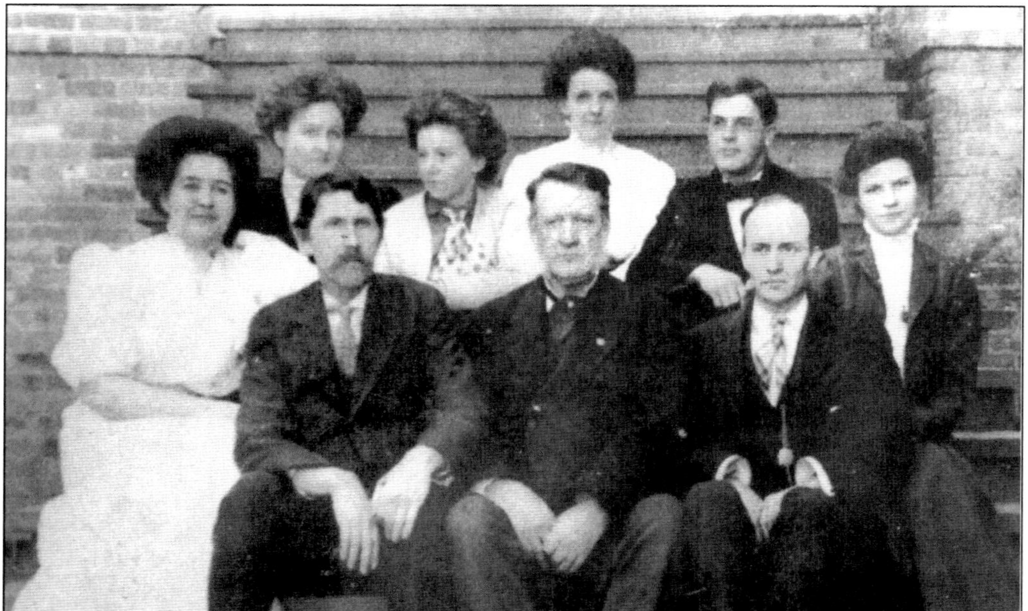

The 1908–1909 faculty included the following, from left to right: (front row) Mary Clark Pitts Duncan, F.A. Brown, Baylus Cade, J.D. Huggins, and Besie Atkins Huggins; (back row) Myrtle Dodson Taylor, Mildred McLean Milan, Alma Smith Griffin, and T.N. Farris.

Miss Etta Curtis was "dean of women" for the high school and junior college for 27 years. Respected as a strict disciplinarian, Ms. Curtis instilled moral training along with academics.

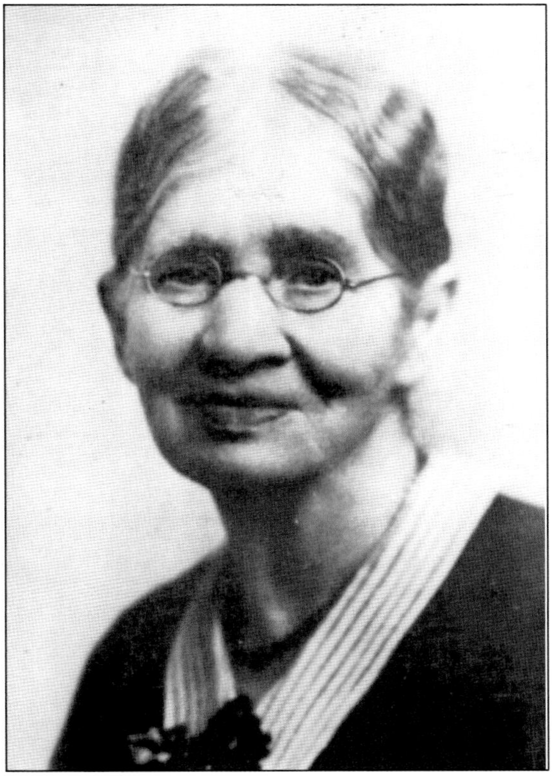

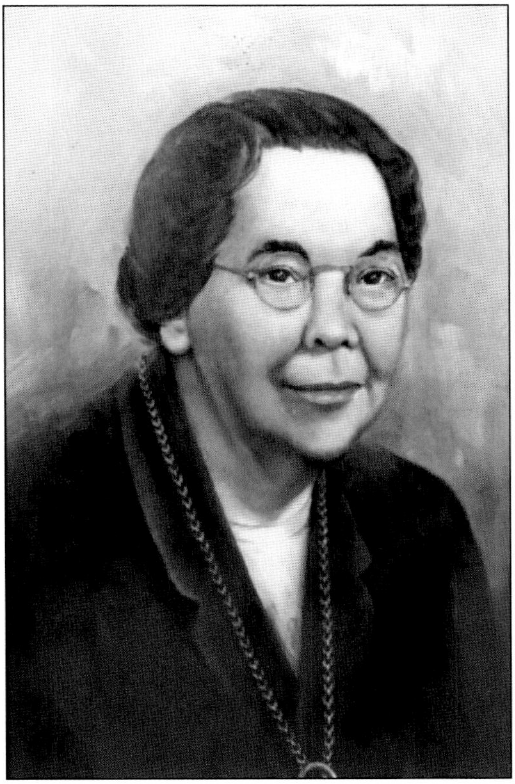

Mrs. Lillian Ritch served the school as matron of dormitories and dietitian from 1915 to 1945. The banquet hall in the Dover Campus Center is named the Lillian M. Ritch Banquet Hall in her honor.

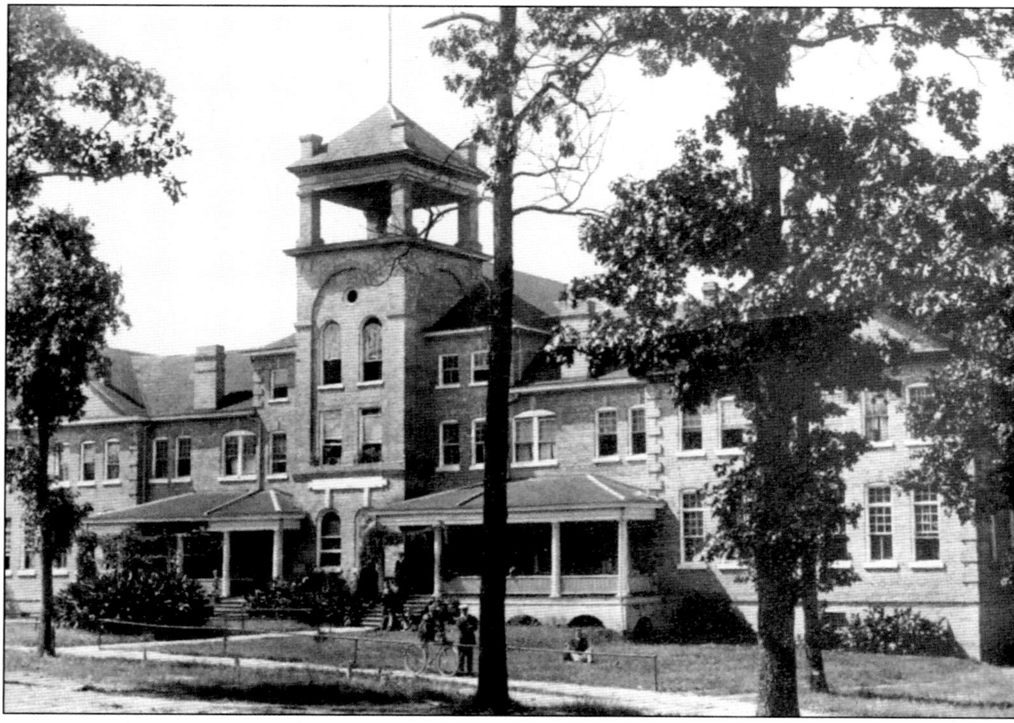

Here is a close-up view of Main Building as it appeared in 1915. The basement housed a large, well-equipped kitchen, a dining room for 250 students, butler's pantries, storerooms, boiler and fuel rooms, a laundry, and lavatories. The first floor consisted of recitation rooms, the library, administrative office, auditorium, two music rooms, two parlors, two cloakrooms, and two society halls. The second and third floors included 44 dormitory rooms for girls with bathrooms and lavatories.

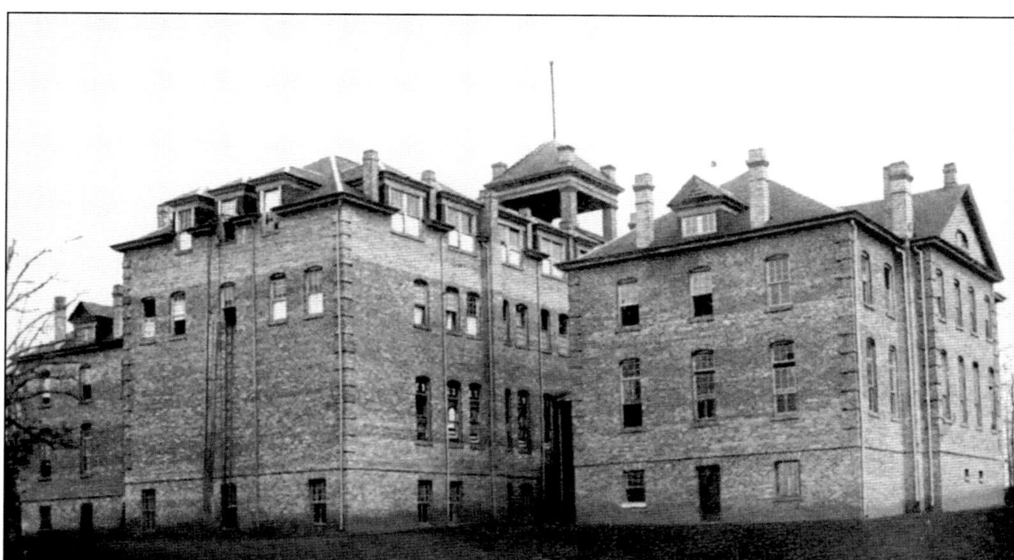

This rear view of Main Building better shows how large a structure it was. Main Building was constructed at a cost of $24,532.

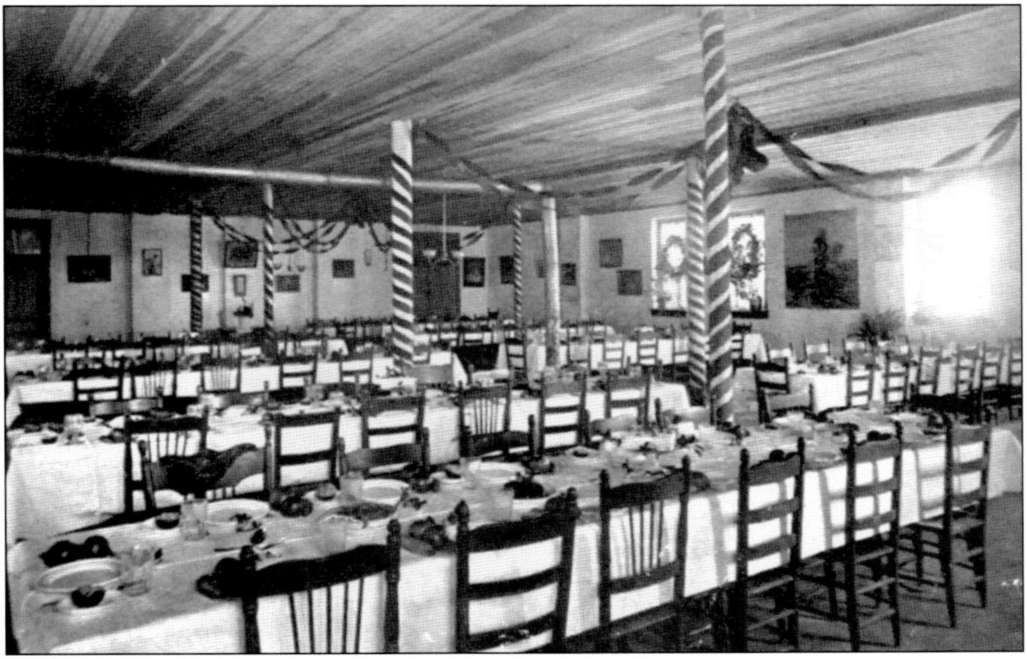

The dining hall in the basement of Main Building is decorated for a holiday celebration.

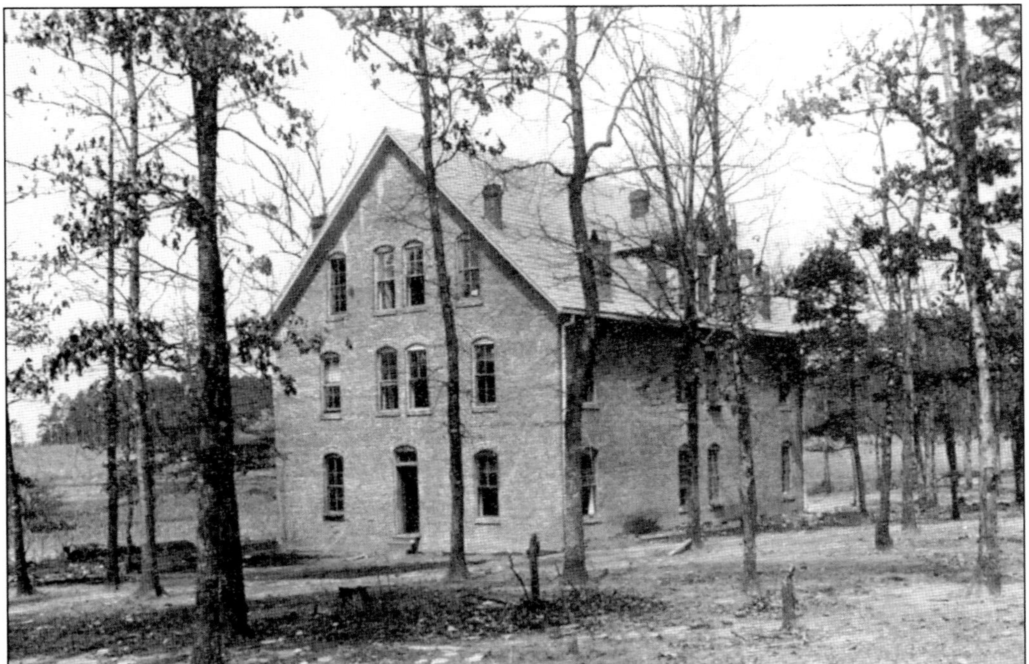

"The Barn" served as the boys' dorm. The building could accommodate 48 students. Many boys roomed in private homes in the community in the early days of the school.

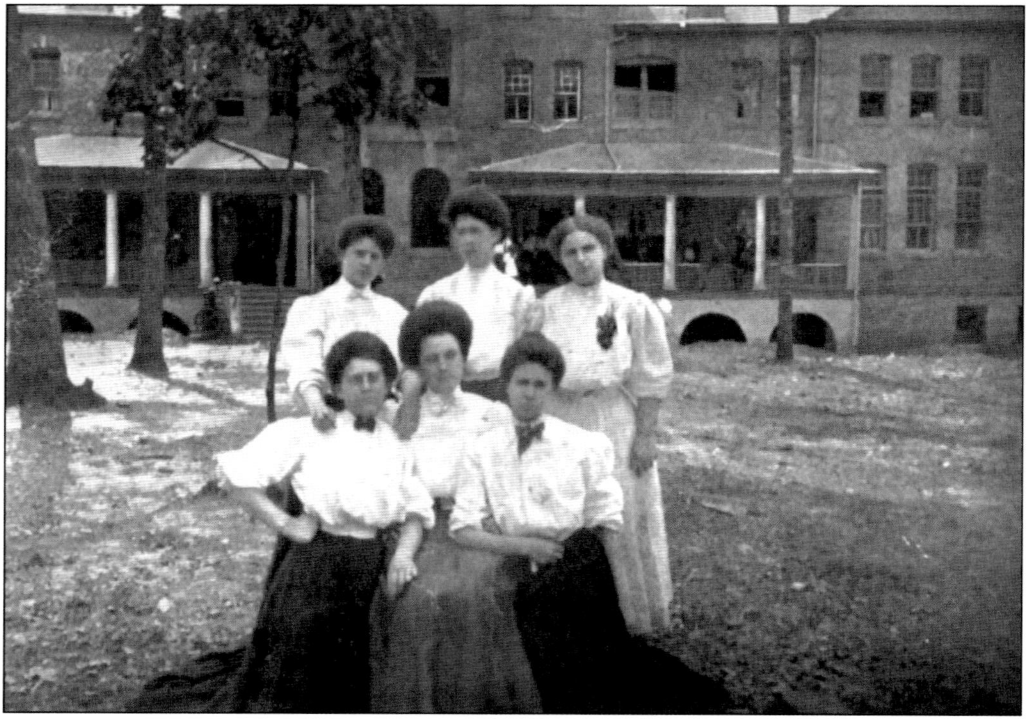

In this photo, from the original school catalog of 1907, are officers of the Rhamsaeur Literary Society, named for Minnie Ramsaeur, an early supporter of the school.

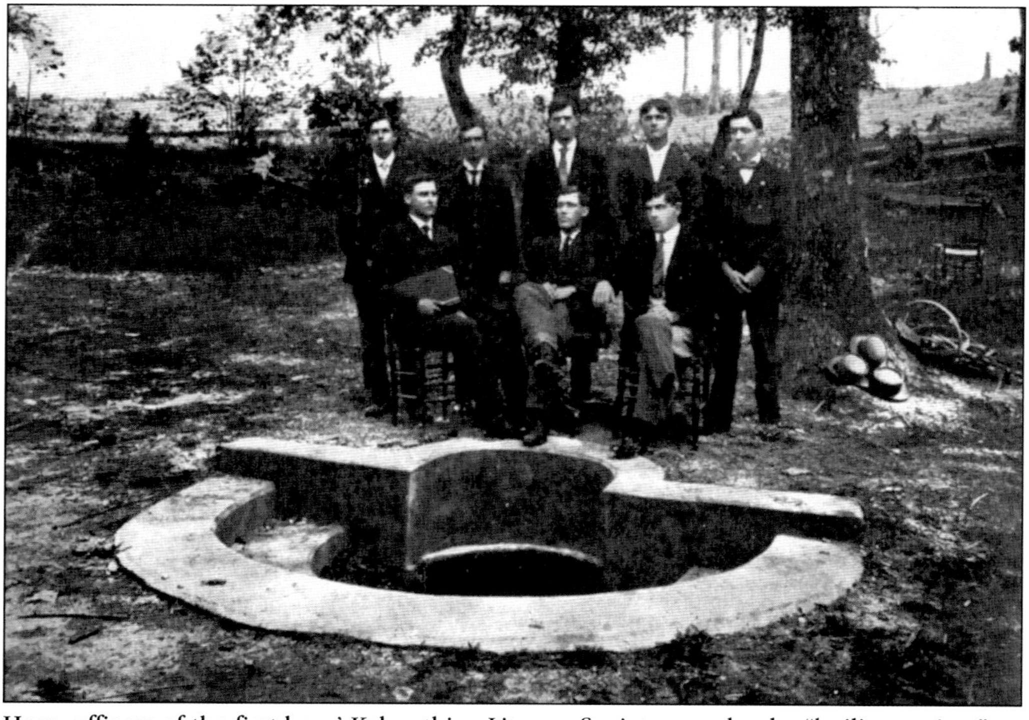

Here, officers of the first boys' Kalagathian Literary Society pose by the "boiling spring."

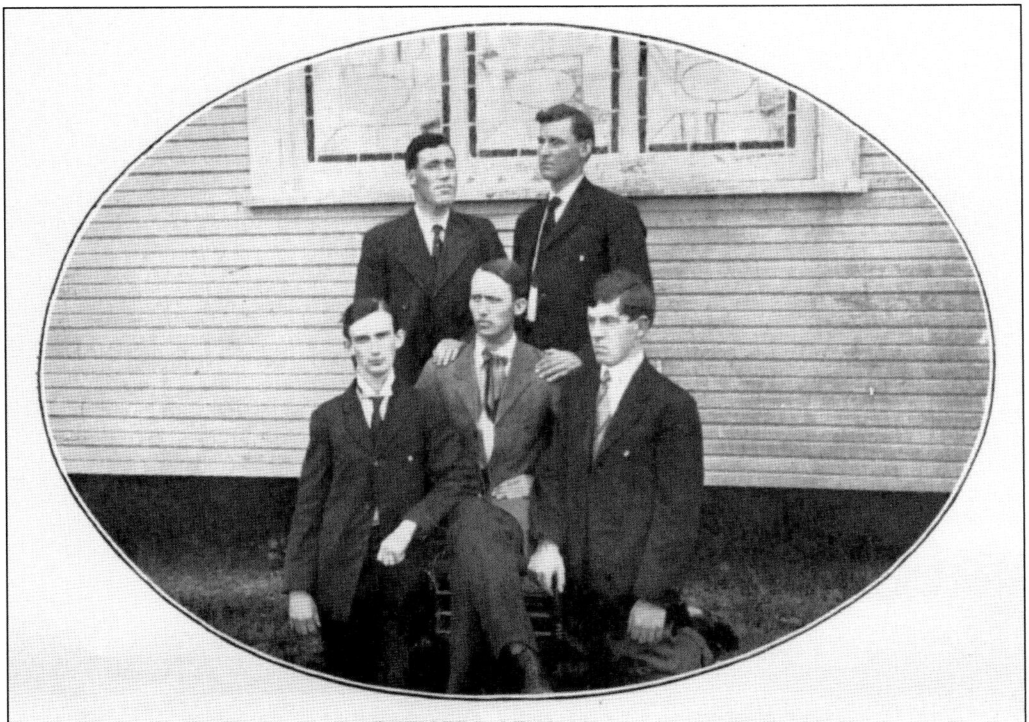

OFFICERS OF Y. M. C. A.

Officers of the first YMCA at Boiling Springs High School are pictured in this 1907 image. No one could have imagined that 97 years later, GWU would offer academic programs to prepare students for careers in YMCAs across the country.

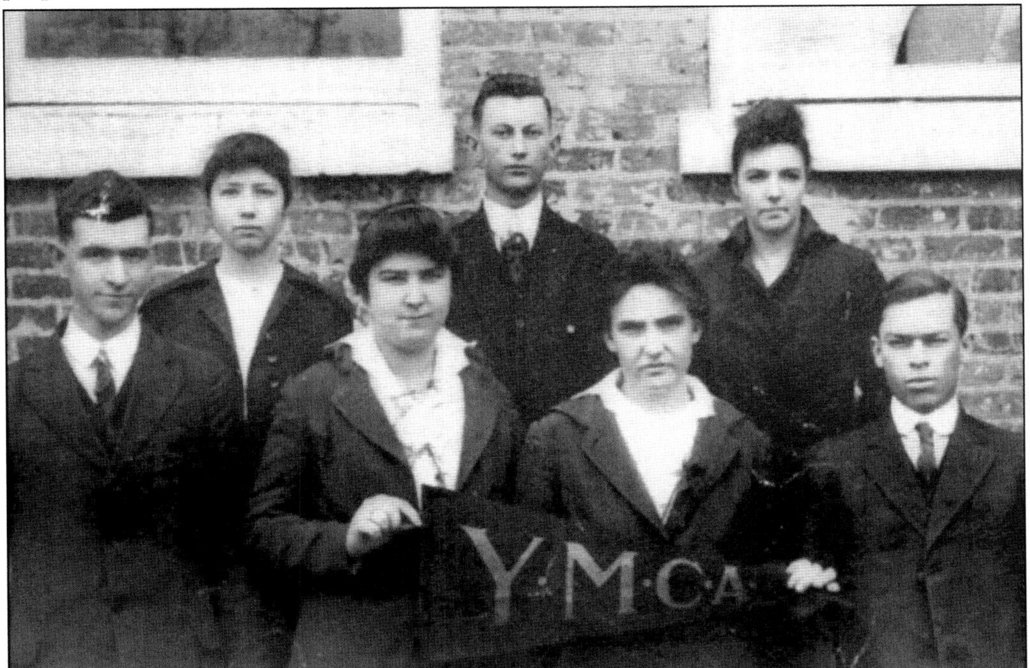

Officers of the high school's YWCA and YMCA are shown in this 1916 photo.

GRADUATES

1910

Atkins, Louise	College Preparatory
Farris, T. N.	College Preparatory
Holland, T. C.	College Preparatory
Moore, Ollie	College Preparatory
Moore, Lelia	English-Scientific
Wilson, T. L.	Commercial

1911

Cade, Bettie Lee	College Preparatory
Hamrick, O. P.	College Preparatory
Hamrick, Mrs. Dr. C. T.	Music
Lovelace, O. N.	College Preparatory
Stroup, M. A.	College Preparatory

1912

Jones, J. B.	College Preparatory
Calton, J P.	English-Scientific
Moore, Kate	College Preparatory
Huskey, Frette	College Preparatory
Lattimore, Lucy	College Preparatory
Ware, J. O.	College Preparatory
Harris, T. F.	College Preparatory
Hamrick, A. V.	College Preparatory
Tate, W. T.	College Preparatory
Wilson, T. L.	College Preparatory

1913

Plummer, Era	College Preparatory
Kendrick, Garrie	College Preparatory
McSwain, Beecher	English-Scientific
McSwain, Dorus	College Preparatory
Hudson, E. V.	College Preparatory
Dalton, J. W.	College Preparatory
Falls, Laura	College Preparatory
Matheney, C. C.	College Preparatory
Quinn, Mabel	Music and English-Scientific
Roberts, Katherine	Music
Green, Alda	Music
Green, Gertrude	Music
Atkins, Louise	Music
Lovelace, Aquilla	Music and College Preparatory
Lattimore, S. C.	English-Scientific
Lattimore, D. D.	English-Scientific

The school catalog from 1914 listed graduates of Boiling Springs High School for 1910 through 1913.

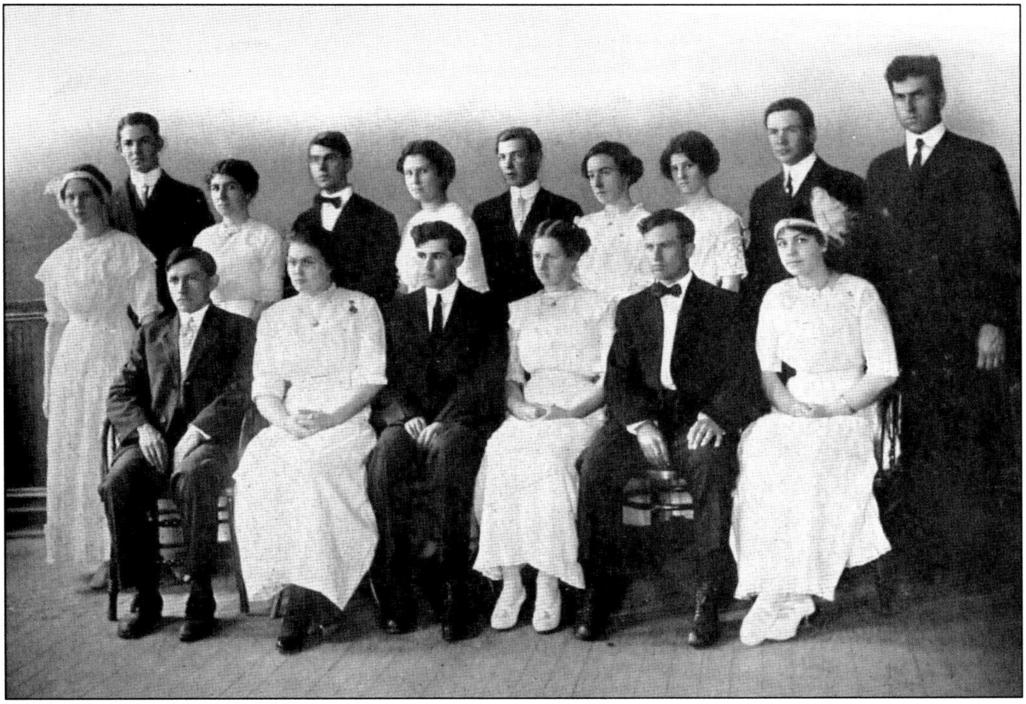

The graduating class of 1913 is shown in their vintage dress.

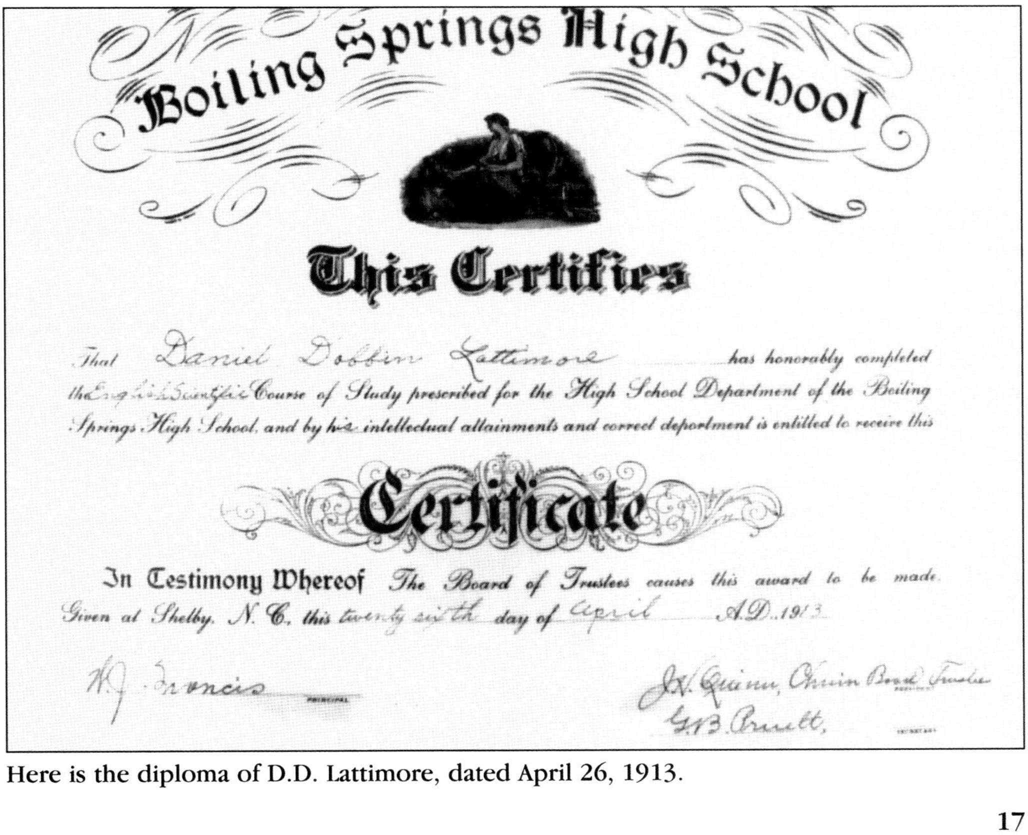

Boiling Springs High School

This Certifies

That Daniel Dobbin Lattimore has honorably completed the English Scientific Course of Study prescribed for the High School Department of the Boiling Springs High School, and by his intellectual attainments and correct deportment is entitled to receive this

Certificate

In Testimony Whereof The Board of Trustees causes this award to be made.
Given at Shelby, N. C. this twenty sixth day of April A.D. 1913

W. J. Francis, Principal

J. V. Quinn, Chairm Board Trustee

G. B. Pruett, Secretary

Here is the diploma of D.D. Lattimore, dated April 26, 1913.

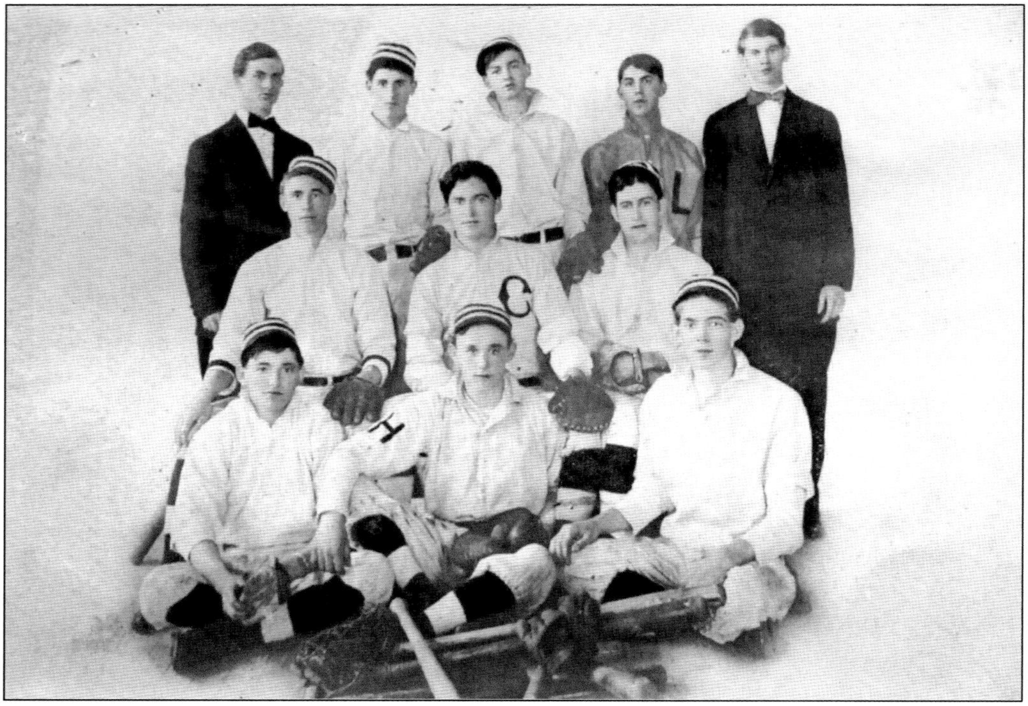

The baseball team of 1910 posed in the Harris Studio in Shelby for their team picture.

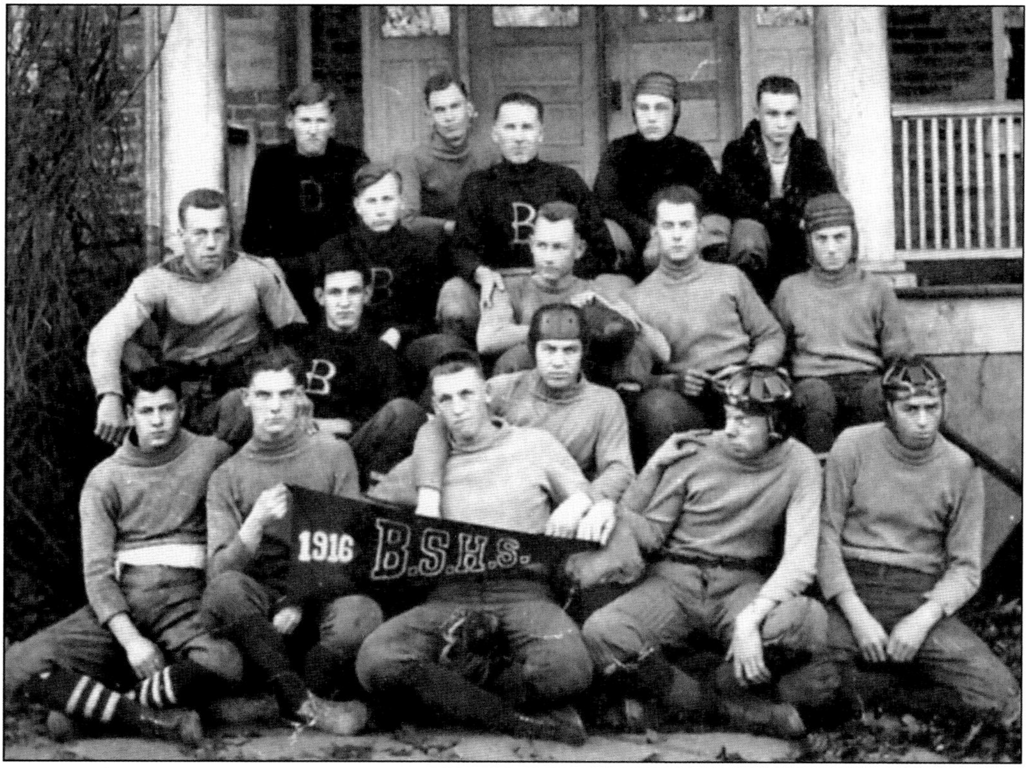

The 1916 football team posed on the steps of Main Building for their team picture. Note the minimum of safety gear.

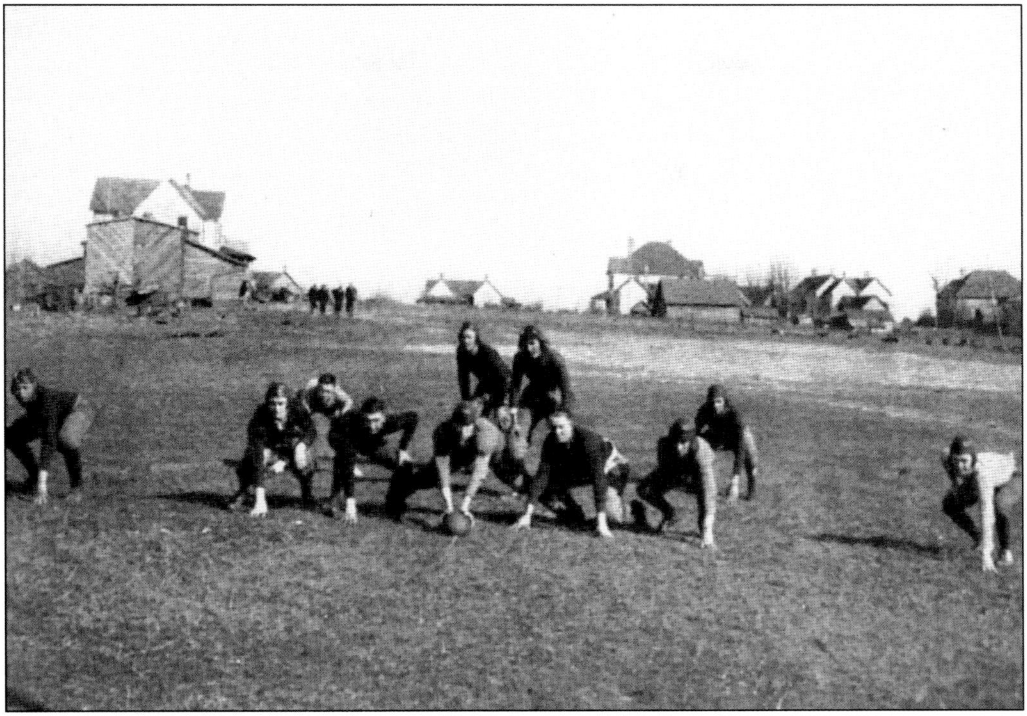

From the practice field we see the team photo from 1917. In the early days, the football team played in Shelby. The photo may have been taken in Shelby, at the ballfield at the intersection of West Graham and Martin Streets.

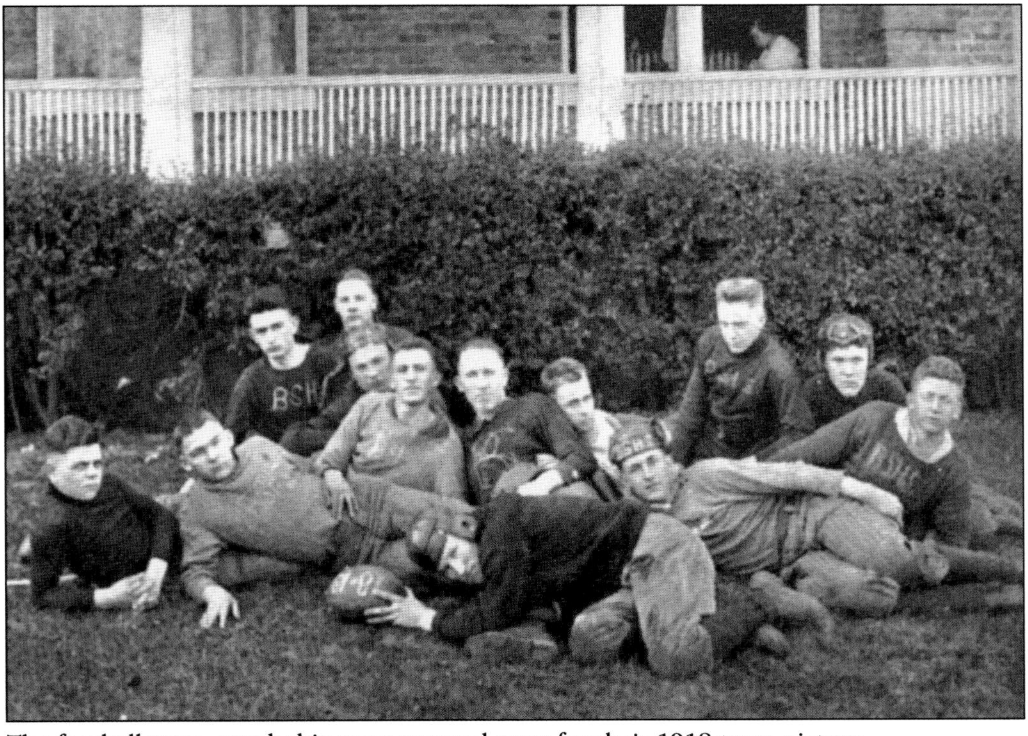

The football team struck this most unusual pose for their 1918 team picture.

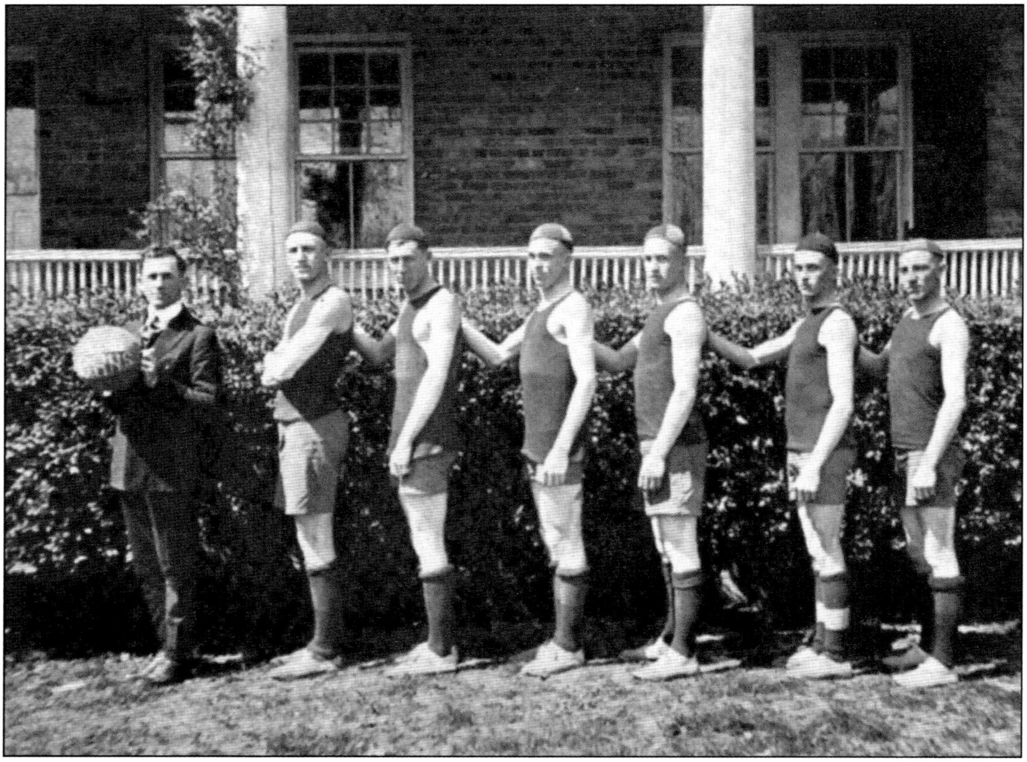

The men's basketball team of 1920–1921 is shown in the uniforms of the day. The team was comprised of a coach and six players.

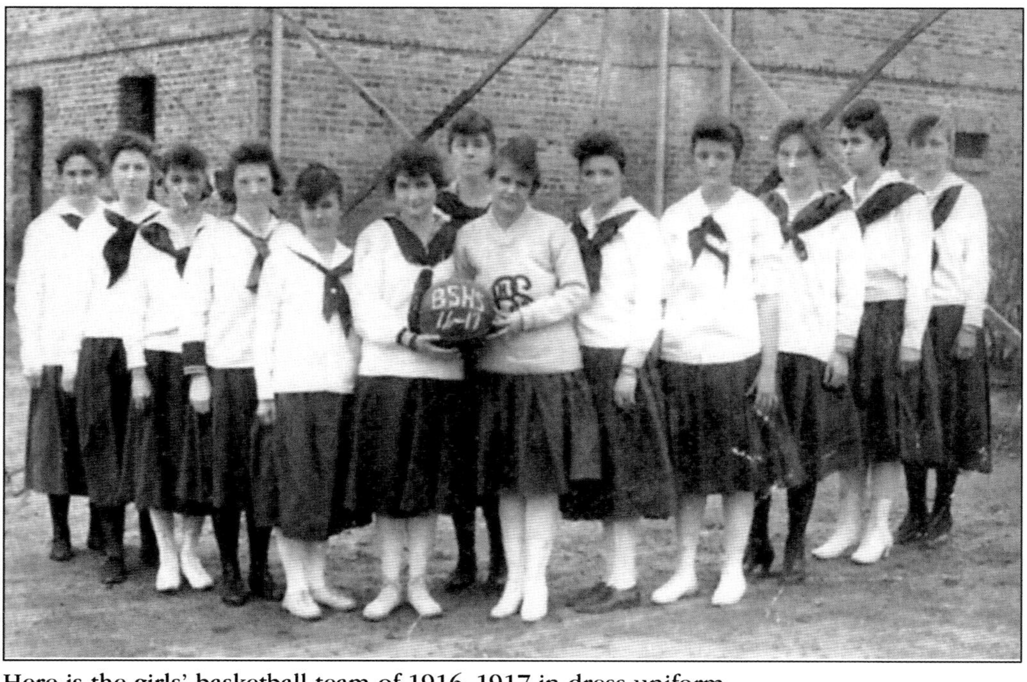

Here is the girls' basketball team of 1916–1917 in dress uniform.

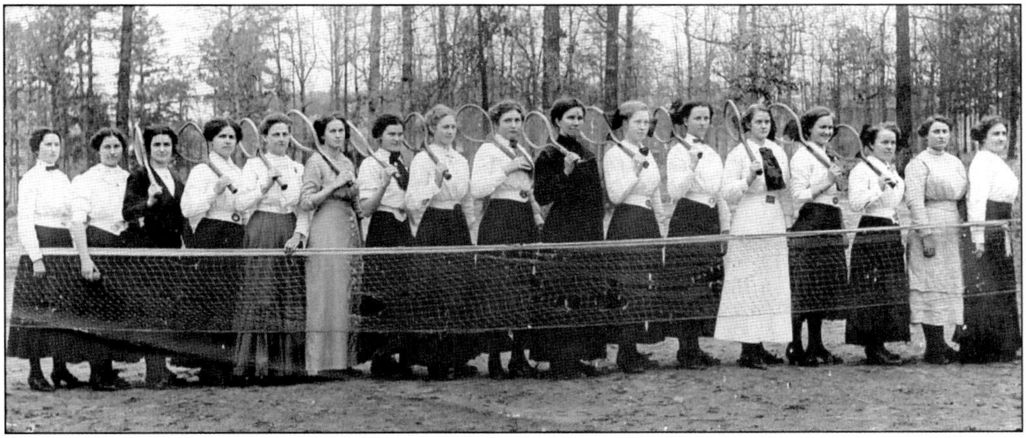

Shown here is the girls' tennis team of 1913. Tennis was a ladies' game in this era. The long dresses were more proper. Wooden racquets were standard equipment.

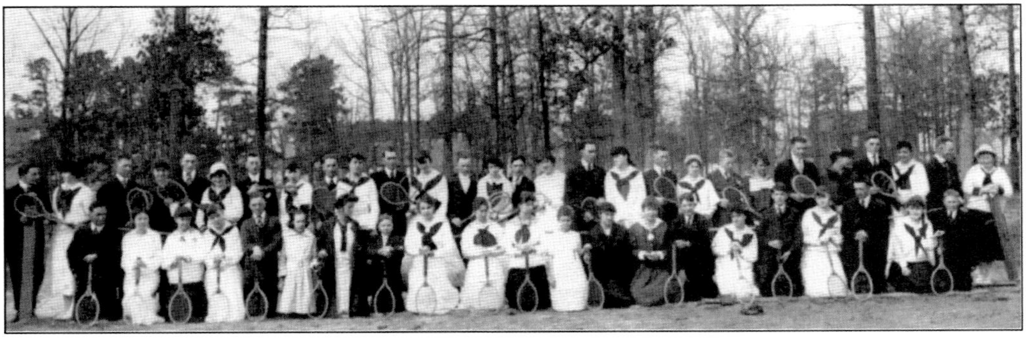

The boys' and girls' tennis clubs are shown here in 1915. Athletic programs were encouraged but were not allowed to interfere with the students' progress in their studies. "We believe that athletics under limitations is conductive to good scholarship." Discussion of the roles of academics and athletics seems to have been an issue 90 years ago, just as it is today.

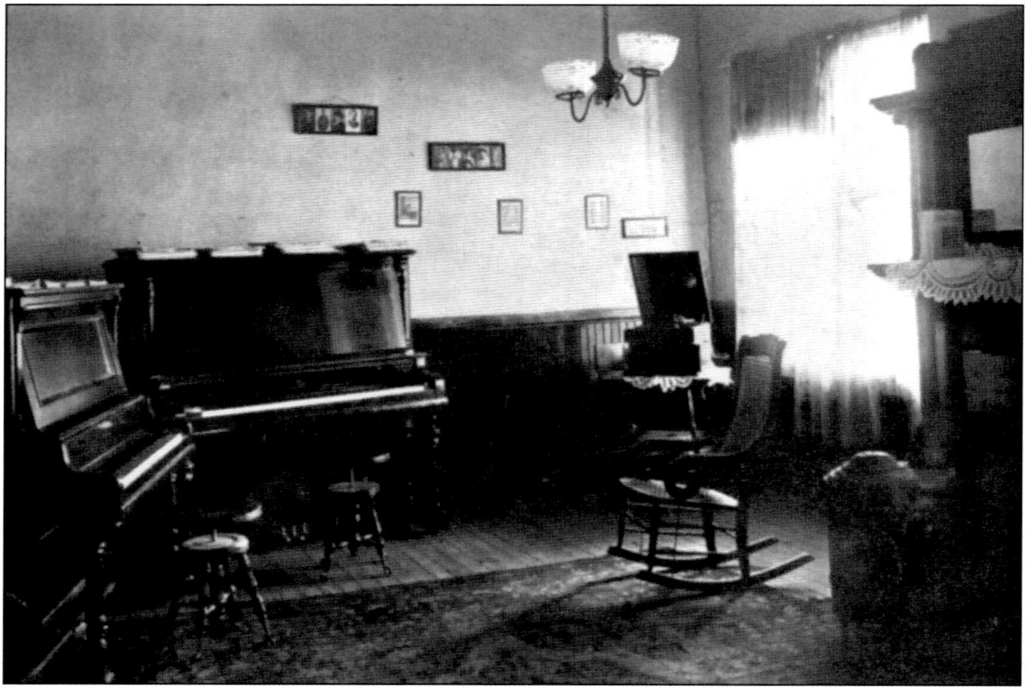

Here is the music room in Main Building as it first appeared in 1909.

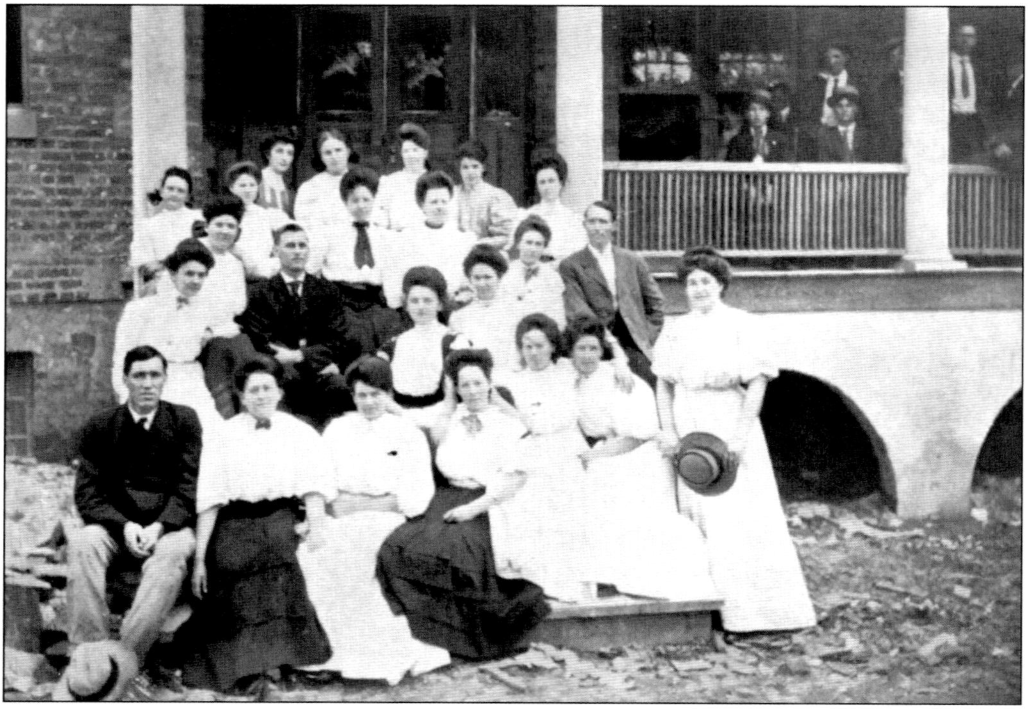

The music class of 1909 is shown in front of Main Building. From the school's inception, music has played in integral role in student development.

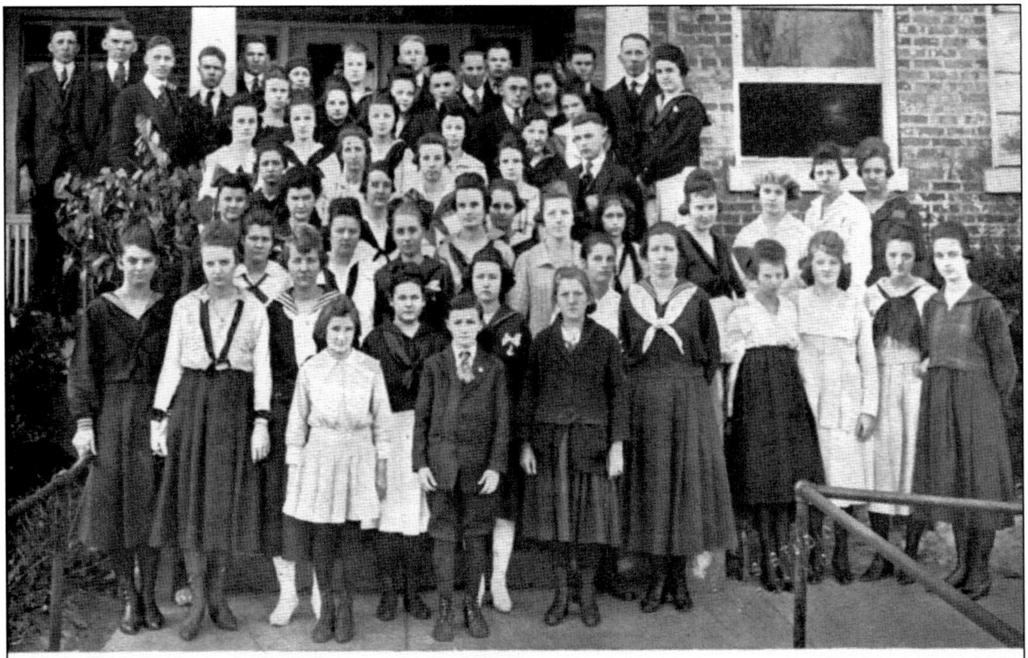

CHORUS CLASS

Pictured by Main Building is the chorus class of 1918. The music department offered instruction in piano, voice, and theory.

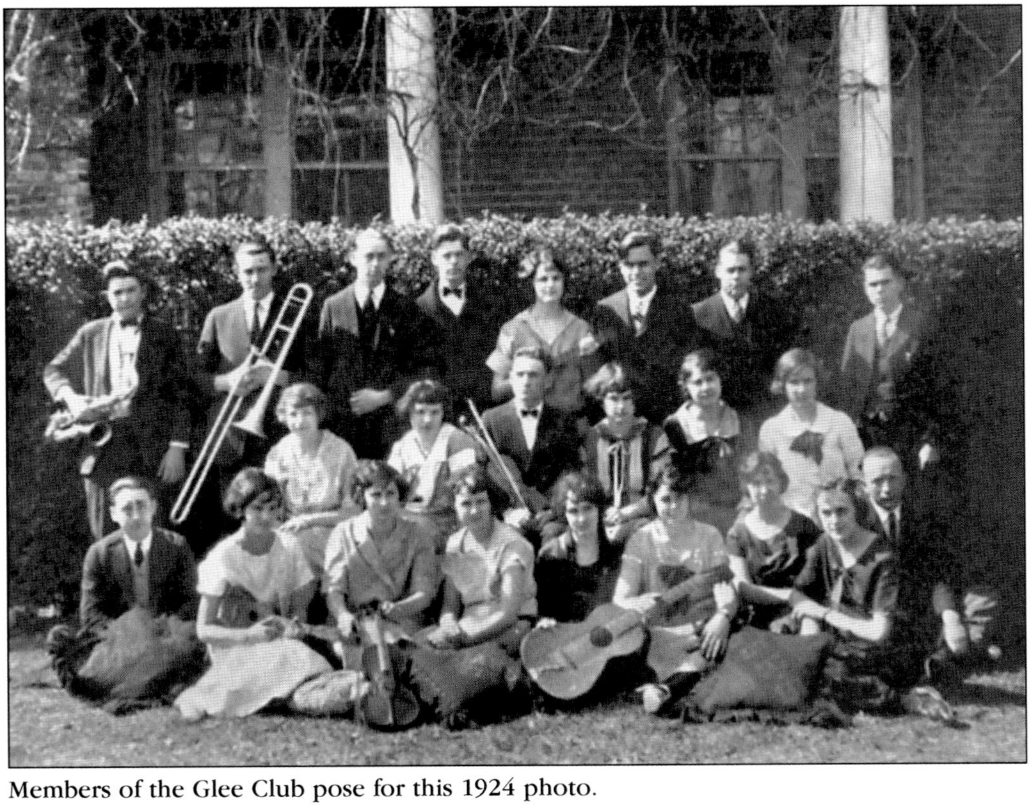

Members of the Glee Club pose for this 1924 photo.

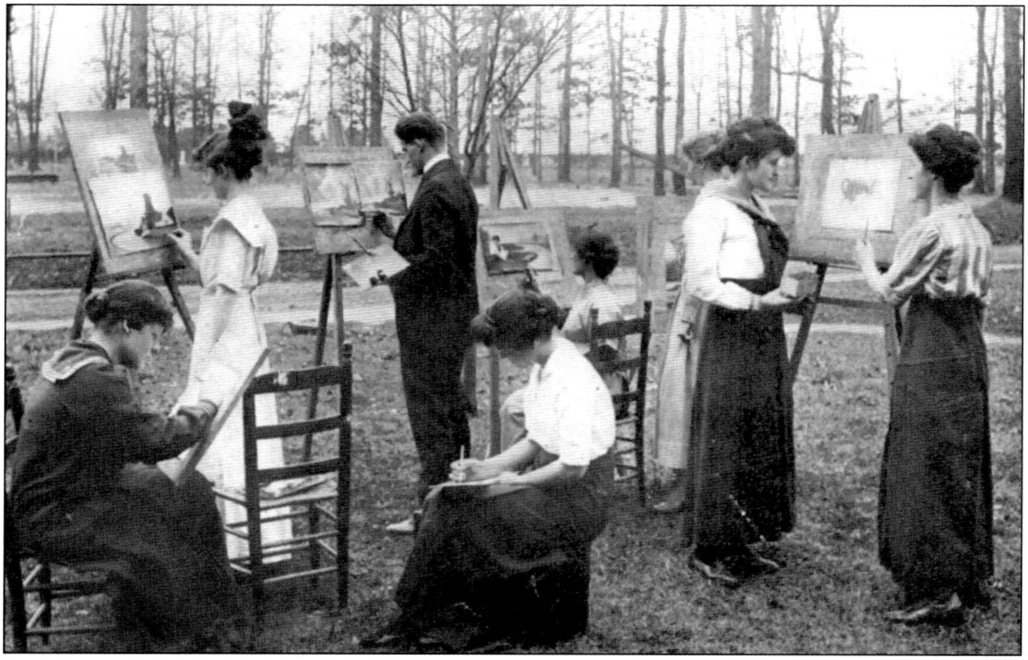

Shown here is the art class of 1915. The following is from the catalog of that year: "we have provided a thorough, practical and interesting course in art. The course is intended to create an appreciation of art, to develop the power of observation and the skill to copy nature and to create beautiful things."

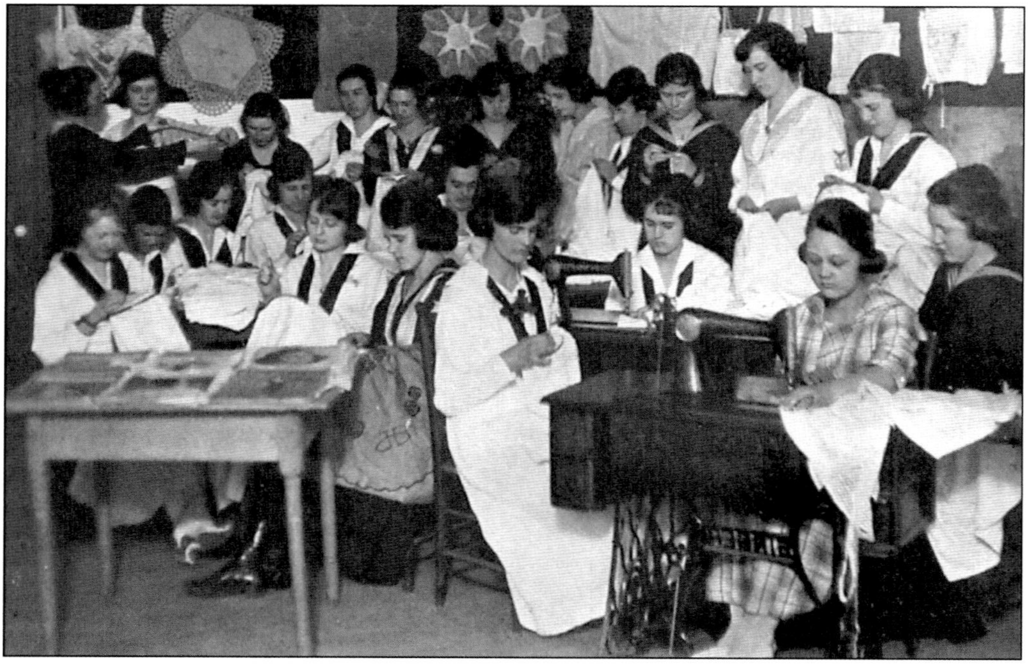

The department of household arts offered classes in domestic art. This image is from the 1919 catalog that explained, "domestic art gives the student a practical knowledge of hand sewing of both elementary and decorative stitches. The course teaches the drafting of patterns, for the construction of dresses, and costumes."

Domestic science, also a part of household arts, provided "instruction that will enable students to become efficient homemakers or matrons and housekeepers in public or private institutions."

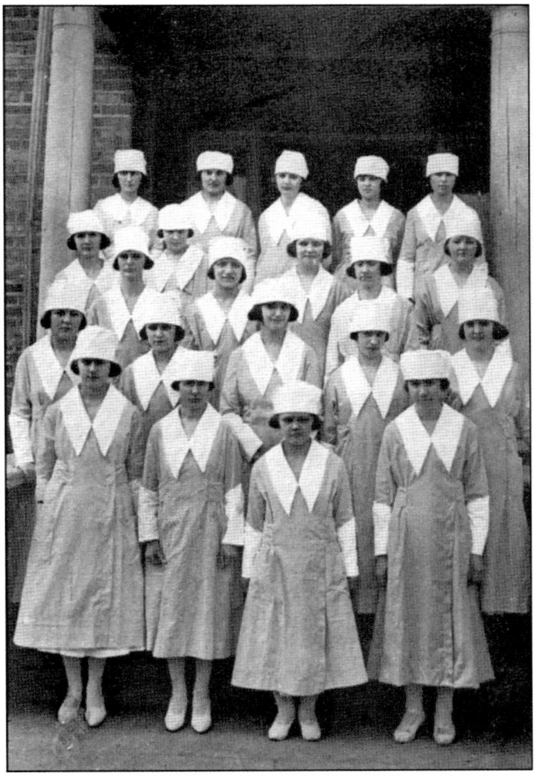

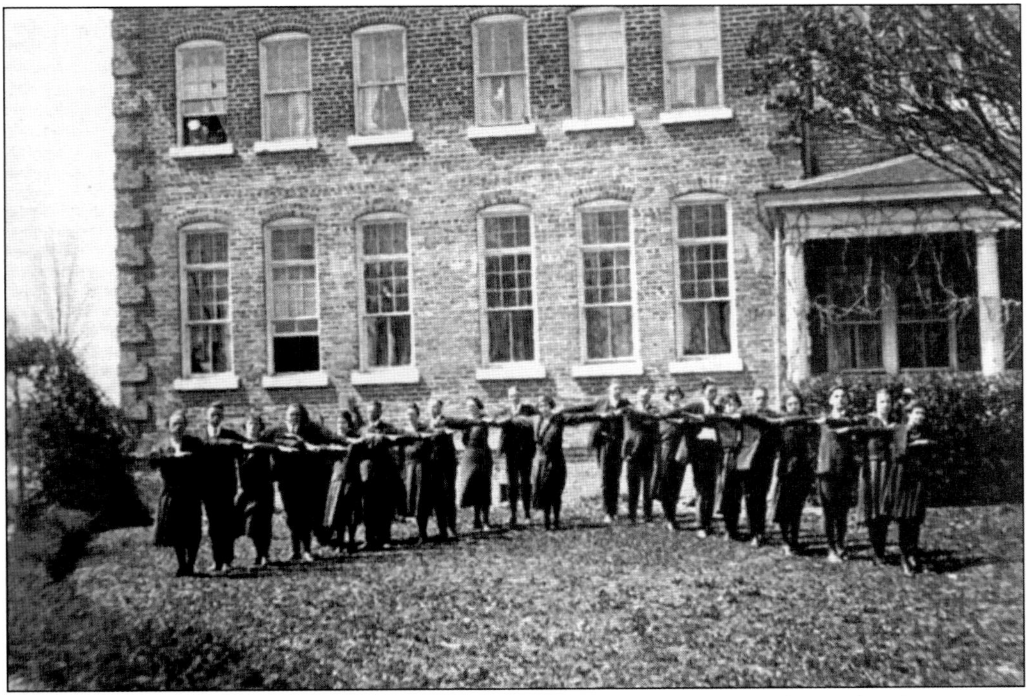

This is a 1919 photo of the expression class in front of Main Building. "The study of expression seeks to awaken in the students a realization of their own potentialities to develop a clear, magnetic voice, graceful and easy manner and the virtue of sincerity and simplicity."

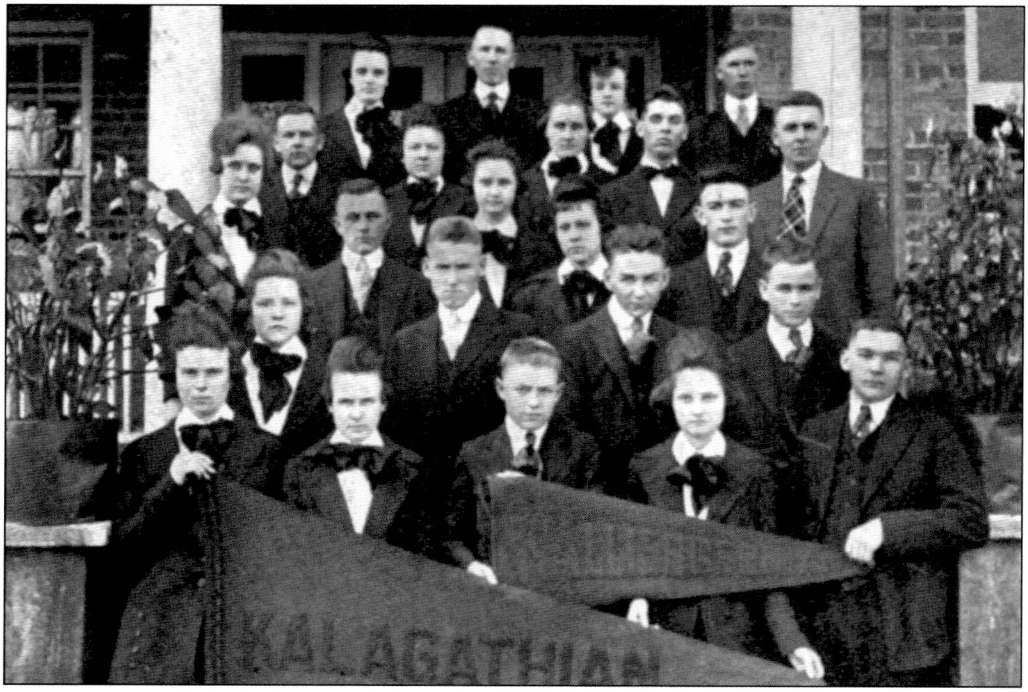

Officers of the 1919 Kalagathian and Kalliergeonian Literary Societies pose for this group photo. Literary societies conducted competitions in debates and speeches. The competition was keen and promoted academic excellence.

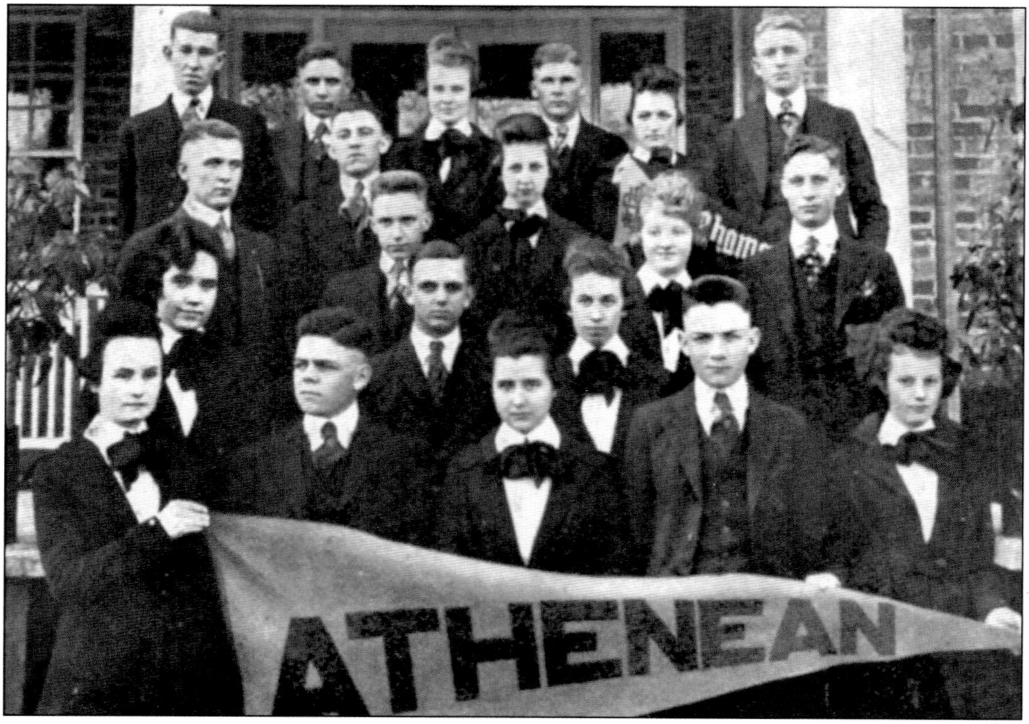

Pictured are officers from the 1919 Athenean and Rhamsaeur Literary Societies. Weekly meetings were held to discuss and exchange ideas from literary and political studies.

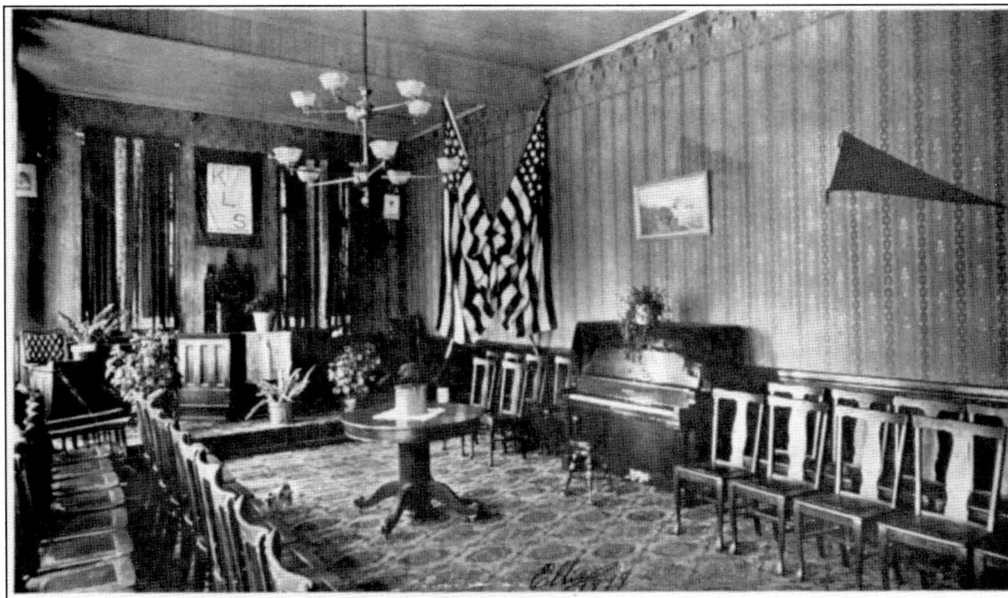

HALL OF KALAGATHIAN AND KALLIERGEONIAN LITERARY SOCIETIES

The hall of the Kalagathian and Kalliergeoian Literary Societies was decorated by students.

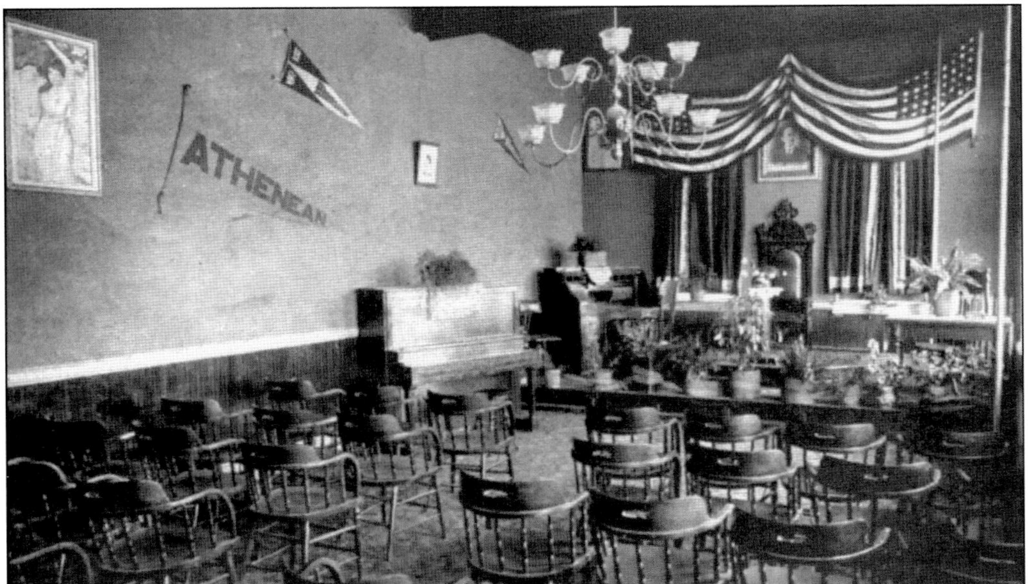

Students took great pride in their association with literary societies. Pictured is the hall that housed the Athenean and Rhamsaeur Societies.

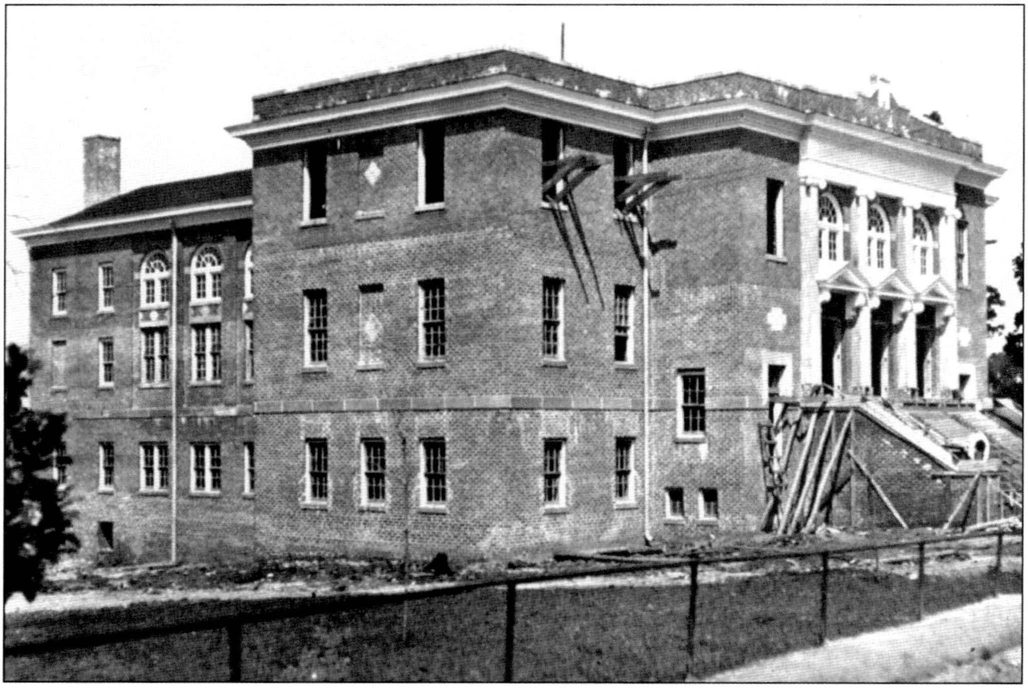

This 1922 image shows Memorial Auditorium under construction. Notice the different style of roofline from the current building.

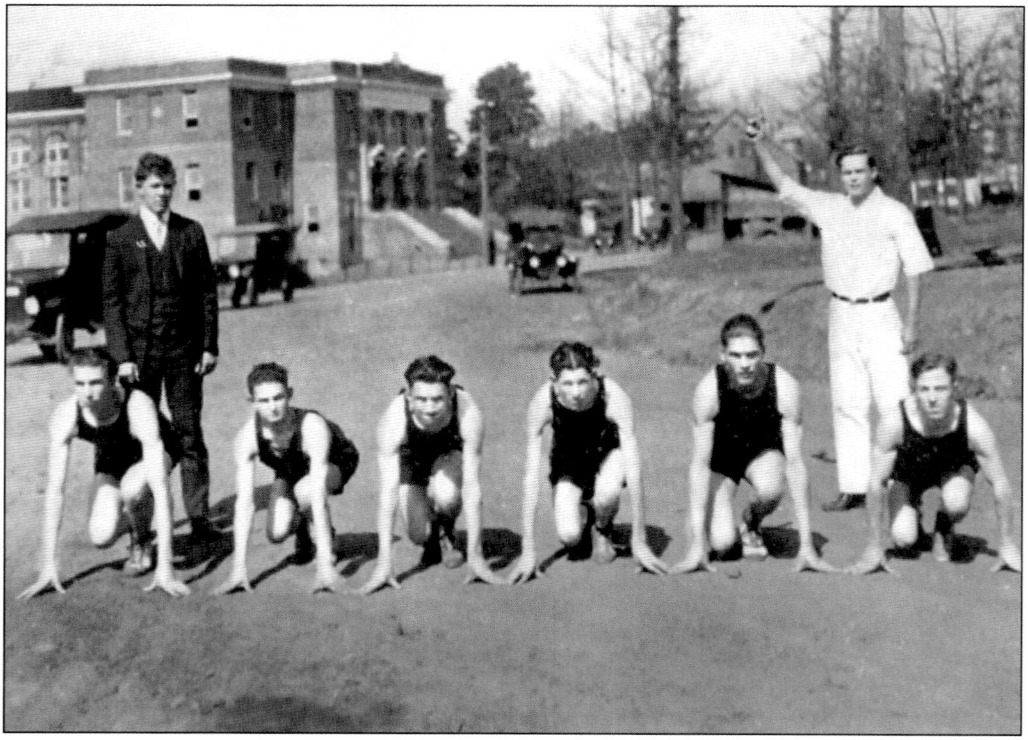

The track team of 1924 is pictured with the newly constructed Memorial Auditorium in the background.

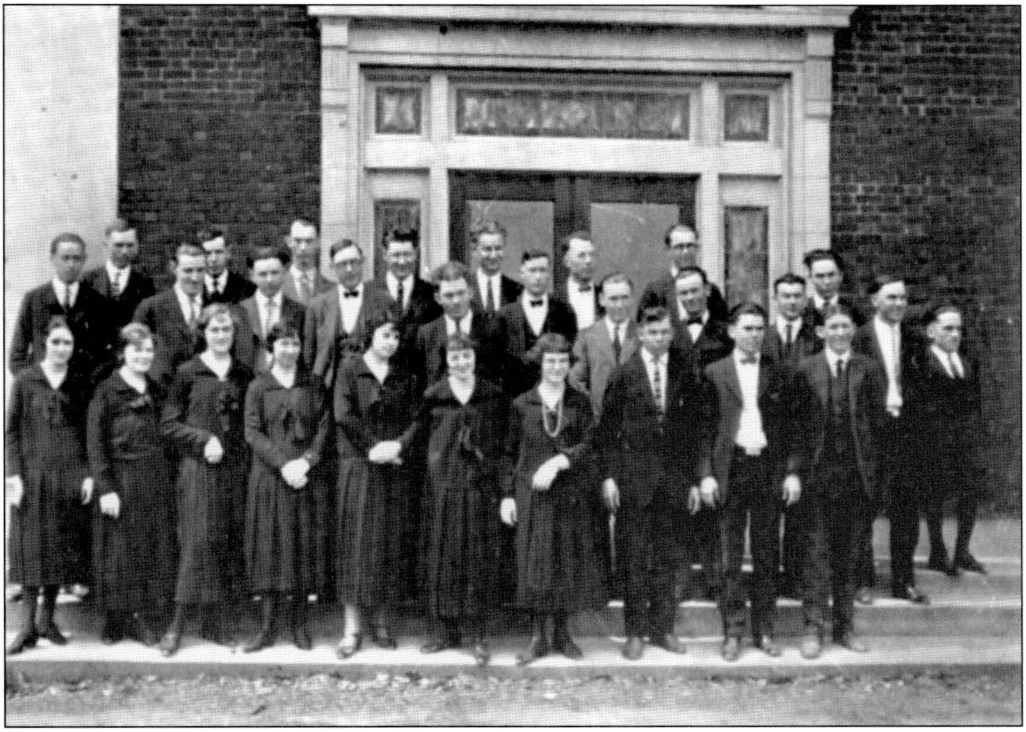

The 1924 ministerial class and others who planned to seek church work pose in front of Boiling Springs Baptist Church.

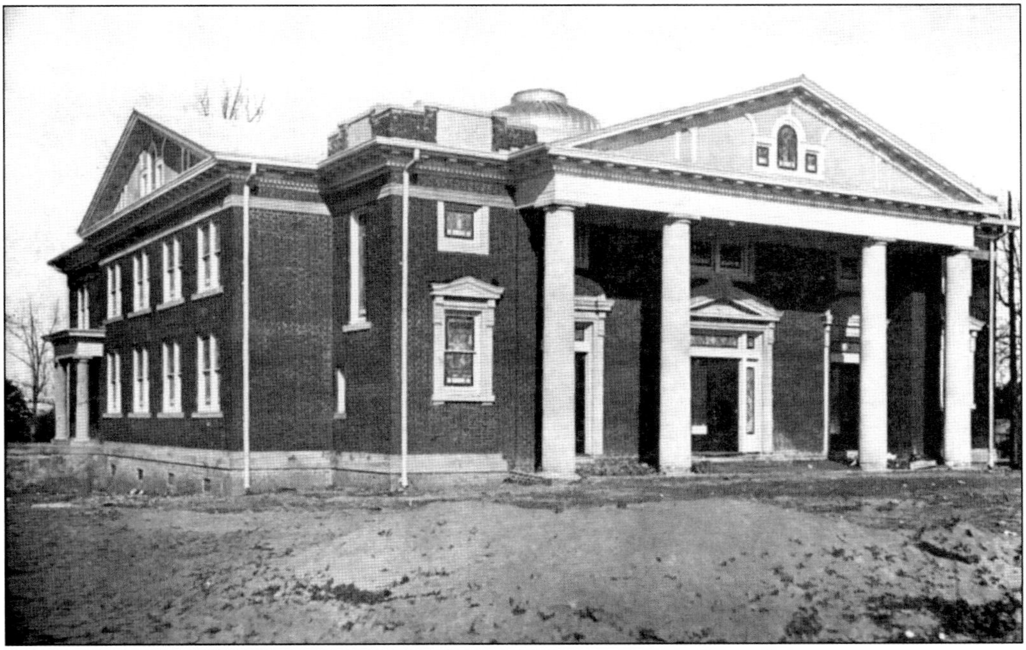

Here is Boiling Springs Baptist Church as it appeared in 1921. The church originally deeded the land to establish the high school.

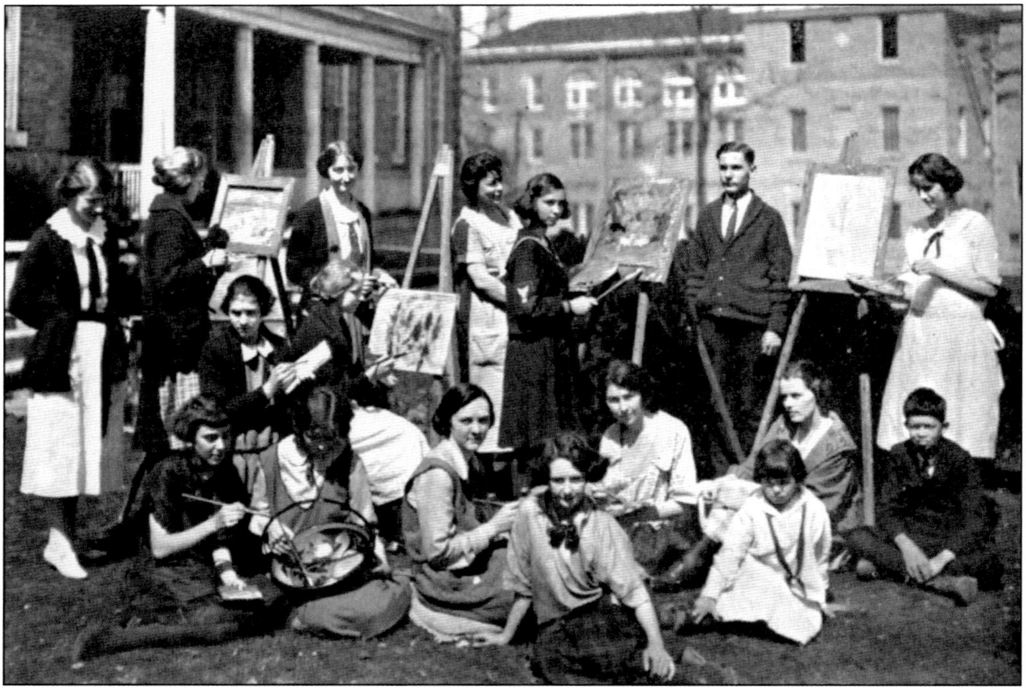

The art class is captured in this 1922 campus scene. Memorial Auditorium is in the right background in the image.

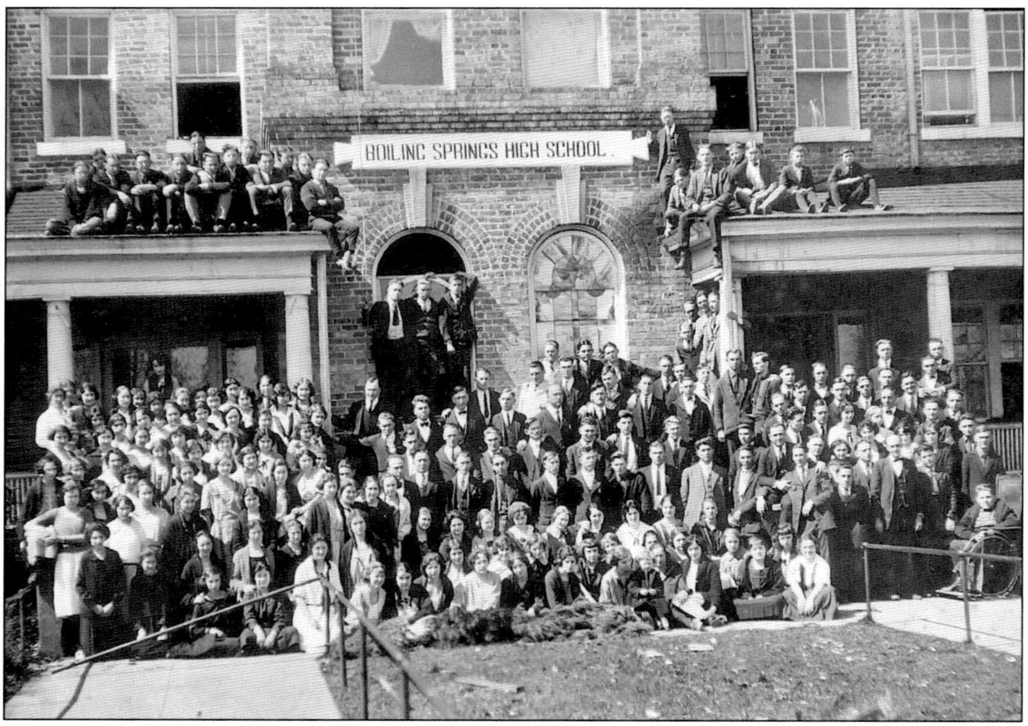

Faculty and students gather for this *c.* 1924 group photo in front of Main Building. Main would soon be renamed the Huggins Curtis Building in honor of Professor and Mrs. Huggins and Ms. Etta Curtis.

Two

BOILING SPRINGS JUNIOR COLLEGE

The Junior College before World War II

James Blaine Davis served as the first president of Boiling Springs Junior College when it opened on September 3, 1928. In that first year, the college had an enrollment of 61 students while the high school had an enrollment of 176 students. The original college had seven departments: Bible, education, English, foreign language, mathematics, natural science, and social science.

The early years of the college coincided with the Great Depression. The college struggled as economic conditions threatened its survival. Several Baptist ministers served as president in the early years, often for little or no pay. Other presidents to serve the college included Zeno Wall (1930–1932), James Linebury Jenkins (1932–1935), Arsola Crawford Lovelace (1935–1936), George Jackson Burnett (1936–1939), and John R. Cantrell (1939–1943).

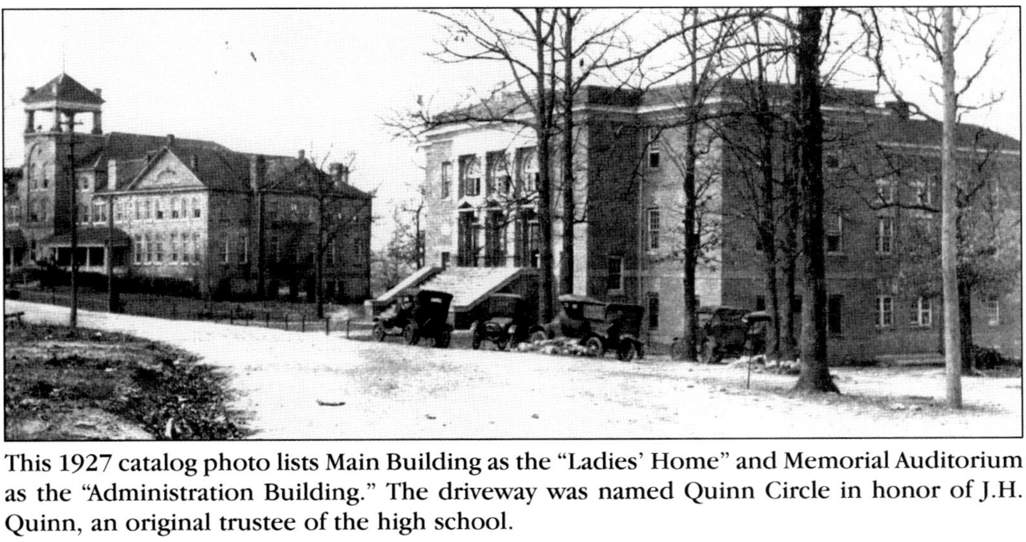

This 1927 catalog photo lists Main Building as the "Ladies' Home" and Memorial Auditorium as the "Administration Building." The driveway was named Quinn Circle in honor of J.H. Quinn, an original trustee of the high school.

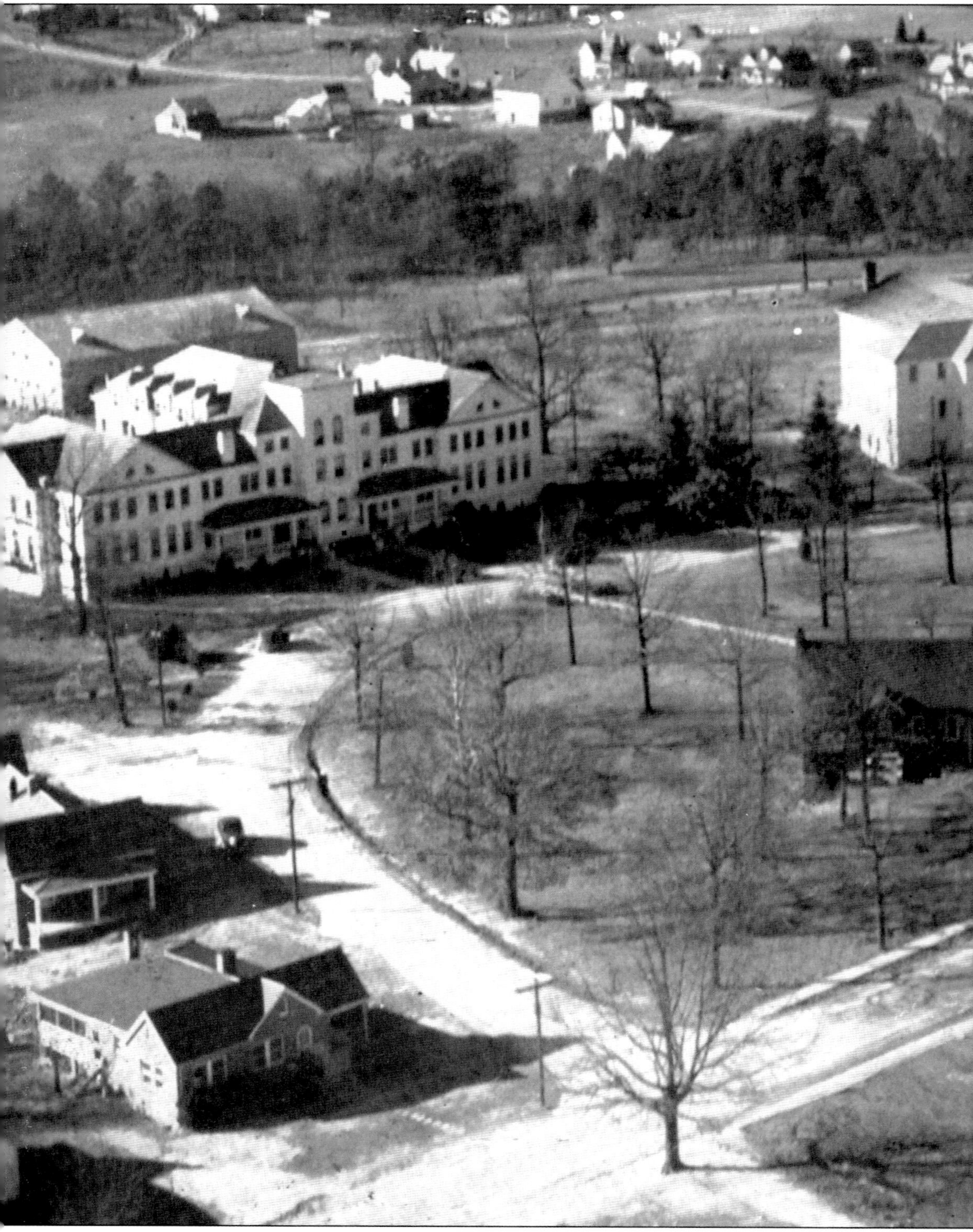

Main Building is to the upper left in this *c.* 1930 aerial view of campus. The "Rock Gym" is behind Main Building. To the right of Main Building are Memorial Auditorium and

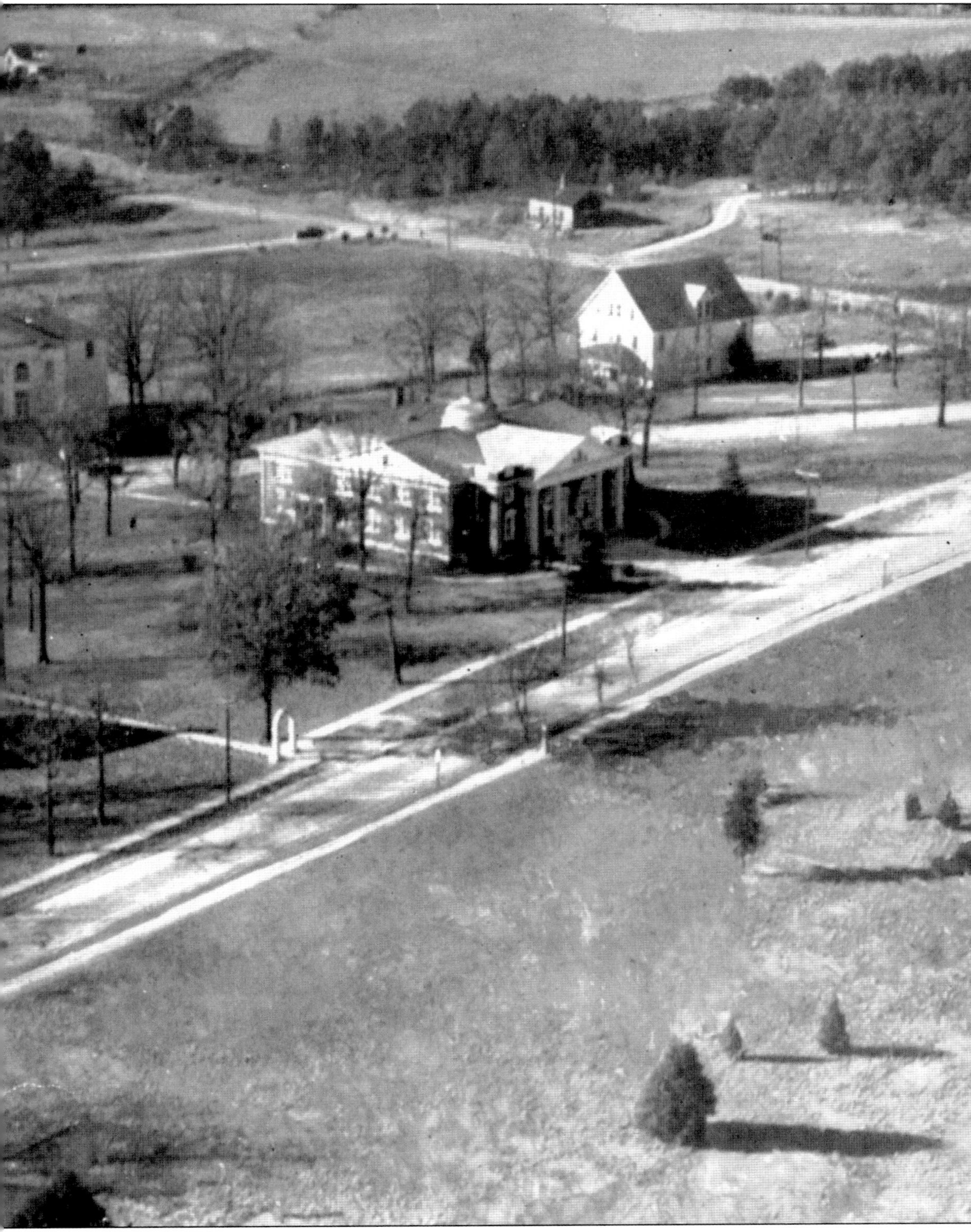

"the Barn" dormitory. Inside Quinn Circle are the Washburn Library and Boiling Springs Baptist Church.

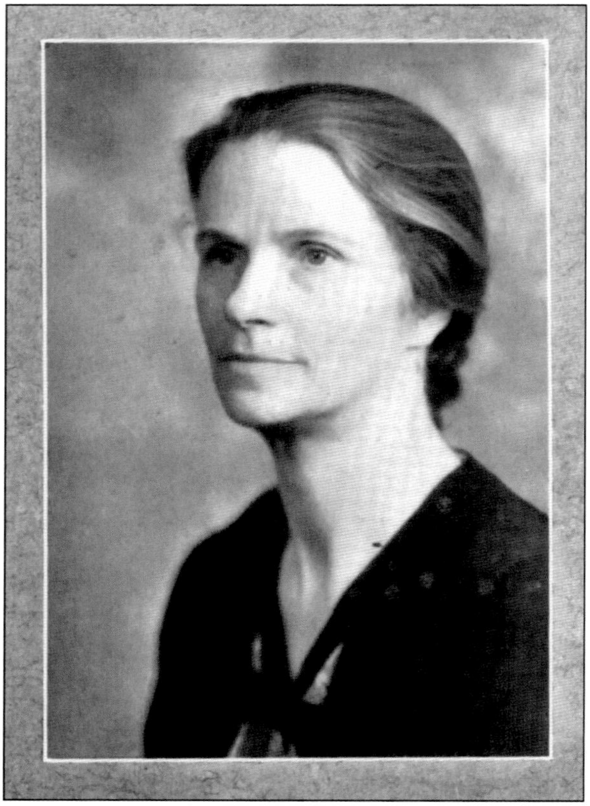

The 1934 edition of the annual *Bubbles* was dedicated to Bessie Huggins. The editors wrote, "In appreciation for the spirit of whole-hearted co-operation which she has always shown toward Boiling Springs College: for her warm friendship and love; for her unselfish service she has so loyally rendered it; and for her life as a visible embodiment of the ideals upon which our College was founded, we dedicate this first volume of BUBBLES."

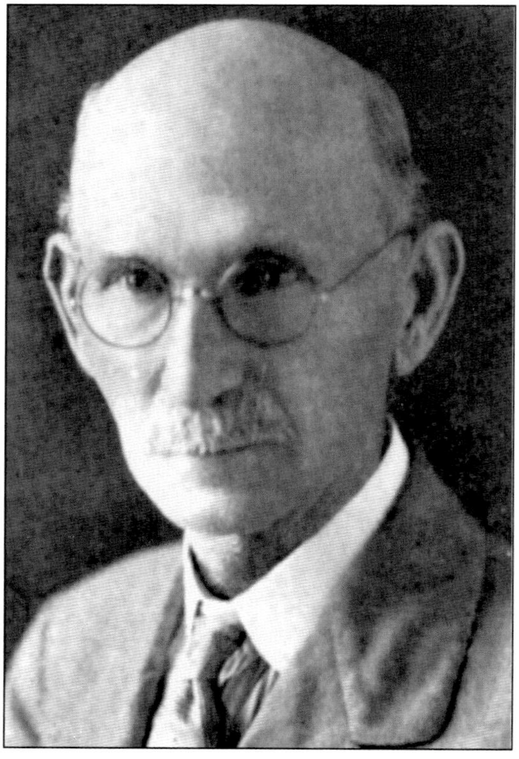

The 1937 edition of *Bubbles* was dedicated to local businessman and longtime school supporter E.B. Hamrick. In part, the dedication stated the following: "Time covers monuments of bronze with patina and shafts of marble with mould. But the monument a man builds for himself in a well-lived life shines with an ineradicable glory in the faces of youth and in the hearts of his friends. So to you, Mr. Hamrick, whose life has been vital for thirty years to the on-going of Boiling Springs College as trustee, patron and friend, we dedicate this volume."

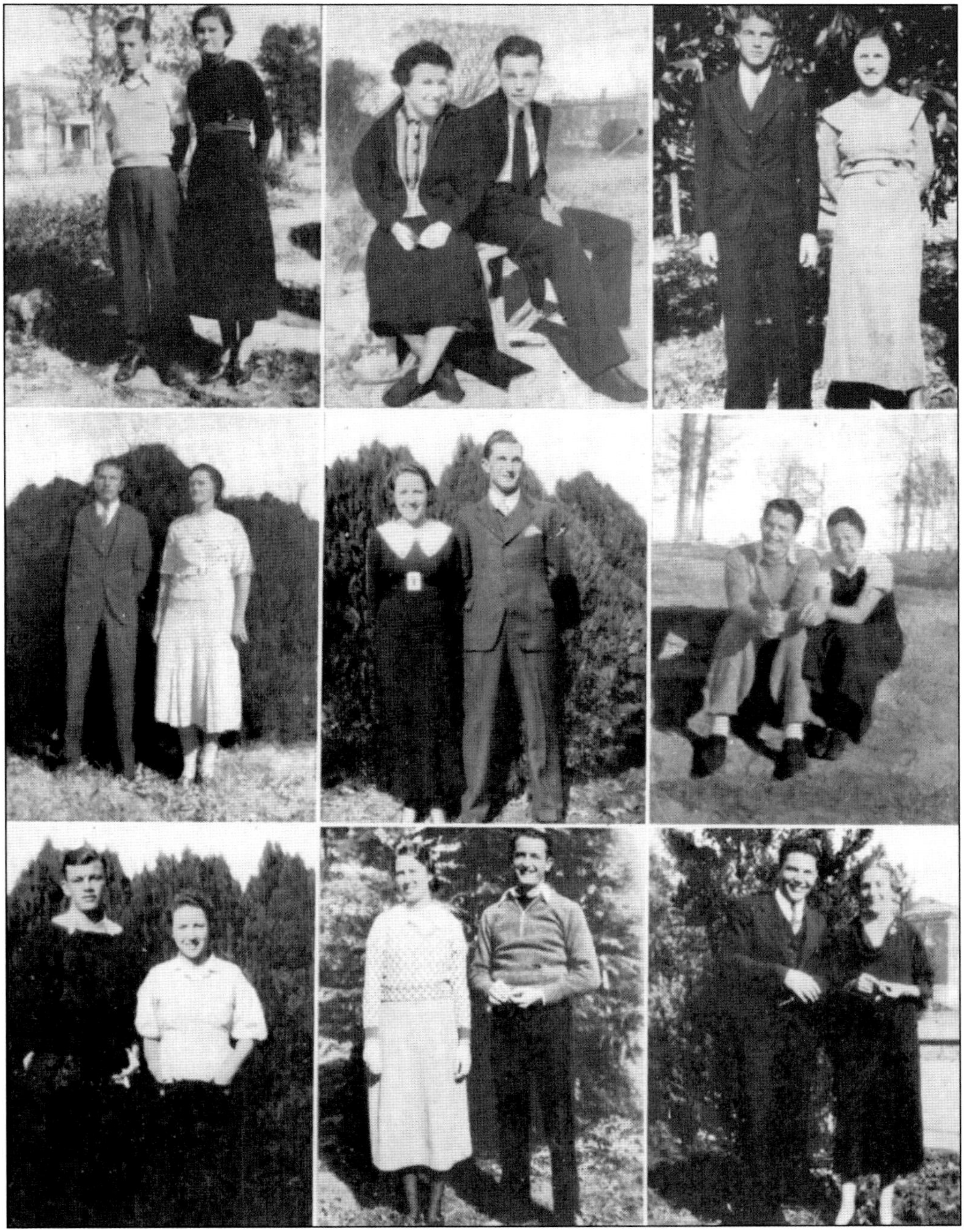

The 1934 edition of *Bubbles* recognized senior superlatives. From left to right are as follows: (top row) best all-around John Hendricks and Mary Sue Mulinax, most popular Margaret Autrey and Bob Spratt, and most versatile Hayden Camp and Bernice Hauser; (middle row) most intellectual Hayden Camp and Mary Sue Mulinax, best looking Annette Blanton and Ben Moore, and most school spirited Lyman Martin and Lalage Sperling; (bottom row) best athletes George Mauney and Annette Blanton, friendliest Bernice Whitesides and Lyman Martin, and most original Bruce Greenwood and Helen Greene.

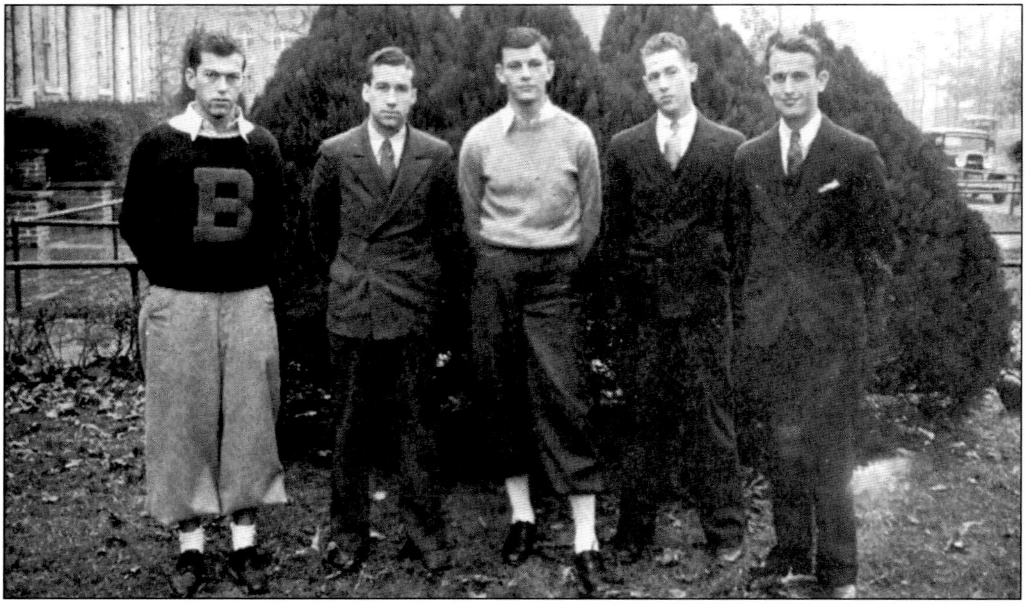

The Boy's Student Government Council of 1934 included Lyman Martin, John Hendricks, George Mauney, George Baker, and Leroy Wahnetah. The faculty advisor was Paul W. Hutchins.

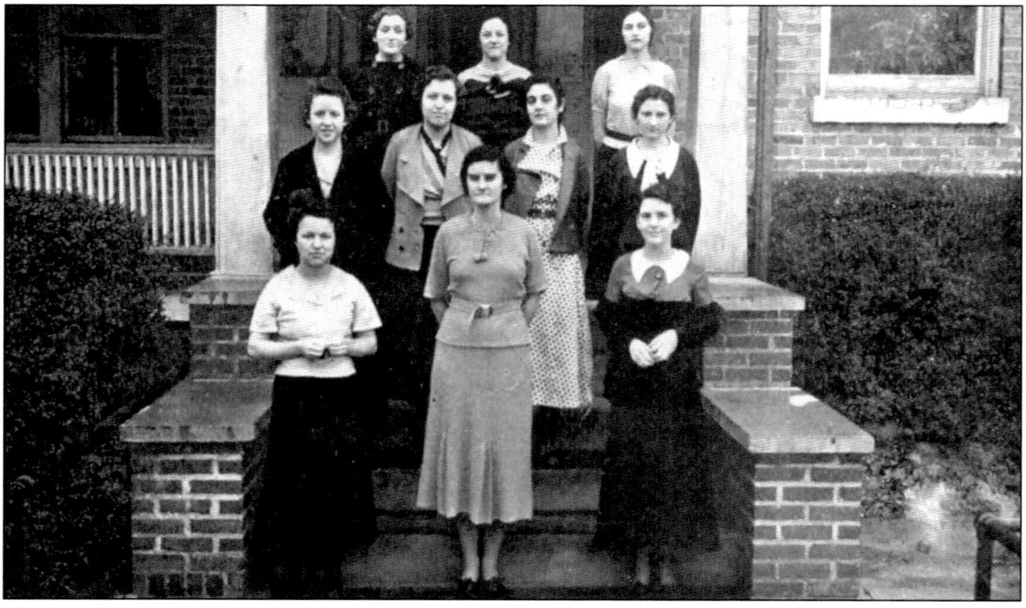

The Girl's Student Government Council of 1934 included Mary Sue Mulinax, Dorothy Washburn, Margaret Autrey, Annette Blanton, Beryl Davidson, Lois Long, Helen Greene, Florence Hamilton, and Julia Renfro. The faculty advisor was Miss Rosalie McMurtrey.

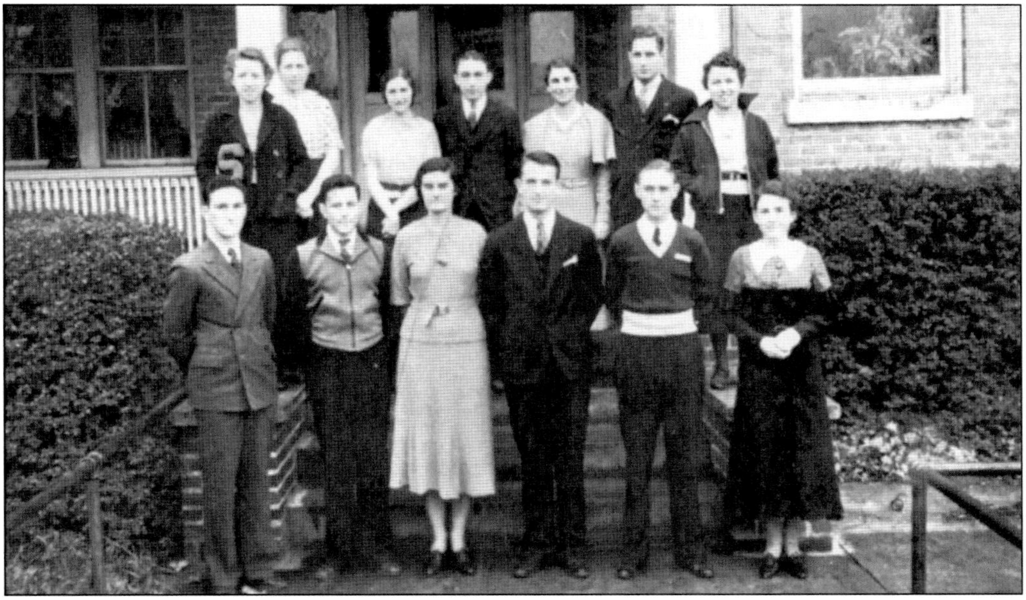

Baptist Student Union (BSU) Council of 1934 included Lyman Martin, Stancill Nanney, Harry Arrowood, Mary Sue Mulinax, Louis Lynch, Minnie Grey Lester, Lois Long, Lalage Sperling, Annette Blanton, Felix Hamrick, Margaret Autrey, Rowell Lane, and Dorothy Washburn. Miss Mary Lee was their sponsor.

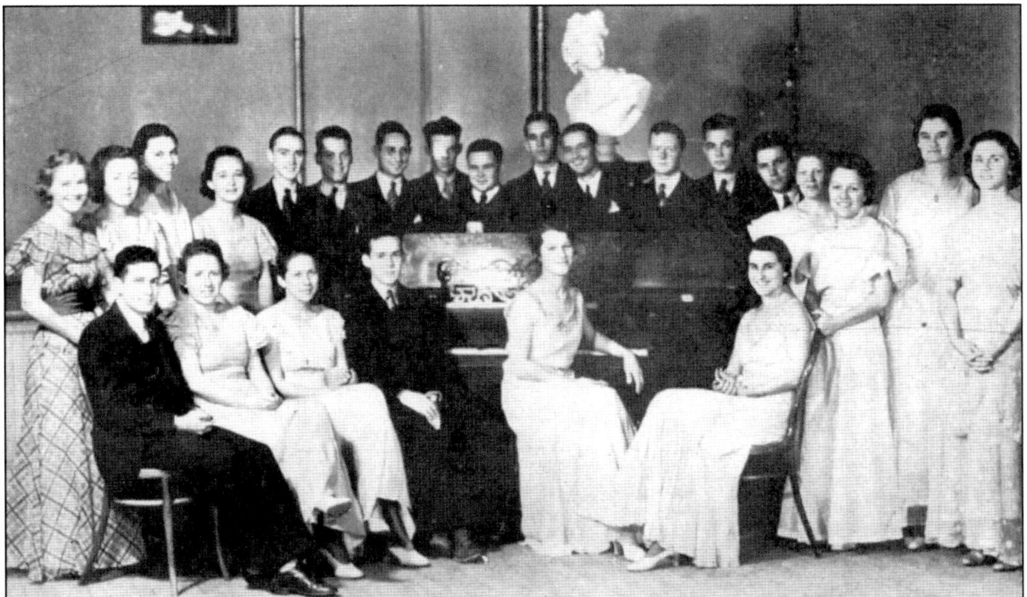

The Glee Club of 1934 included Bob Spratt, Alex Ross, Anna Coble, Annette Blanton, Florence Hamilton, Helen Hamrick, Mary Hamrick, Sibyl Moore, Mary Sue Mulinax, Margaret Autrey, Cathereen Fuller, Macie Lee Hamrick, Bernice Houser, Lalage Sperling, Jean Moore Thompson, Mary Sue Holland, Harry Arrowood, Thomas Lattimore, Rowell Lane, Louis Lynch, Elmo Scoggins, Bruce Arrowood, Somers Collins, Ben Jenkins, Lyman Martin, John Withrow, and Leroy Wahnetah. Miss Mary Lee was the director, and Miss Lucille Johnson was the accompanist.

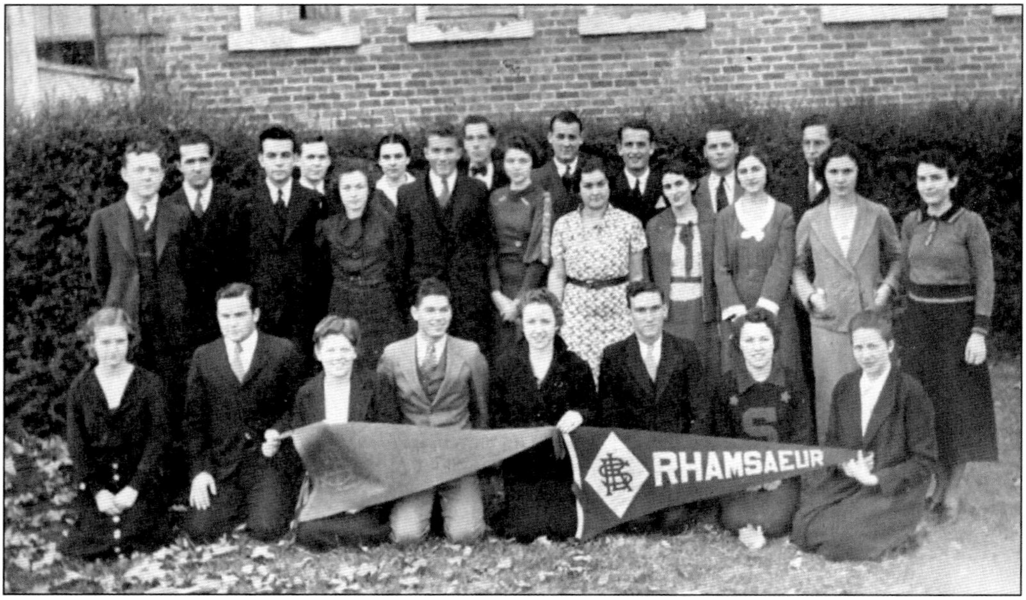

Members of the Athenian-Rhamsaeur Literary Society *c.* 1920 are, from left to right, as follows: (front row) Sybil Moore, Somers Collins, Mary Hamrick, Broughton Ramsey, Annette Blanton, Stancill Nanney, Margaret Autrey, and Lalage Sperling; (middle row) Thomas Lattimore, Robert Spratt, Cathereen Fuller, Hayden Camp, Ruth Wacaster, Sara Lee Norman, Beth Long, Lois Long, Bernice Houser, and Dorothy Washburn; (back row) James Anderson, Alexander Ross, Anna Coble, Marlowe Stroupe, William Harrill, Lyman Martin, Elmo Scruggs, and Rowell Lane.

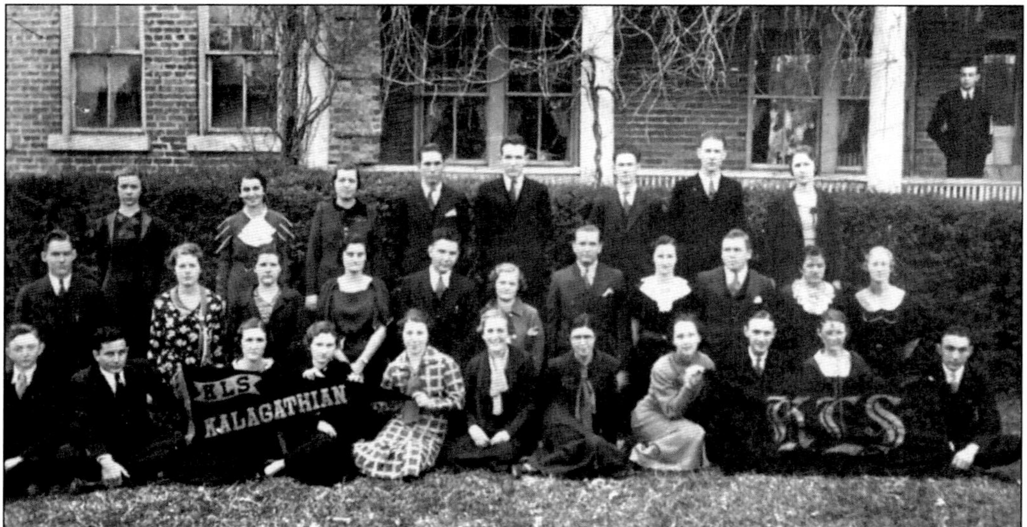

The members of the Kalagathian-Kalliergeonian Literary Society pictured here *c.* 1920 are, from left to right: (front row) Palmer Brooks, Harry Arrowood, Hermina Hamrick, Beryl Davidson, Kathleen Davidson, Helen Greene, Lois Jolley, Helen Hamrick, Lewis Lynch, Margaret Lee, and Felix Hamilton; (middle row) Sam Weir, Hope Finch, Jean M. Thompson, Mary Sue Mulinax, Bruce Arrowood, Lula Phillips, Robert Cook, Mary Russell, Clarence Peeler, Selma Wellmon, and Ruby Lynch; (back row) Delphine Blalock, Mary Lee, Julia Renfro, Ben Jenkins, James Hamrick, Waldon Turner, Roy Greene, and Bernice Whitesides.

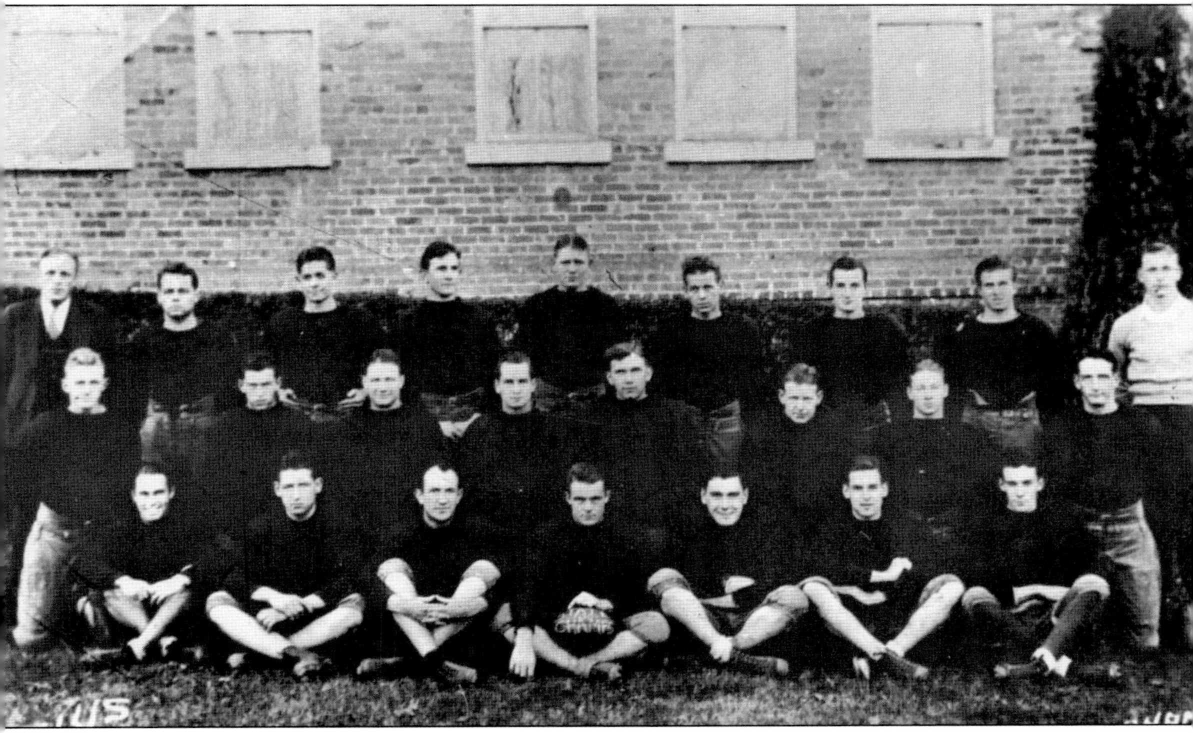

The 1930 Boiling Springs College Football Team won the North Carolina Junior College Football title. Pictured from left to right are as follows: (front row) Wall (quarterback), Cooley (guard), Harrison (tackle), Moore (guard), Faulkenberg (tackle), Vaughn (guard), and Forney (end); (middle row) McCraw (end), Hendrick (halfback), Stroud (halfback), Boney (halfback), Scarborough (fullback), Harris (fullback), Hunt (tackle), and Jolly (center); (back row) Blainey Rackley (coach), Waters (guard), Hemby (sub), Mulinax (center), Wall (sub), Bridges (end), Lattimore (sub), Bridges (sub), and Falls (manager).

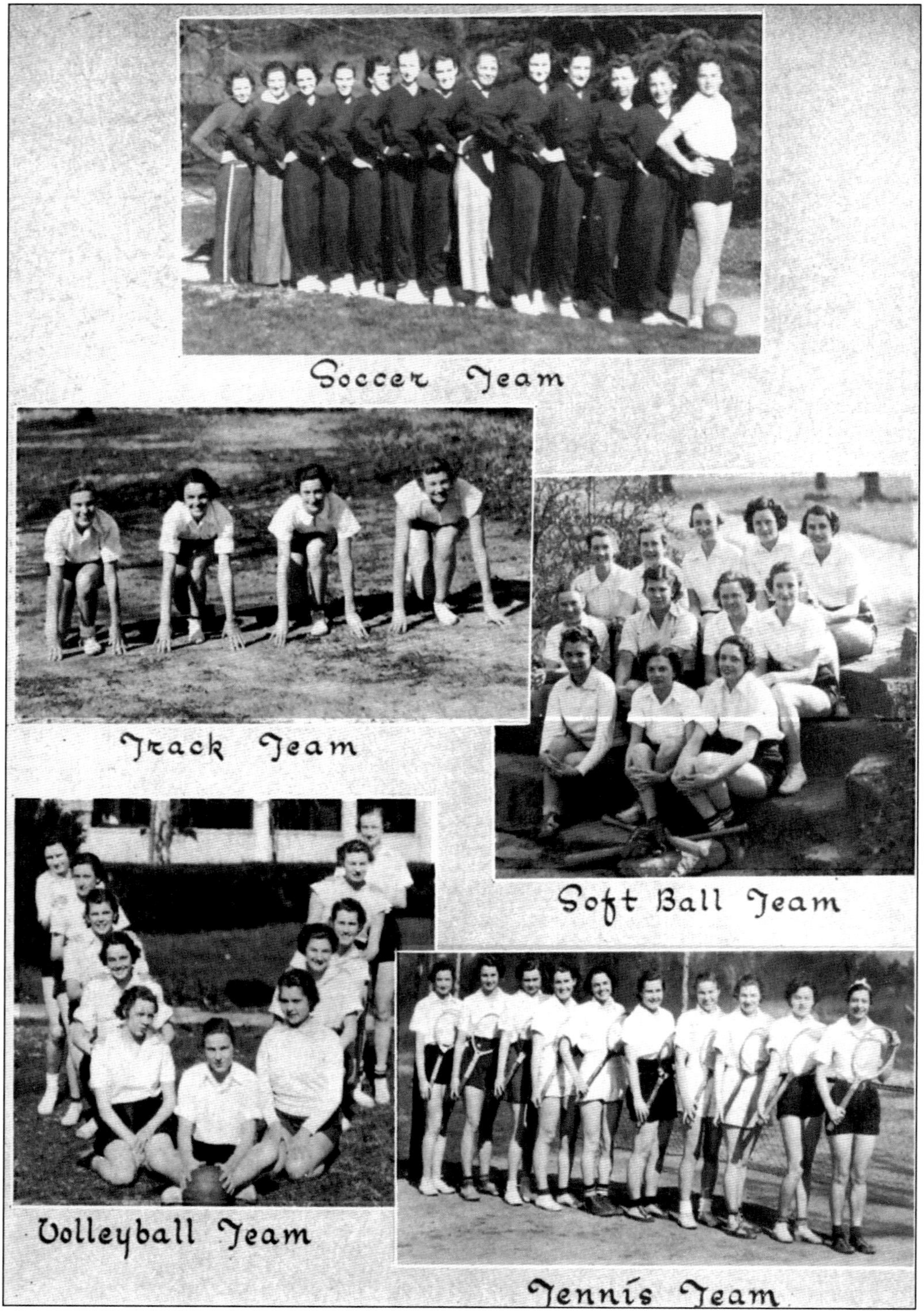

Before the days of Title IX, the Girls Athletic Association was alive and well. Girls' team sports included soccer, track, softball, volleyball, and tennis.

Coach Marjorie Crisp was a pioneer in coaching girls' sports. Coach Crisp moved on to Wake Forest College for an illustrious career in coaching.

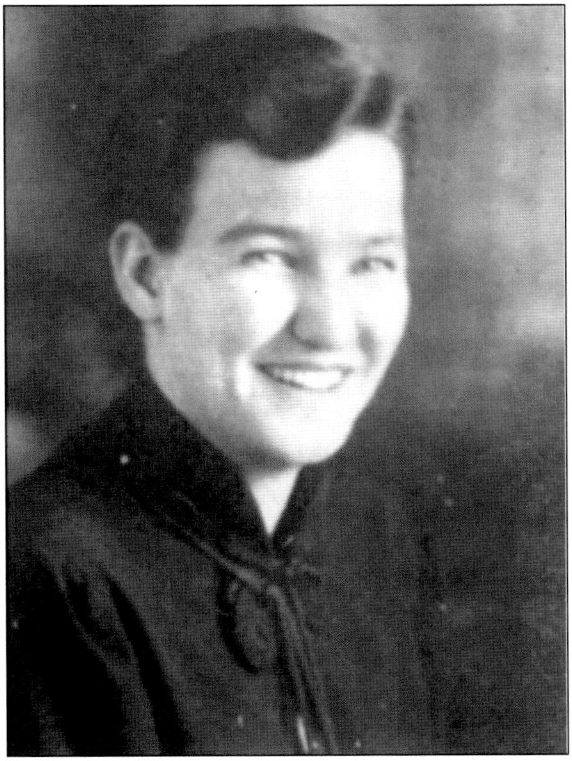

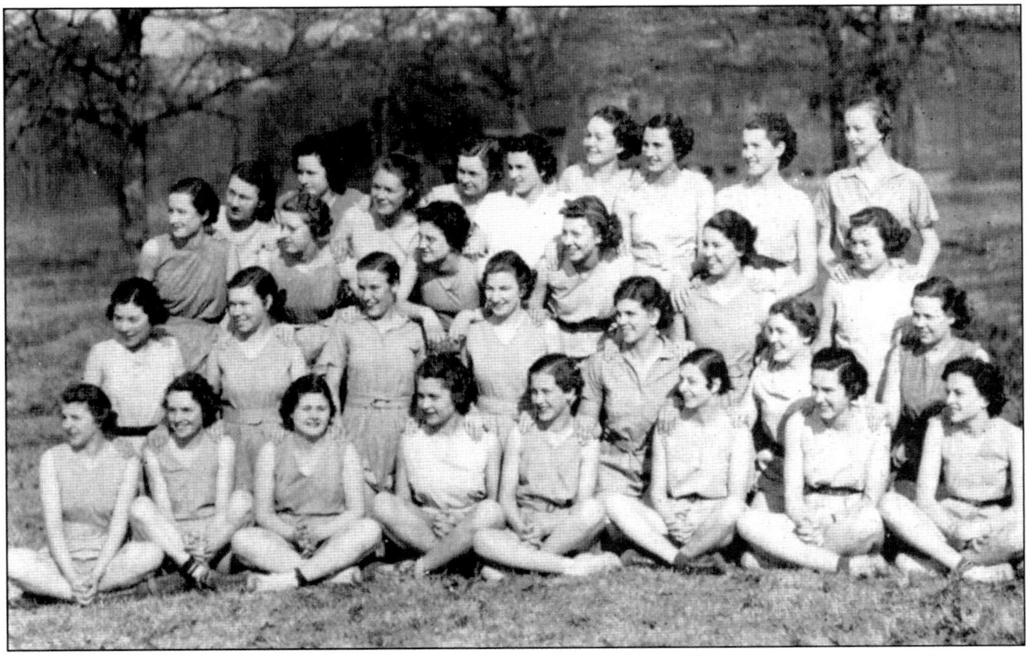

Officers of Girls Athletic Association were Lucy Crisp, president; Margaret Herndon, vice president; and Frances Jones, secretary and treasurer. Katherine Hamrick and Nellena Jones were co-captains.

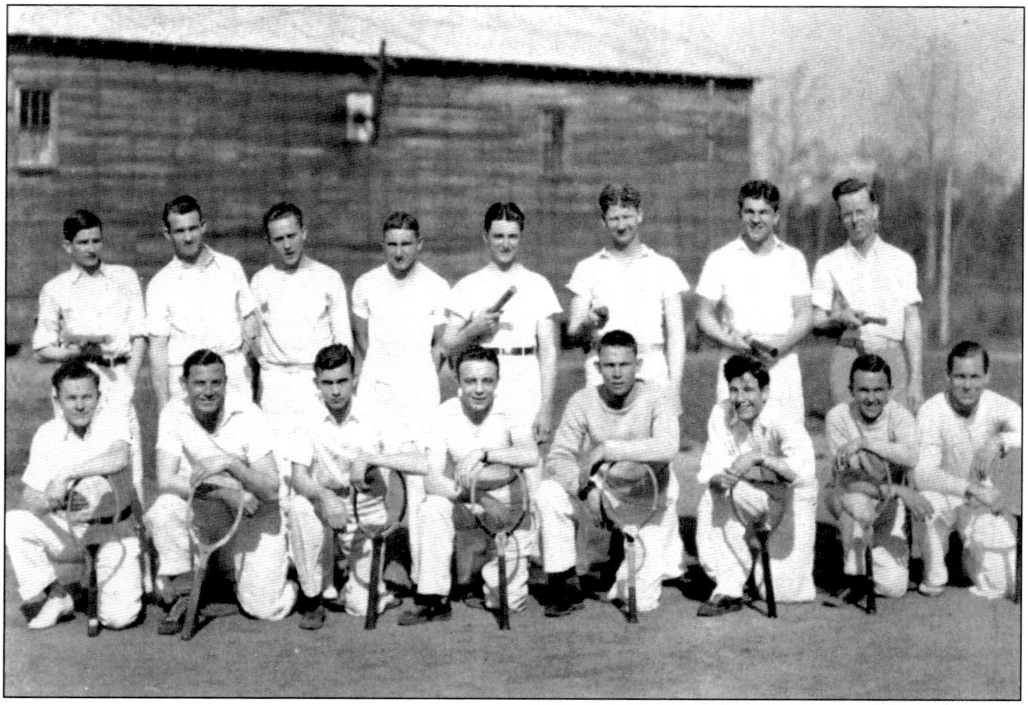

The Boiling Springs College tennis team posed for this *c.* 1936 picture.

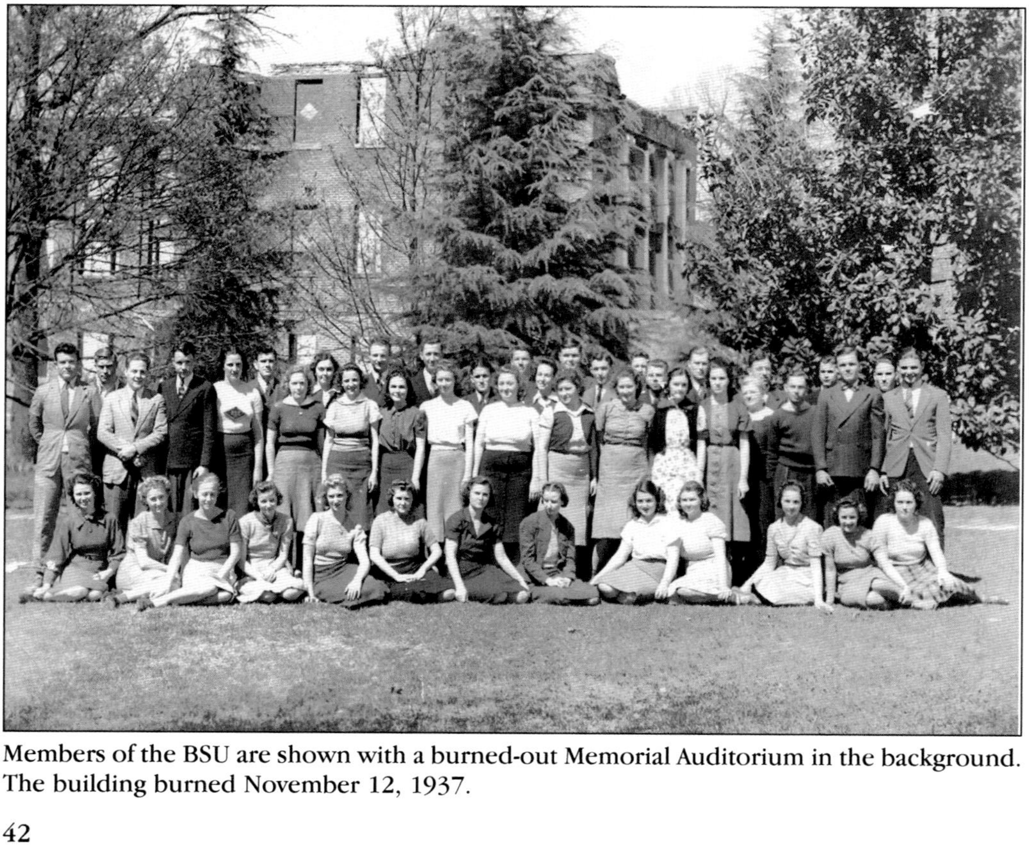

Members of the BSU are shown with a burned-out Memorial Auditorium in the background. The building burned November 12, 1937.

Three

Gardner-Webb College

The Phil Elliott Era of the Junior College: 1943 to 1961

The 1940s would bring new life to the school. It had survived the Great Depression even though there were times it appeared the college would close. It was now a two-year college, with the high school becoming a part of history. Ahead was a war that would seriously deplete the male population on campus.

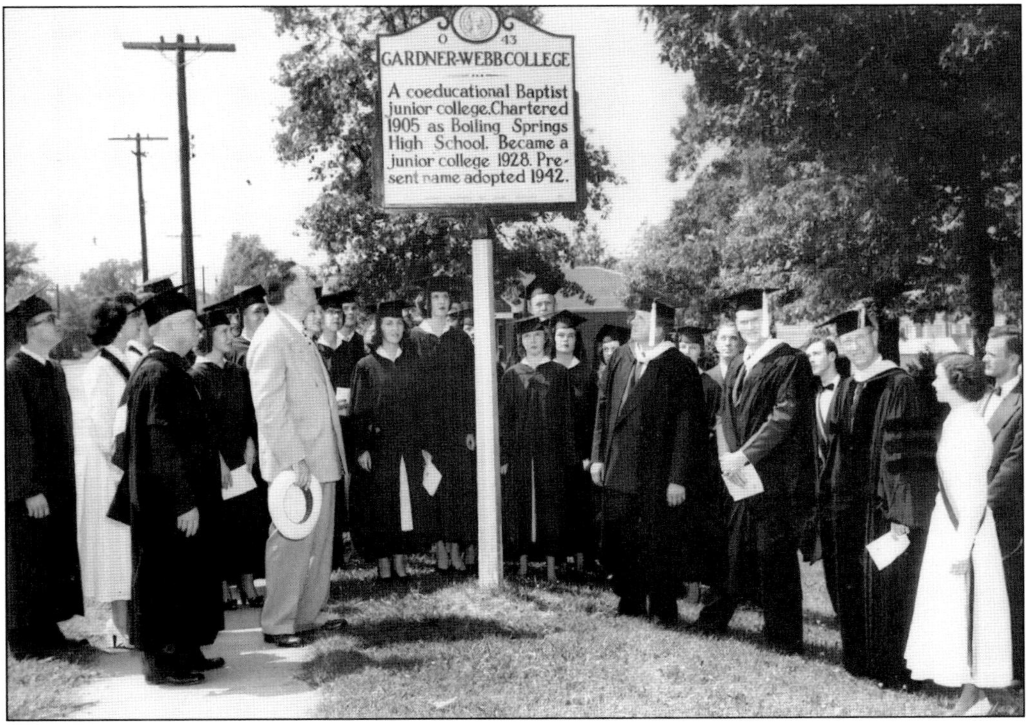

Here, *c.* 1944, graduates look at the new state historical marker showing the name change to Gardner-Webb College (GWC). Dr. Elliott is on the right, and the pastor of First Baptist Church of Shelby, Dr. Zeno Wall (with hat in hand), is one the left. Dr. Wall was one of the many pastors who served as president of the institution in the 1930s.

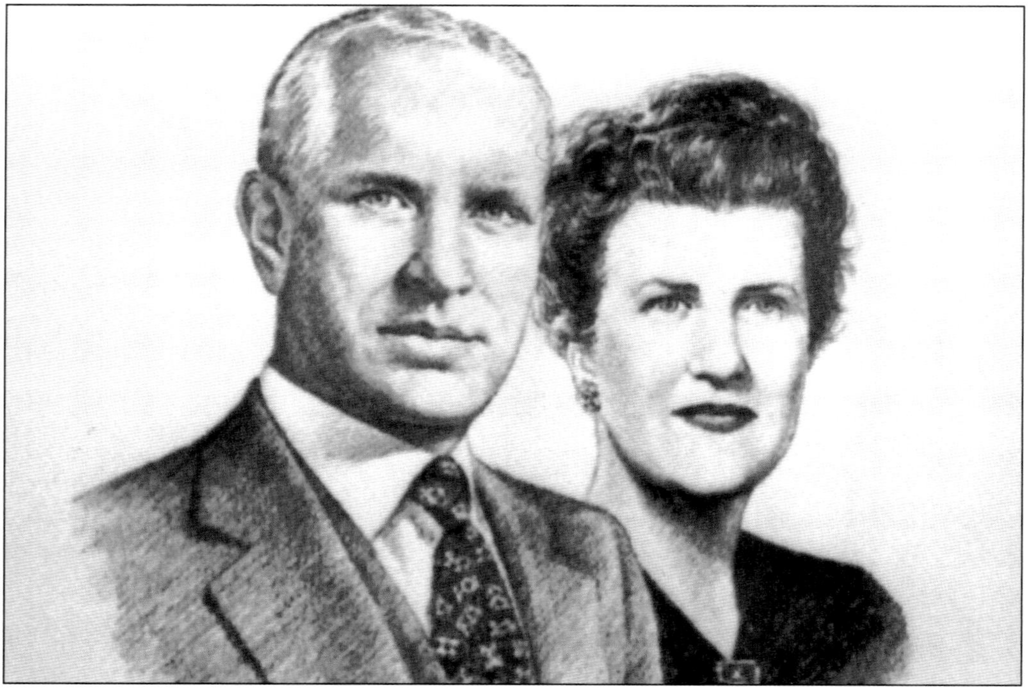

Former North Carolina governor O. Max Gardner of Shelby took an interest in the college, and in 1942, Boiling Springs Junior College became Garner Webb College. Gardner's wife, Fay Webb, was a member of a prominent Shelby family.

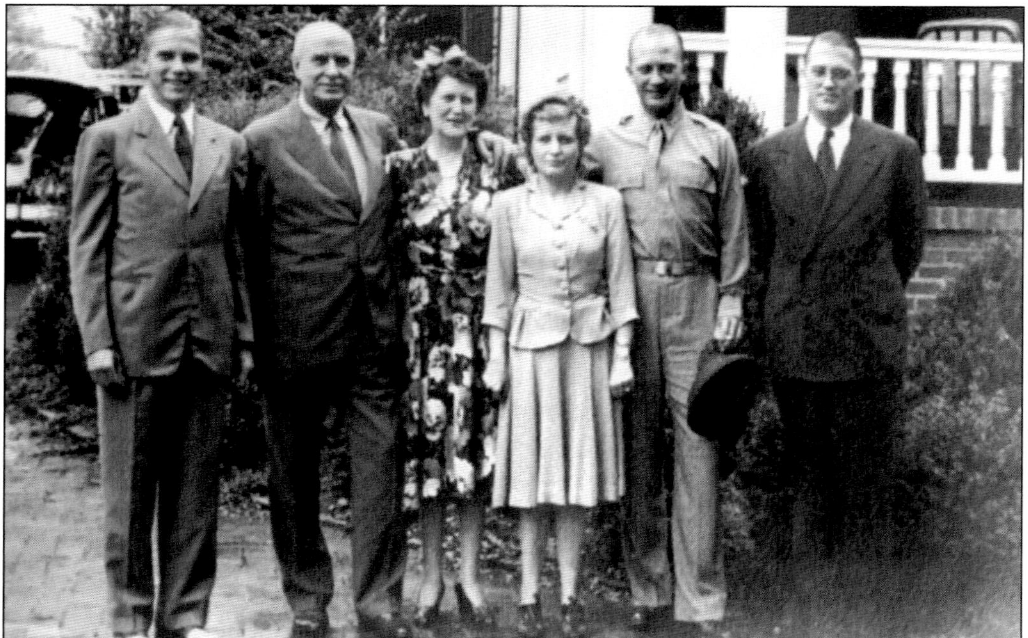

This 1943 photo taken at Webbly—the Gardner home on South Washington Street in Shelby—shows, from left to right, O. Max Jr., Governor and Mrs. Gardner, Margaret Love Gardner Burgess, Ralph Gardner, and James Webb "Decker" Gardner. Three of these six would have buildings on the Gardner-Webb campus named for them.

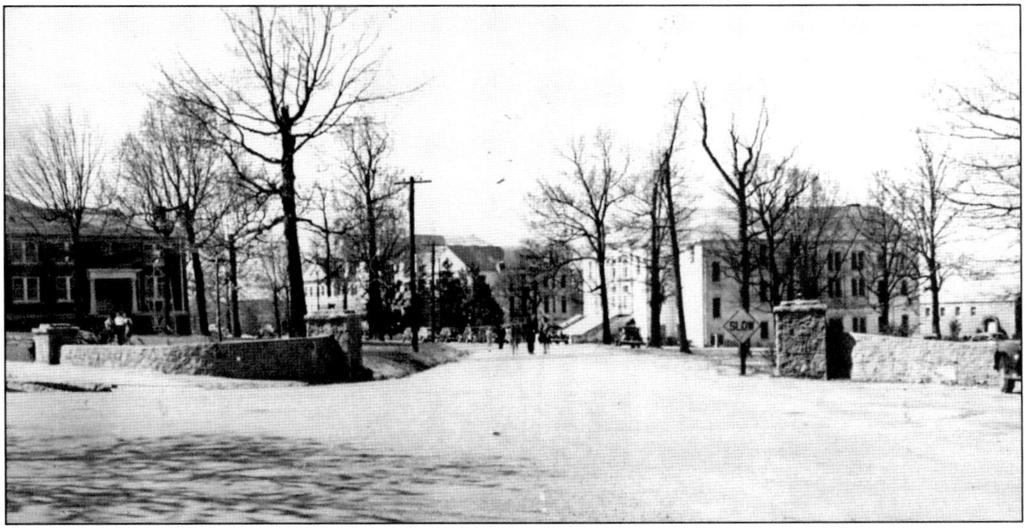

One looking down Quinn Circle in the 1940s would have seen the rebuilt Memorial Building, renamed Hamrick Hall, and the Main Building, by then the Huggins Curtis Building, on the right. The Old Rock Gym can be seen behind Hamrick on the right. Boiling Springs Baptist Church stood where the Dover Chapel is today.

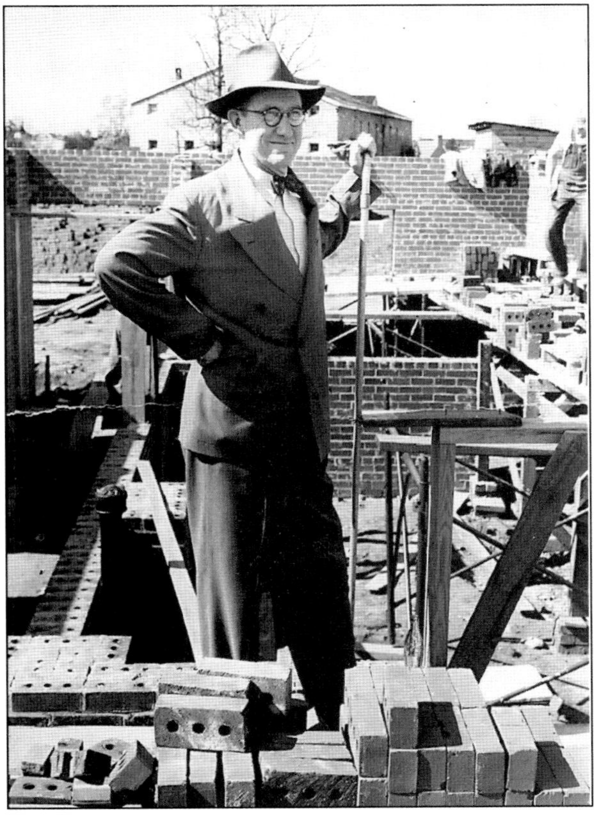

In 1943, Gardner-Webb secured a Western Carolina College English professor named Philip Lovin Elliott to be its fulltime president. Dr. Elliott would lead the college for a record 18 years. This 1949 photo, taken by a young student named John Roberts, shows Dr. Elliott standing in the Decker Dorm construction site. The Old Rock Gym is seen behind the tree.

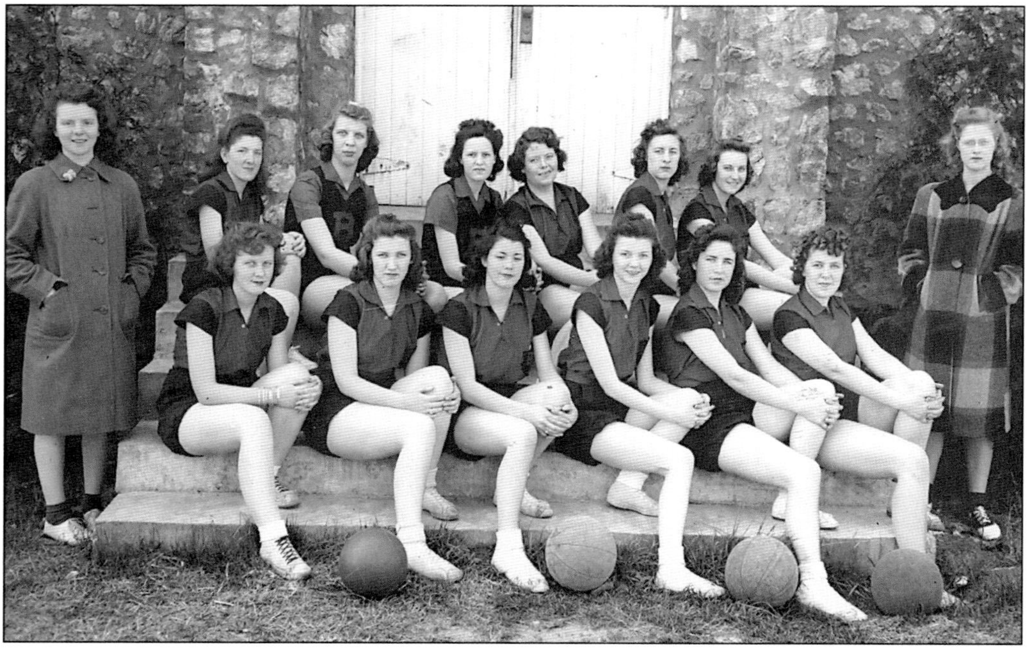

As alumni look at photos of yesteryear, we hope it will give some a chance to find friends or even oneself. This is the 1942 women's basketball team posing on the steps of the Old Rock Gym. Many today do not realize GWU's women's basketball tradition went back this far.

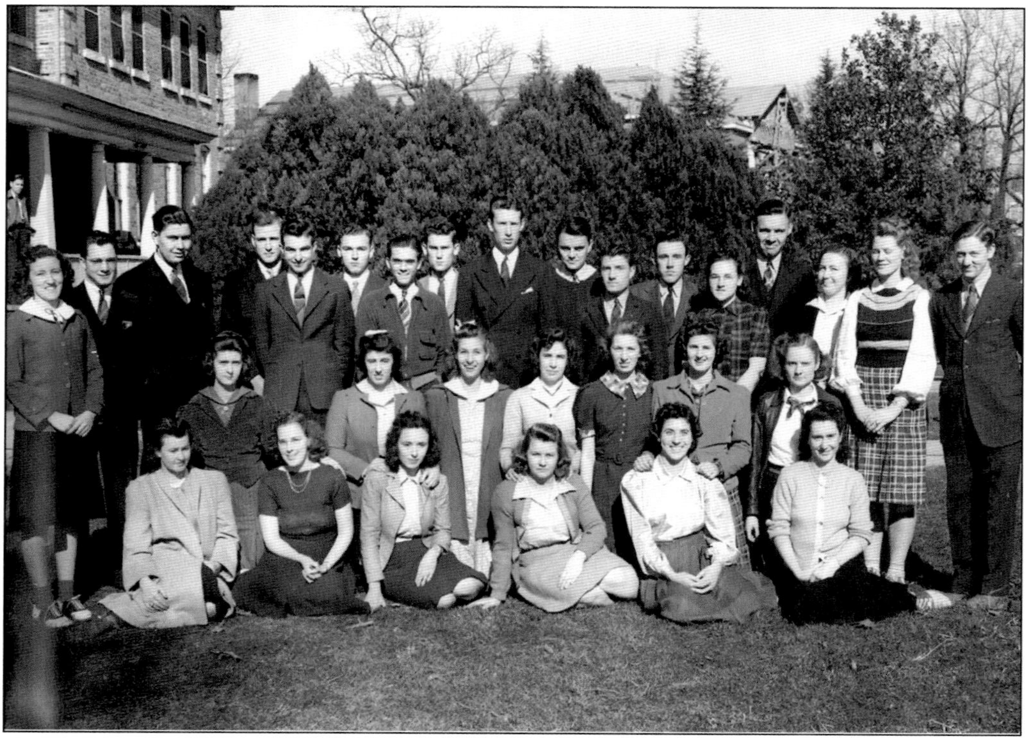

Alumni of the 1940s get another chance to find friends in this photo. This may be a BSU group. Huggins Curtis is on the left, and the Hamrick Building is behind the trees.

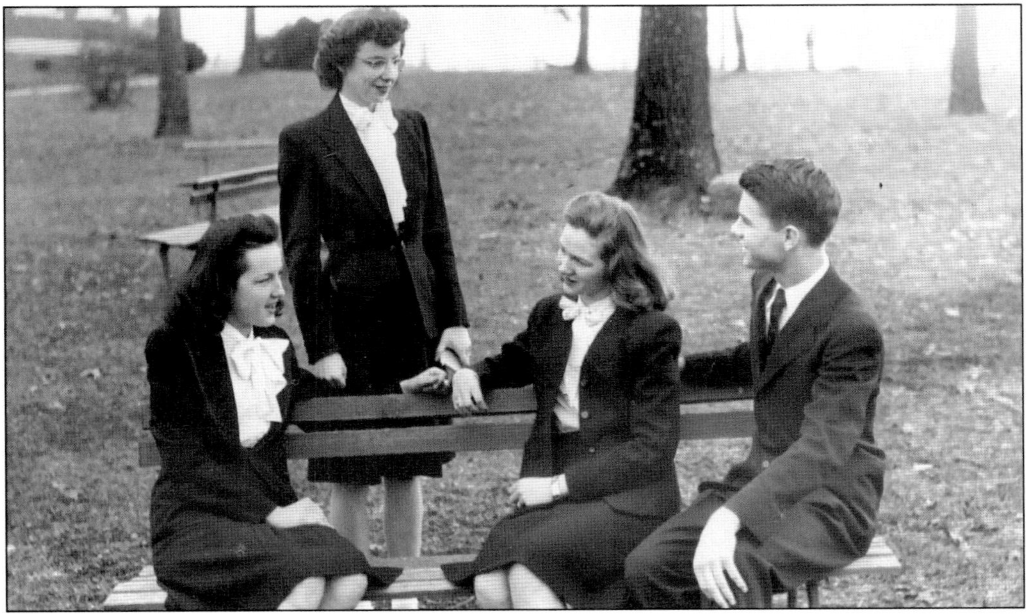

This mid-1940s photo of student government officers was characteristic of World War II days when men were in the minority. Pictured from left to right are Cothenia Jones, Ruth Derry, Eunice Borders, and Clyde McAllister. Ms. Jones met a young student from Boiling Springs named Lansford Jolley. Lansford attended GWC from 1944 to 1945 and then went into service. He claims that the Japanese surrendered the day he graduated from boot camp. He returned after the war and graduated. He married Cothenia, and they still live in Boiling Springs.

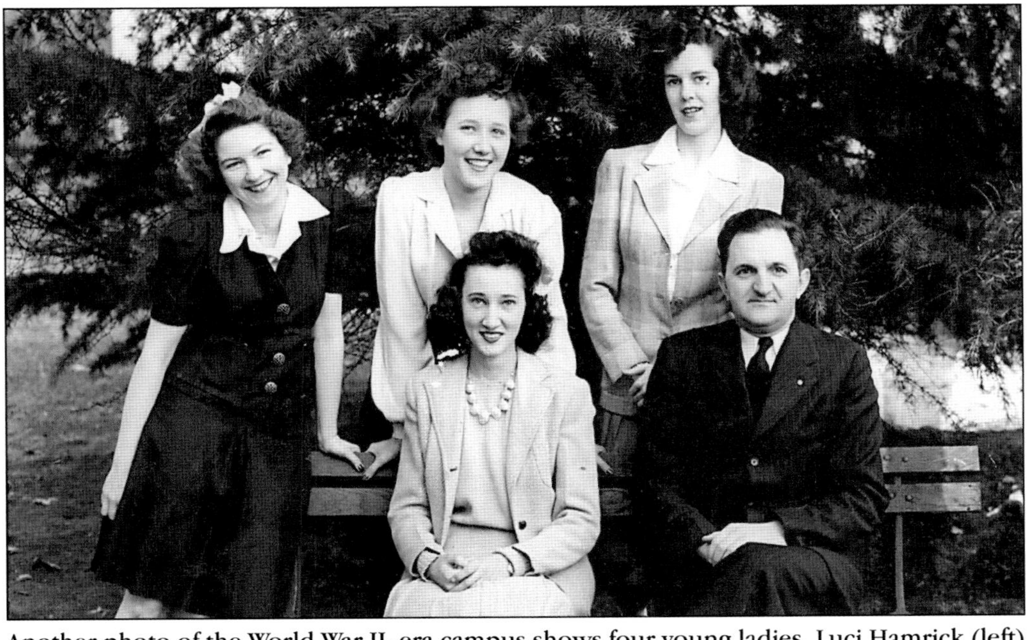

Another photo of the World War II–era campus shows four young ladies. Luci Hamrick (left) is one of those alumni who remain close to the school. Luci and her husband, Weldon Hamrick, have retired in Gastonia, North Carolina, and Luci is active in church and on the GWU Alumni Board.

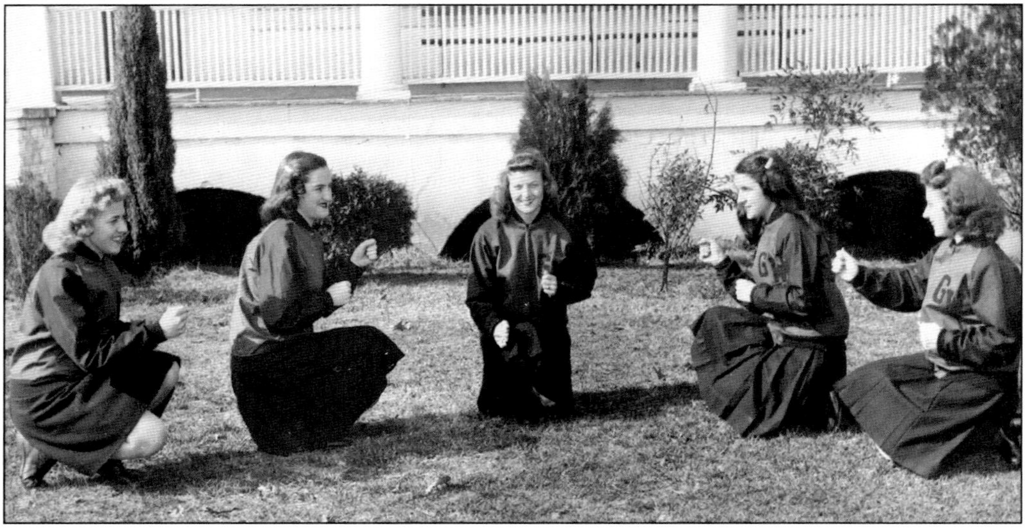

These five young women were cheerleaders during the 1945–1946 school year. Notice the dress style from 60 years ago.

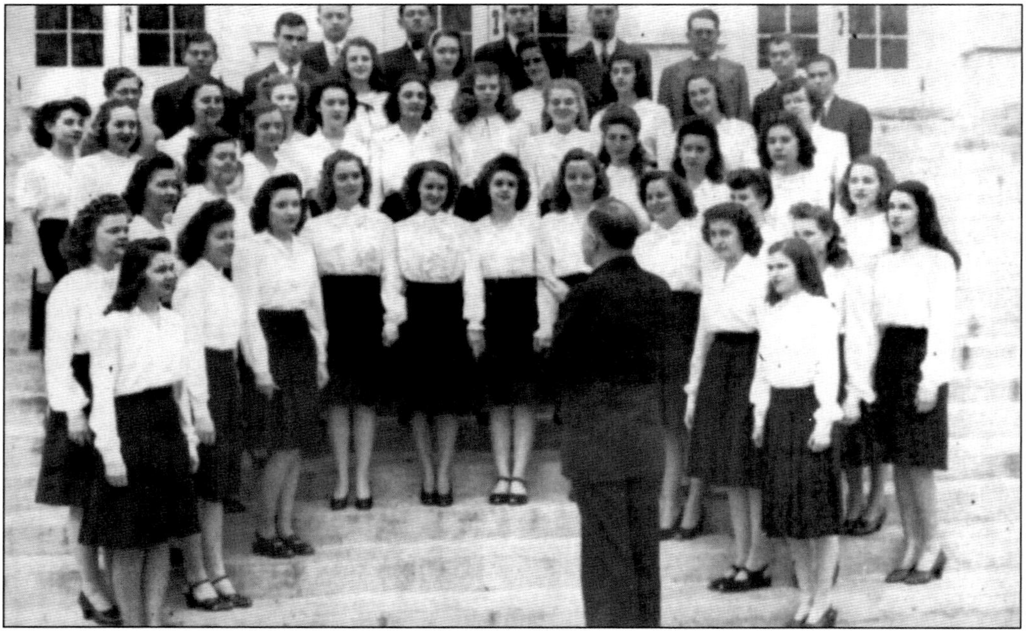

The 1946–1947 GWC choir poses on the steps of Hamrick. The leader was Dr. Stephen Morrisett, who was a multi-talented GWC faculty member. Dr. Morrisett led choirs, played the organ, taught religion, and served as interim pastor in local churches. By the time his vision forced his retirement in 1959, he had memorized large portions of the Bible.

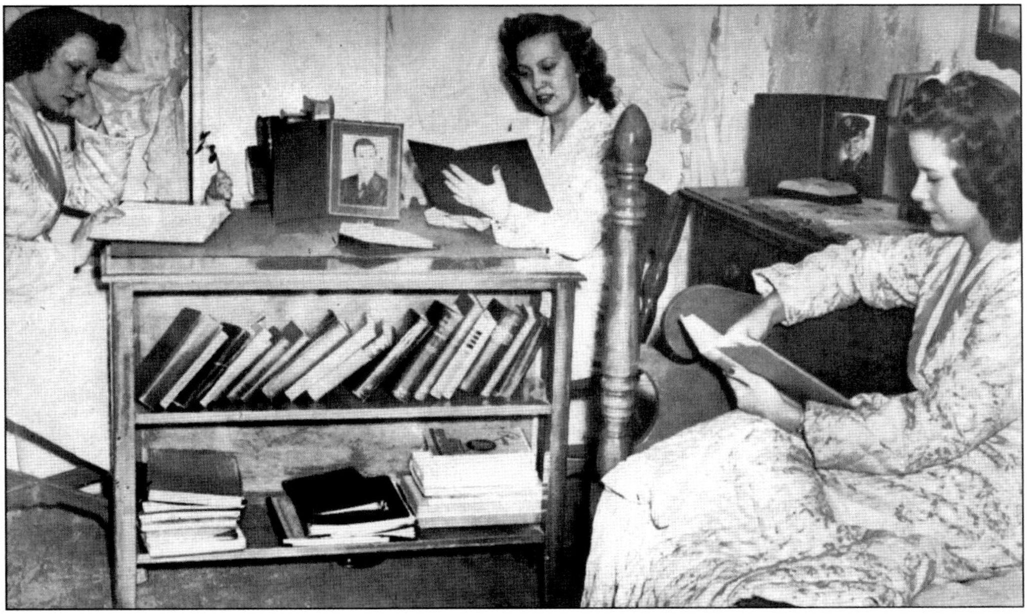

College students of today expect television, air-conditioning, telephones, computers, and even apartments. The girls in 1946 had to be satisfied with beds, desks, and minimal furniture. Even then the guys were in the dorm, but only in pictures.

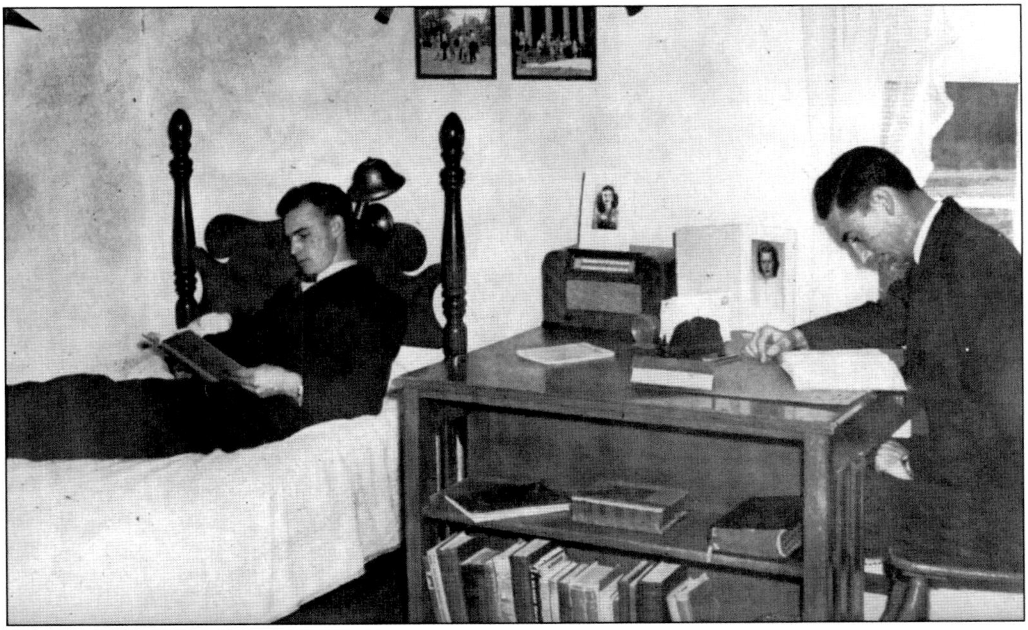

The boys of 1946 had to endure the same sparse rooms. They do have pictures of two young women watching over their studies.

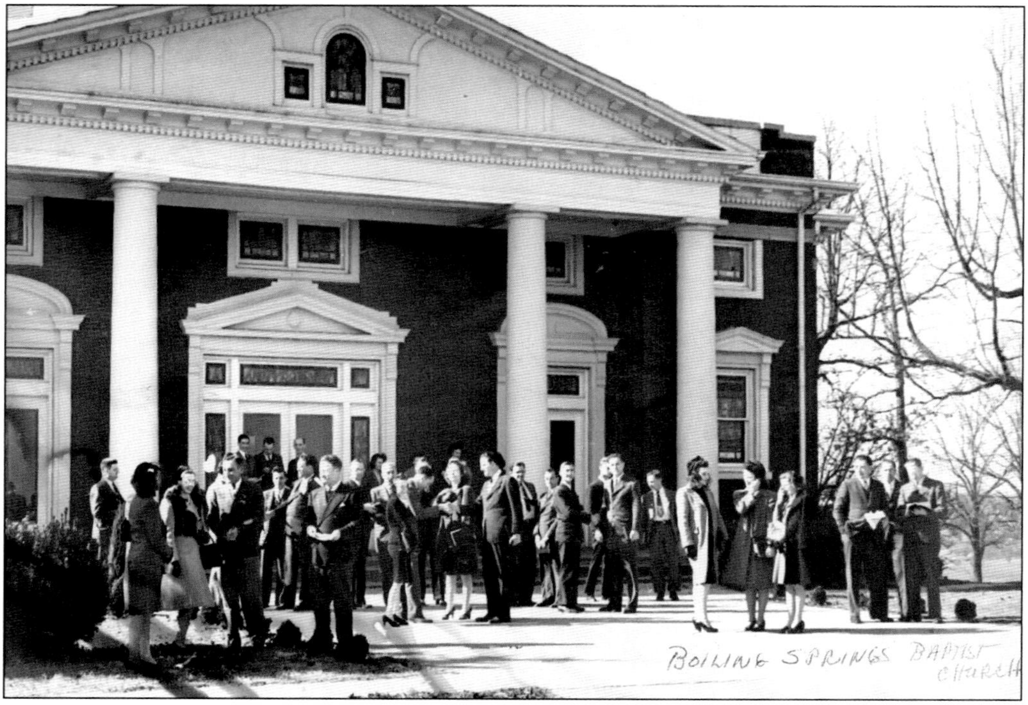

Boiling Springs Baptist Church was located on South Main Street, just off campus, for decades. It was virtually a part of the campus. Students attended church there regularly, and following the practice of that day, many joined the local church while they were in school. This appears to be a typical scene after the Sunday morning worship service during the winter of 1946–1947.

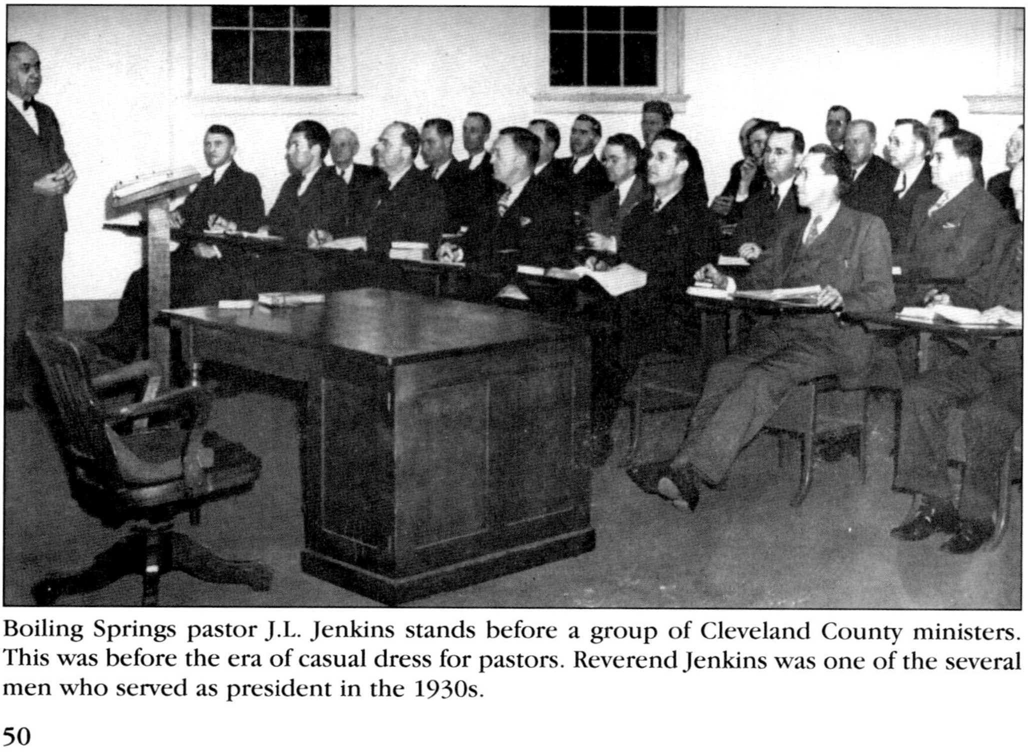

Boiling Springs pastor J.L. Jenkins stands before a group of Cleveland County ministers. This was before the era of casual dress for pastors. Reverend Jenkins was one of the several men who served as president in the 1930s.

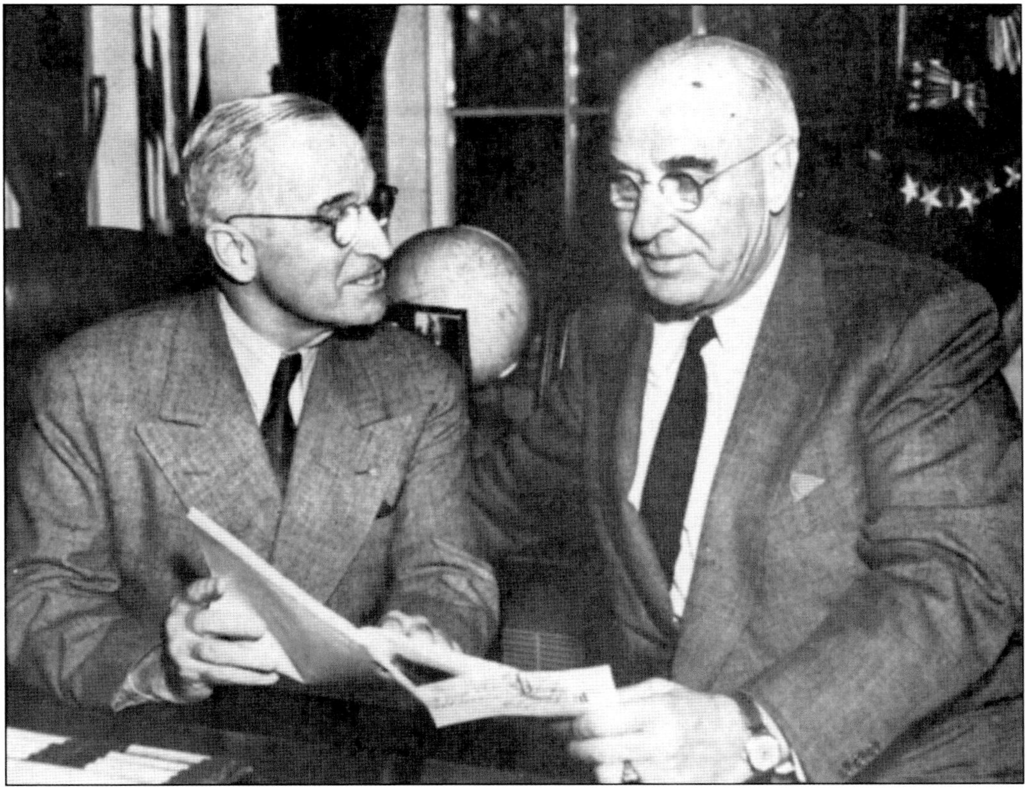

Governor Gardner left Raleigh in 1933. He practiced law in Washington, became a multi-millionaire industrialist, and held appointments from President Franklin Roosevelt as undersecretary of the treasury and as a member of the War Mobilization Board. In 1946, President Harry S Truman appointed him United States ambassador to the Court of St. James (England). Here, the governor chats with President Truman in late 1946.

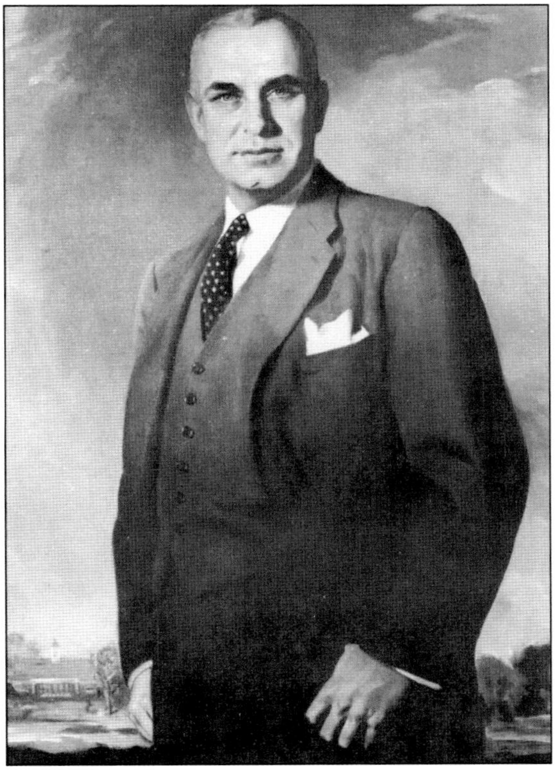

In February 1947, while in New York preparing for the voyage to England, Governor Gardner suffered a heart attack and died. Shelby's First Baptist Church was packed and overflowing as Shelby's number-one citizen and GWC's leading benefactor was mourned.

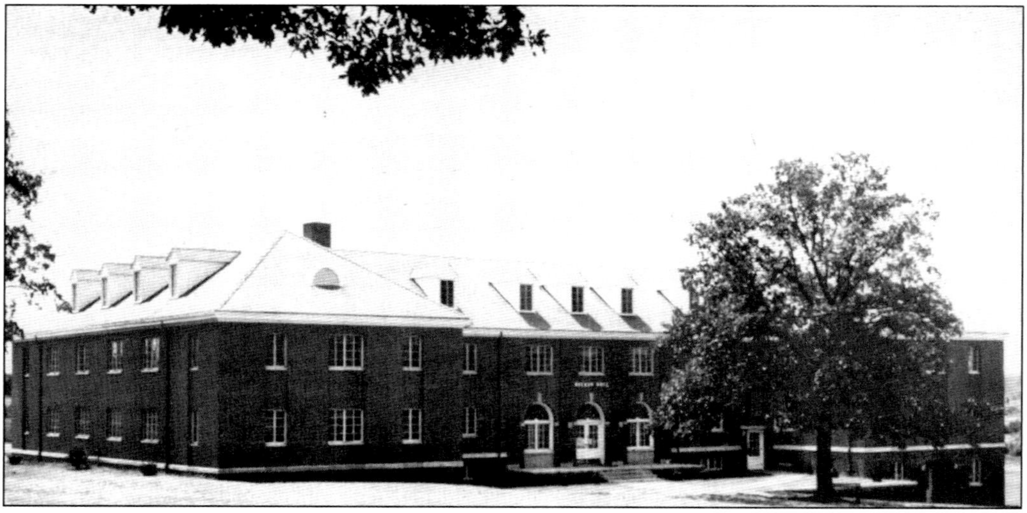

In 1949, Decker Hall for men opened as the "new dorm." James Webb Gardner, known as Decker, had died, and the dorm still stands as a memorial to him. Air conditioning was installed in 1986. The dorm houses young women today.

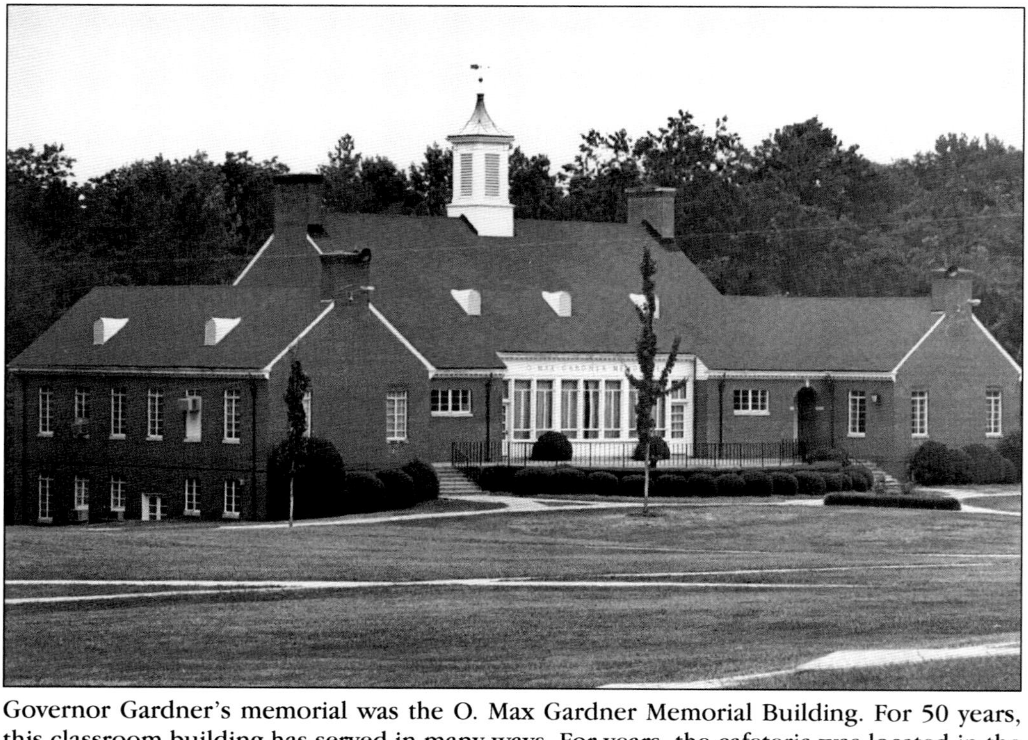

Governor Gardner's memorial was the O. Max Gardner Memorial Building. For 50 years, this classroom building has served in many ways. For years, the cafeteria was located in the basement. Classrooms held classes in English, psychology, French, and speech. Graduates of the 1980s had receptions here. Today it houses the GWU fine arts department.

Students can be seen going through the line in the O. Max Gardner (OMG) cafeteria in the 1950s. Note that food choices were fewer in those days.

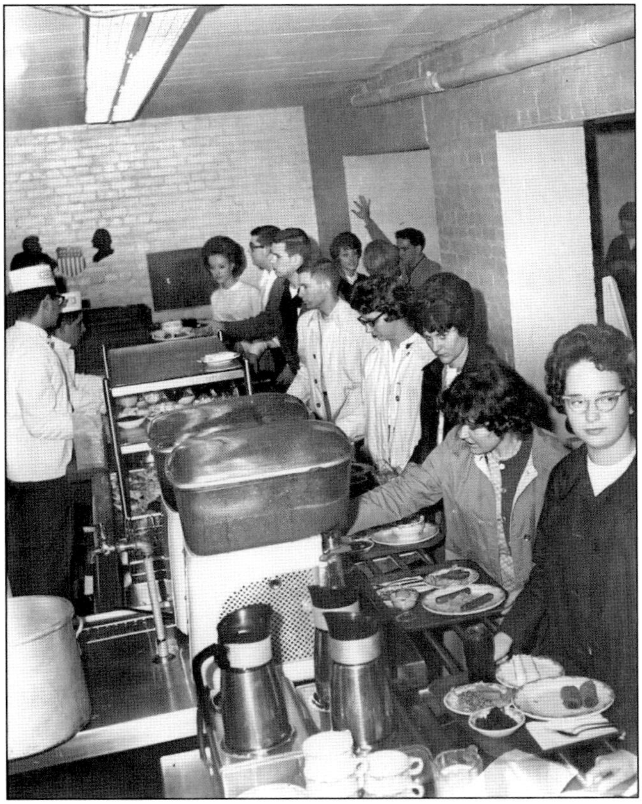

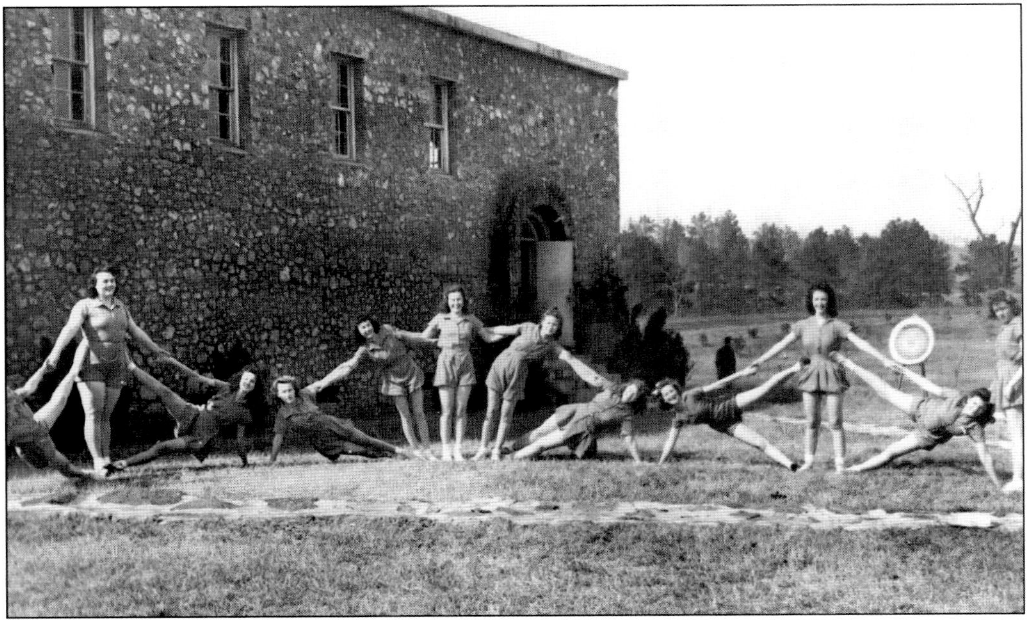

This is not as easy as it looks. GWC women put on an acrobatics display on the lawn outside of the Old Rock Gym.

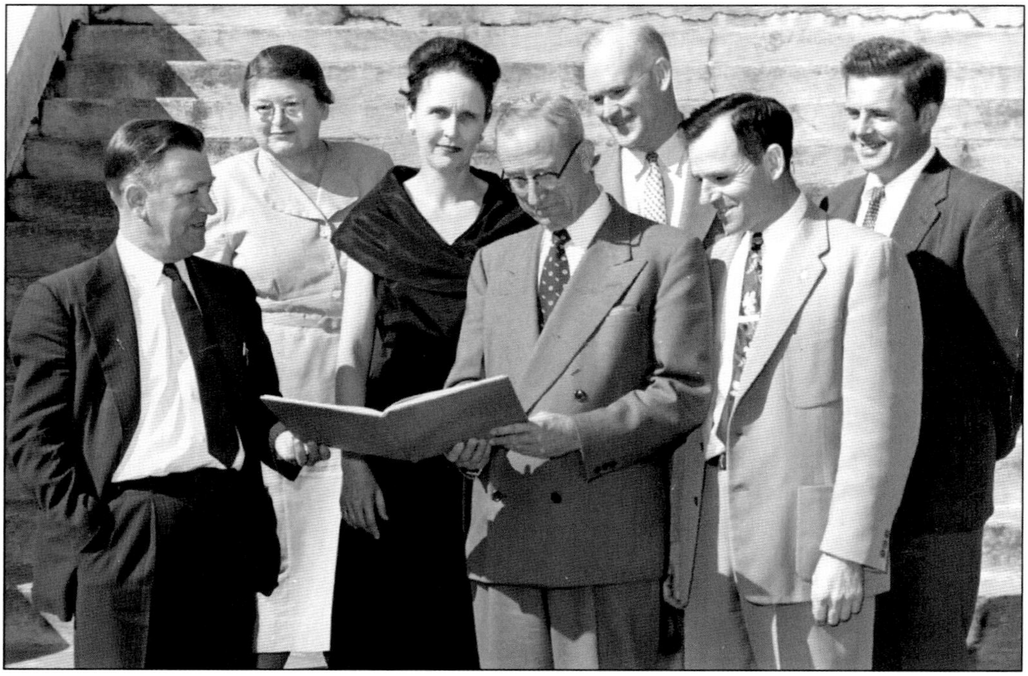

There are pictures of John Roberts elsewhere in this book, but he was always on the other end of the camera. He took this 1956 photo of Dr. Elliott and six faculty members. Graduates of the 1950s should remember the following, pictured here from left to right: Paul Stacy (biology), Elma Pollack (Spanish), Abbie Miller (music), Dr. Elliott, J.O. Terrell (history and dean), Hubert Dixon (math) and J.Y. Hamrick (English).

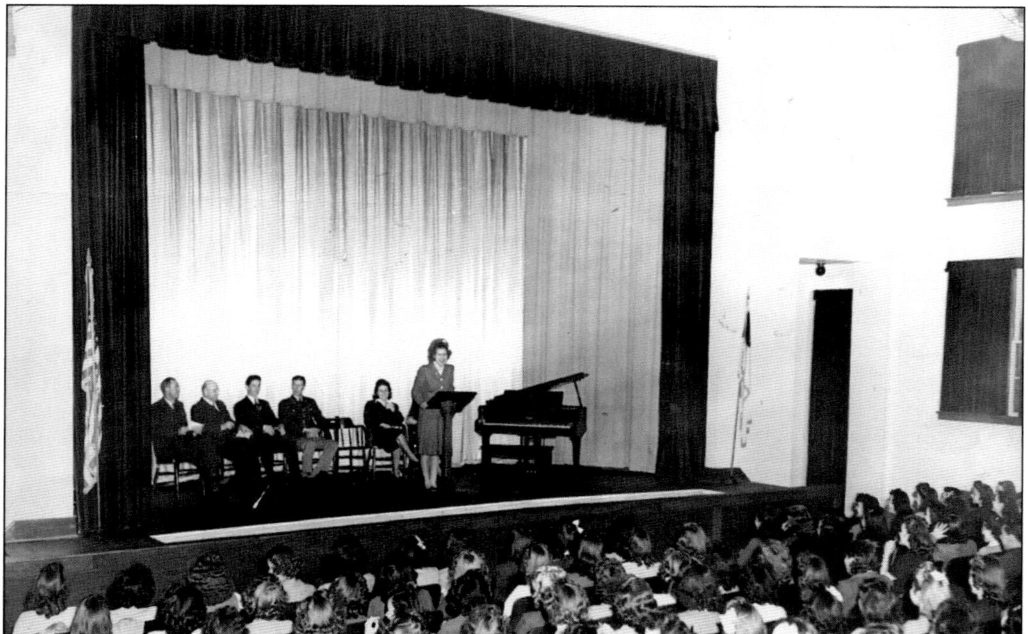

Here it is—chapel. In the 1950s, students went three days a week to sit in assigned seats in Hamrick Auditorium. Most can remember Dorothy Hamrick Edwards walking the aisles next to the walls, carefully checking to be sure students were present.

This campus landmark is over 60 years old and has been moved several times. For years, all graduates marched through the arch on the way to the ceremony. Alumni should take time to read the dedication on the back of the arch. It states, "Erected by the Alumni in memory of Prof. J.D. Huggins. He was the first principal of this institution as a high school and the first dean of the college. His radiant character and his sacrificial life of service for 25 years were an inspiration to thousands of boys and girls. He was the embodiment of greatness without pretense."

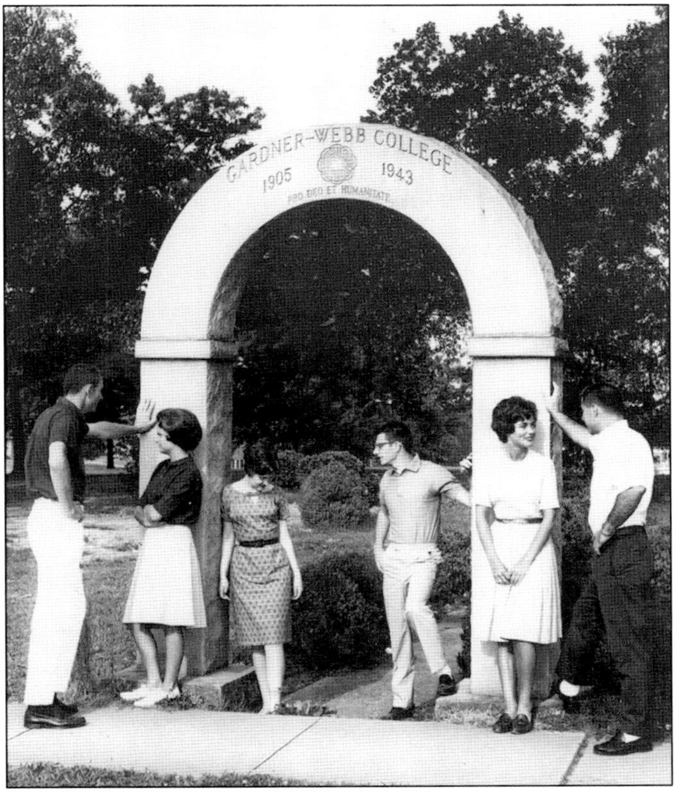

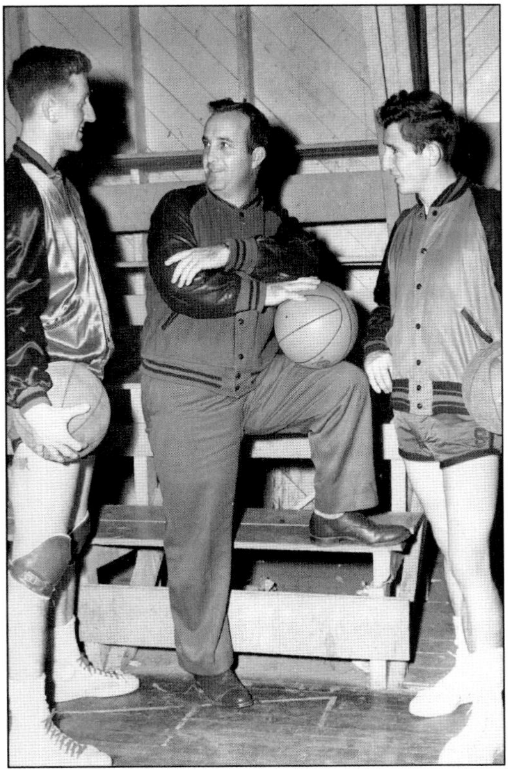

Some 1950s athletes will remember Coach Wayne Bradburn, who coached football and basketball. Can you identify the players?

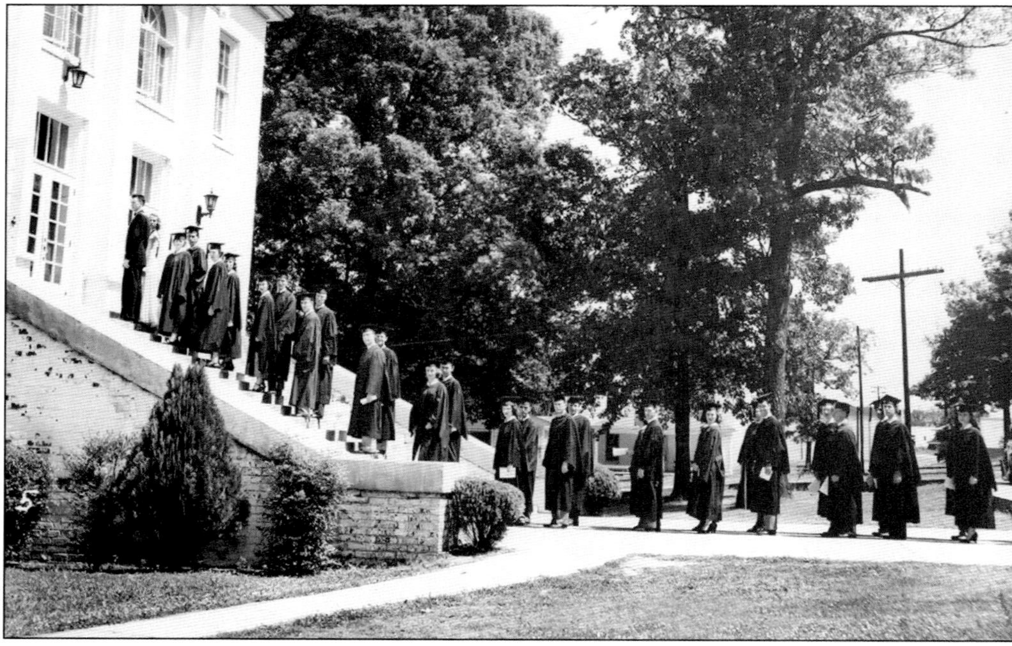

For years, graduation was held in Hamrick Auditorium. This cover photo shows the 1950 lineup. For those who think modern graduations are work, just try a June graduation in a non-air-conditioned Hamrick with a speaker who enlightened the class of 1961 for an hour.

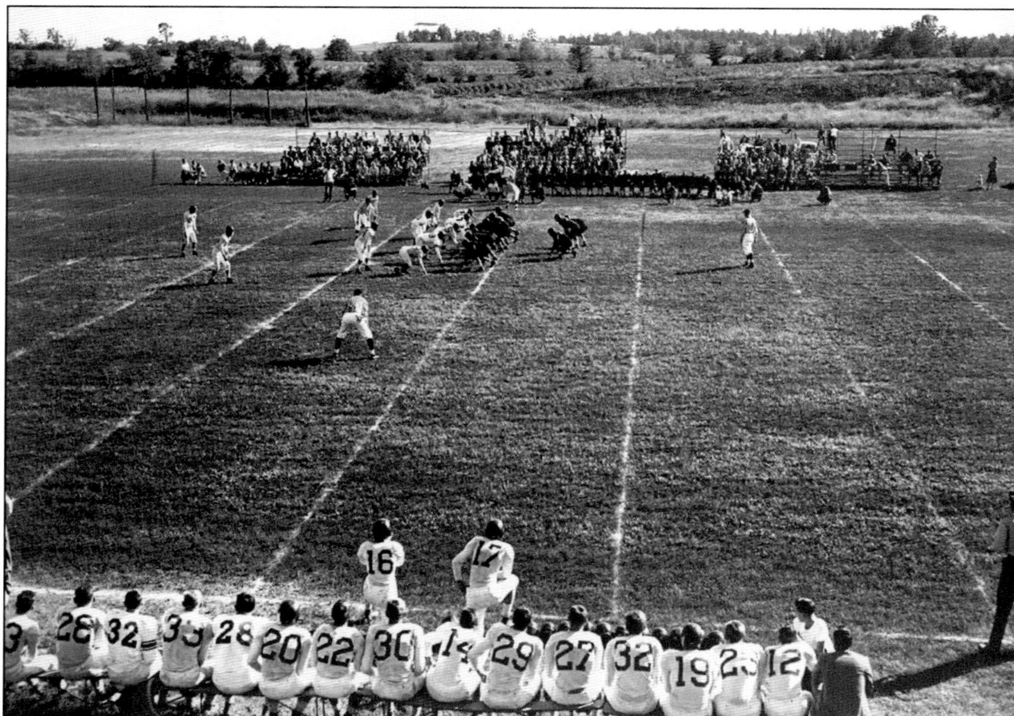

If you attended Gardner-Webb in the last 40 years, football meant Spangler Stadium. However, in the 1950s, football was played on the field where Lutz-Yelton Convocation Center (LYCC) now stands. Note the seating for the visitors.

Since President Cantrell had had the buildings painted white in the 1930s, students attended classes in the white Hamrick Building. This 1955 photo shows students changing classes.

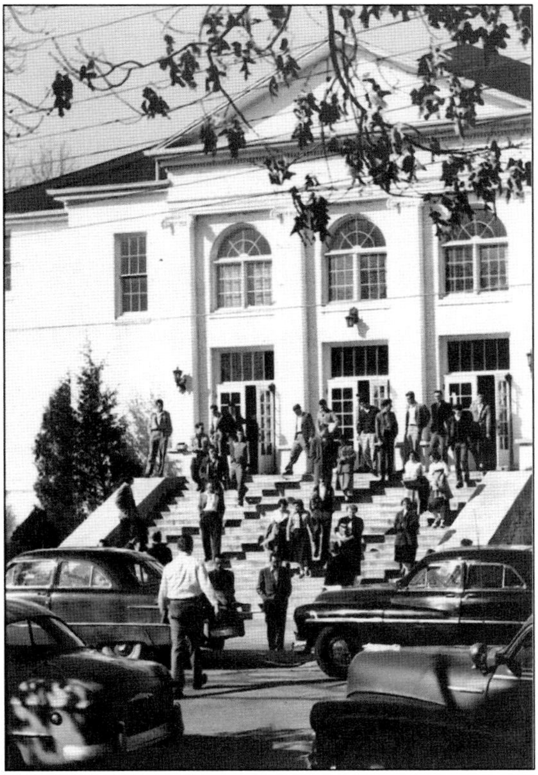

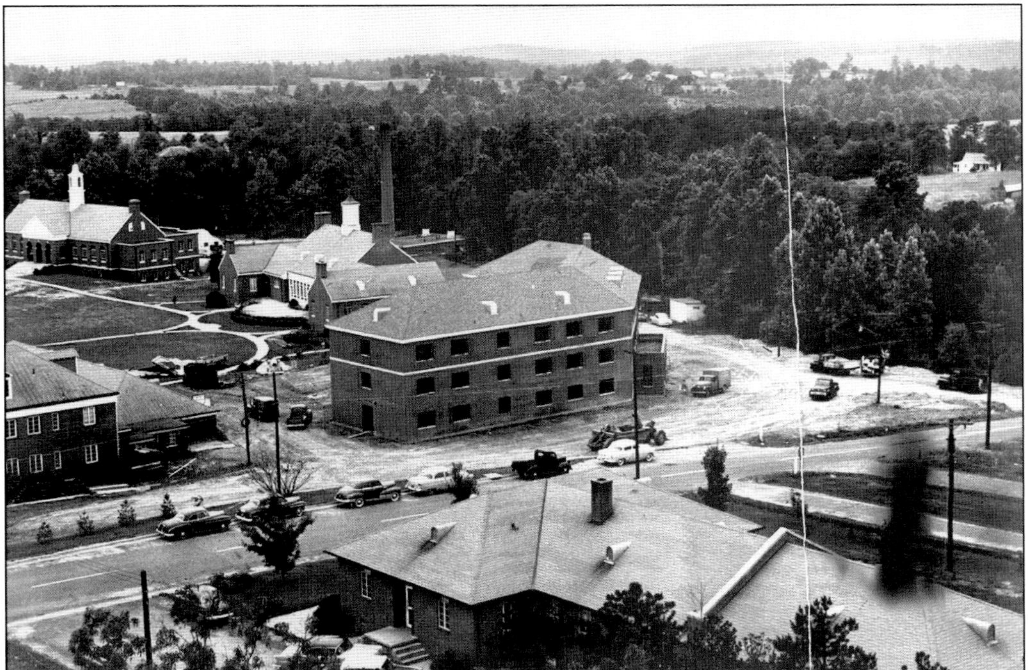

By the mid-1950s, the campus was taking on its modern look. In 1956, a new girls' dormitory, named in honor of Shelby businesswoman Mae Cline Stroup and her late husband, Rush, was under construction. The O. Max Gardner Memorial and John R. Dover Library are seen.

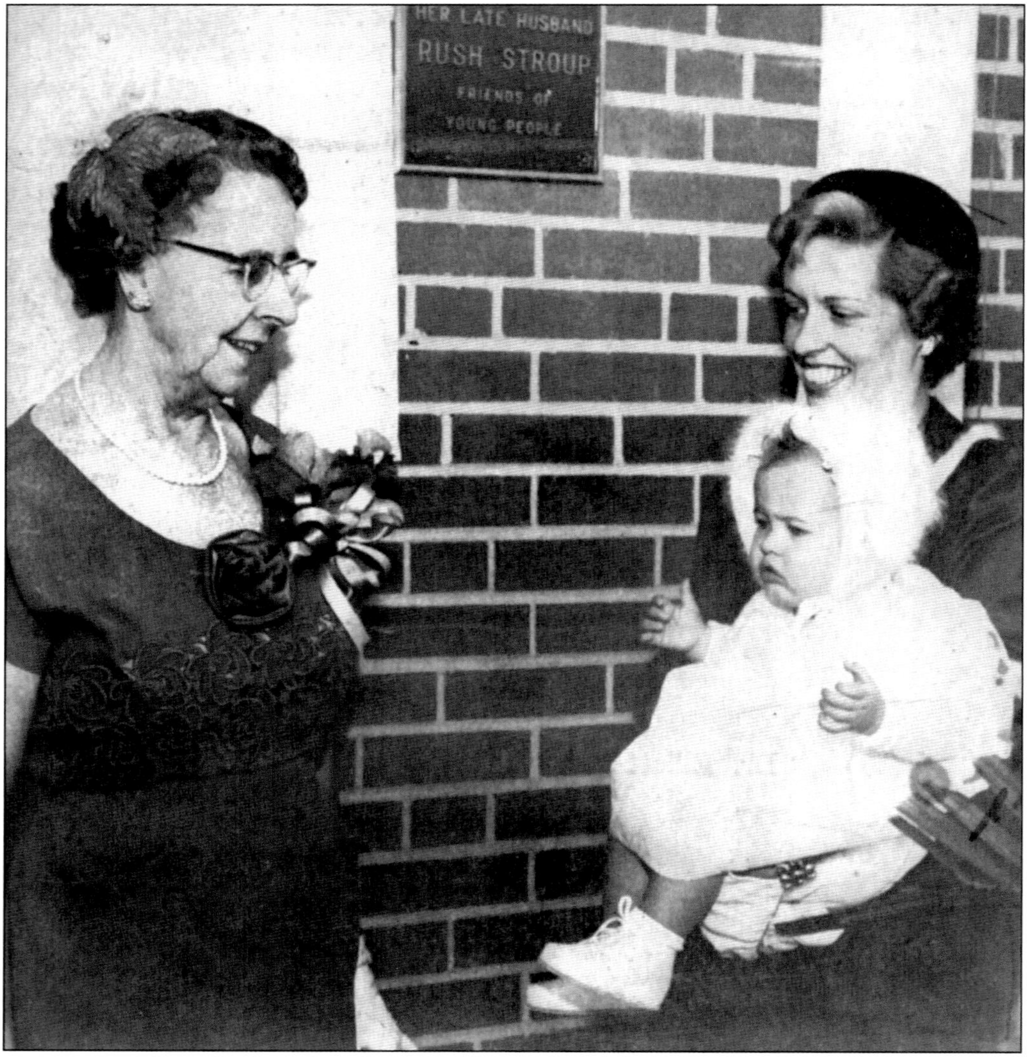

This issue of the *GWC Quarterly* shows Mrs. Rush Stroup in front of Stroup Dormitory with young Sally Hamrick. Sally's mother is Sara Ellen Honeycutt Hamrick, who is Mrs. Stroup's niece. Sara Ellen's husband, Julian, served for a time as Gardner-Webb's business manager. In 1960, Mrs. Stroup would become the first woman elected as chair of a North Carolina Baptist college board of trustees.

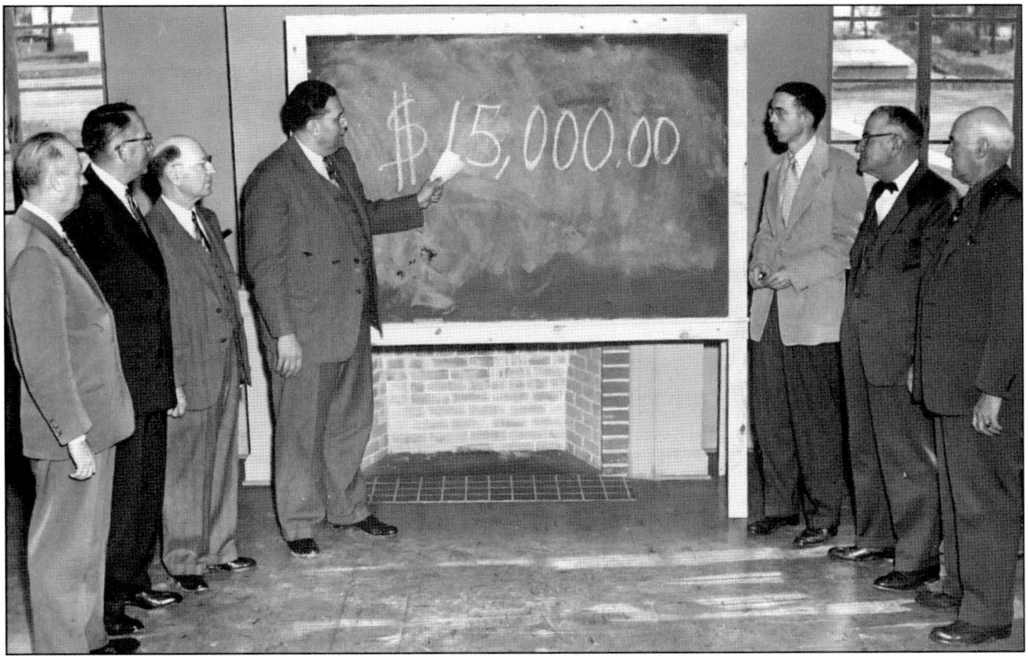

Fund-raising was needed in the 1950s. Goals were lower, however. Baptist leader and then-GWC staff member Ben Fisher speaks to local businessmen including Carlos Young (right of the board) and C. Rush Hamrick Sr. (behind Dr. Fisher). The location was the south end of the then-Dover Library—now Dr. Joyce Brown's office.

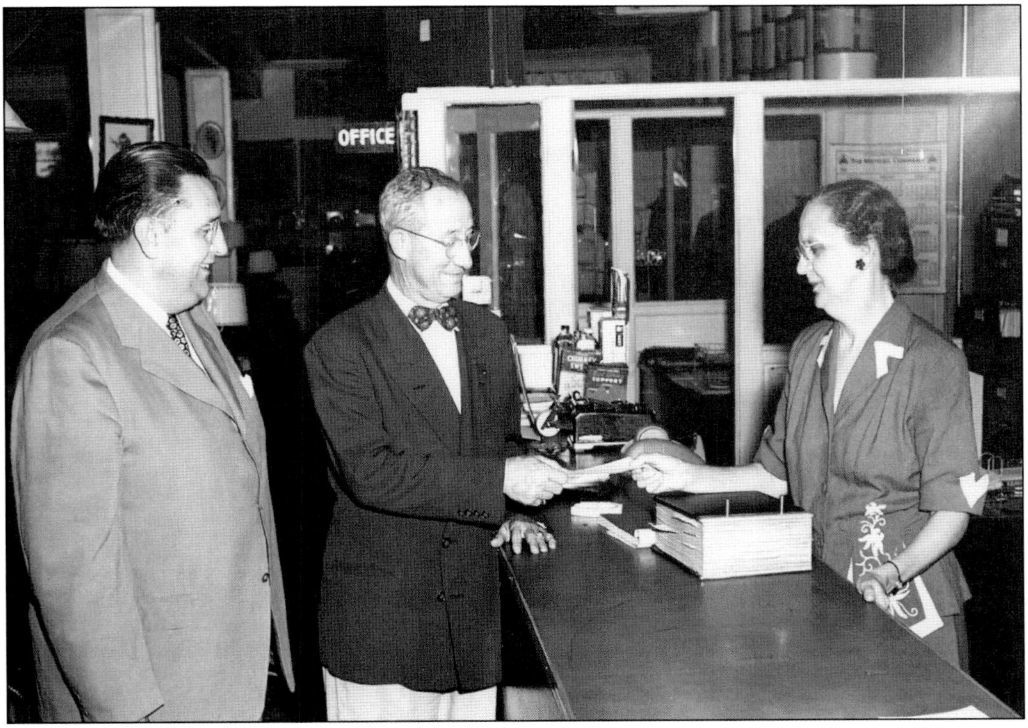

Ben Fisher, Phil Elliott, and Abbie Miller are seen on the main floor of Hamrick. Before Webb Hall was built, the president's office was in the Hamrick Building.

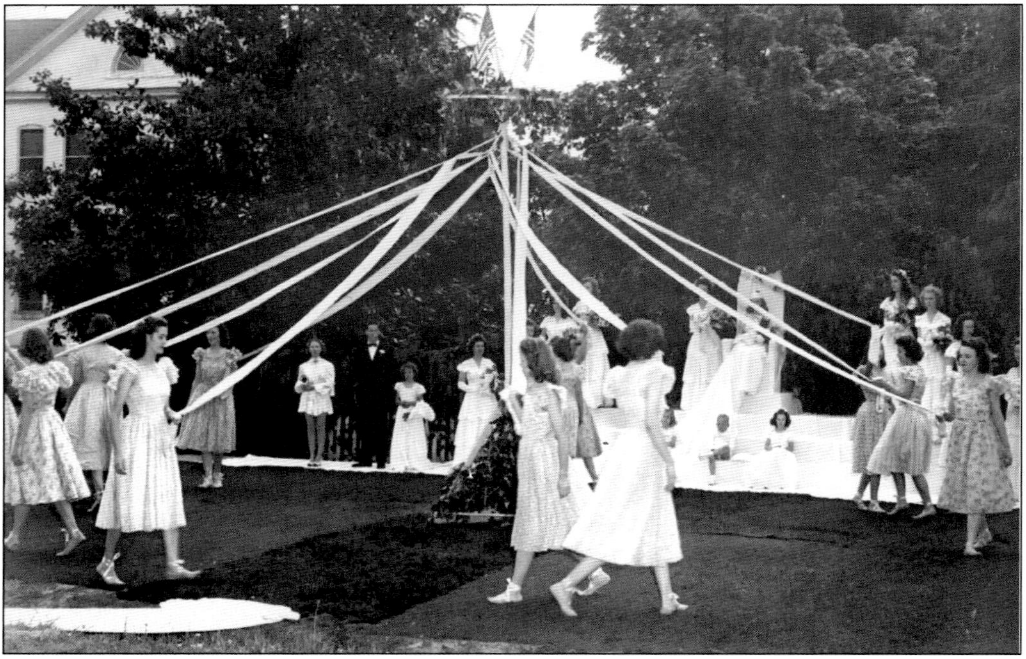

In the post–World War II era, students looked forward to the annual May Day events. This social event, which was so significant a half-century ago, has been lost in time.

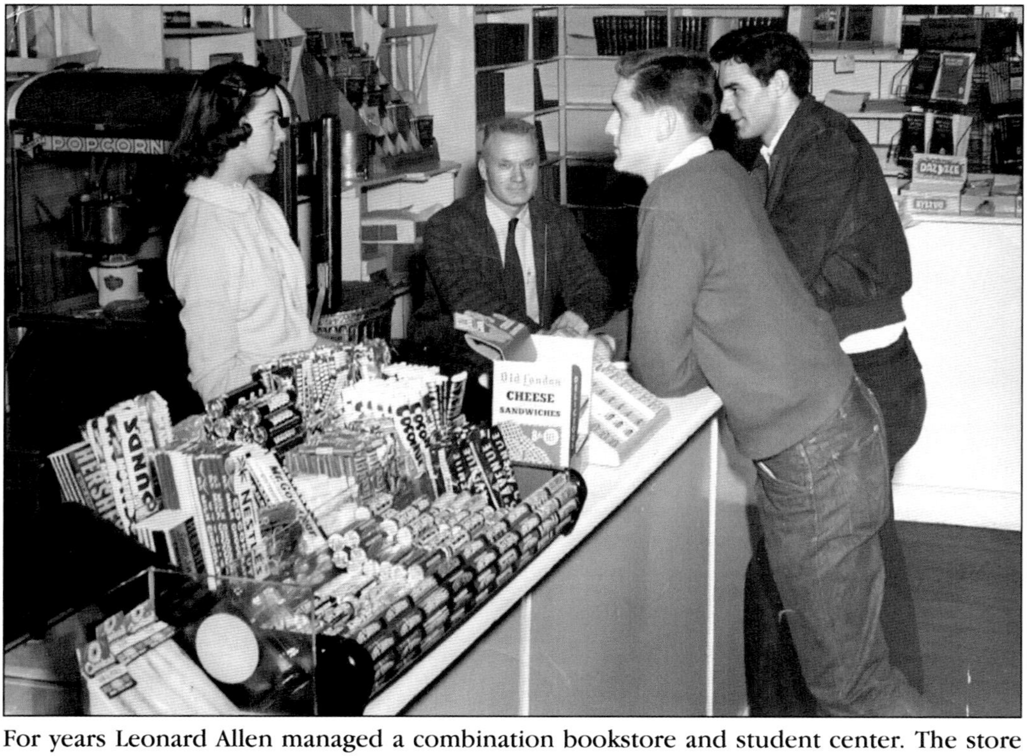

For years Leonard Allen managed a combination bookstore and student center. The store can be seen on the next page. The current GWU bookstore is named in honor of Mr. Allen. At the lower left, note three sandwiches made by the Cleveland Sandwich Company. Jim Beason, who owned the Snack Shop, also managed the local Cleveland Sandwich Company.

In the late 1950s, if one looked from the front of Hamrick to the north, the small building was the bookstore and student center. Beyond this the men's dormitory, the Barn, can be seen. The Barn survived until 1960.

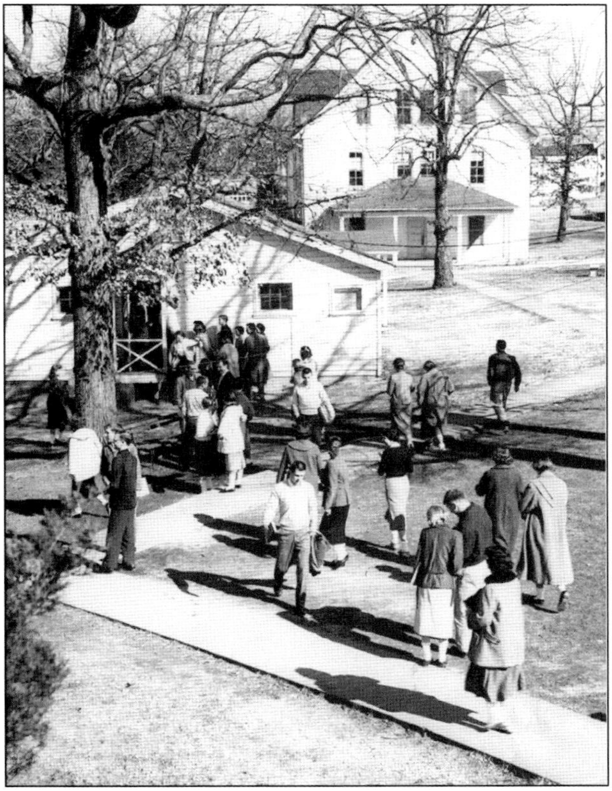

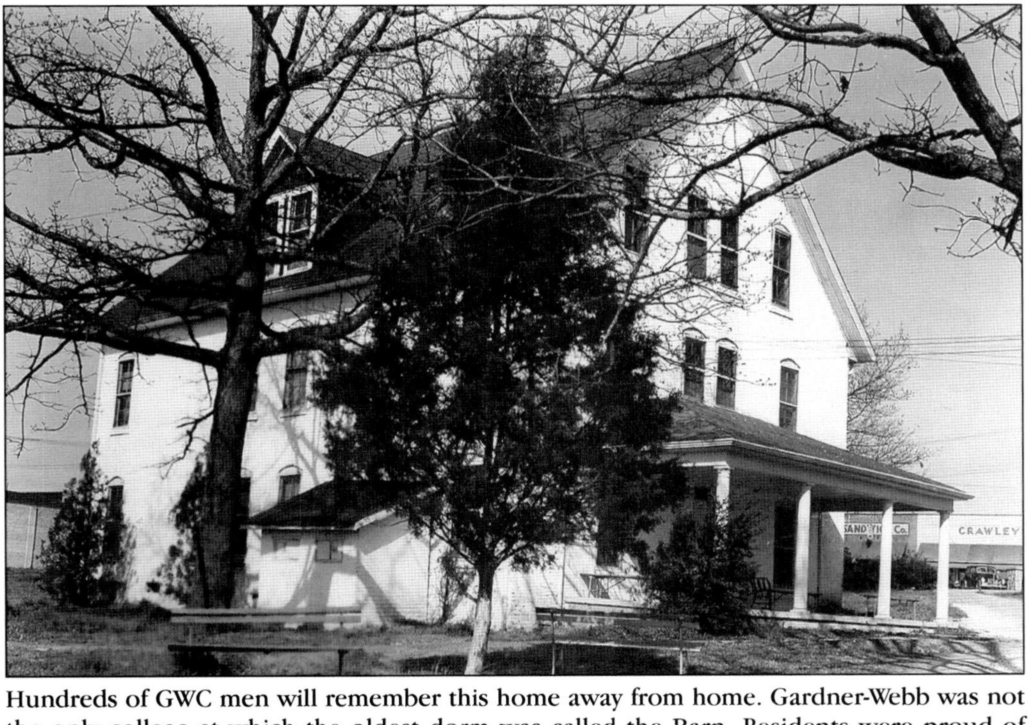

Hundreds of GWC men will remember this home away from home. Gardner-Webb was not the only college at which the oldest dorm was called the Barn. Residents were proud of their home in this building, even if it carried a derogatory name.

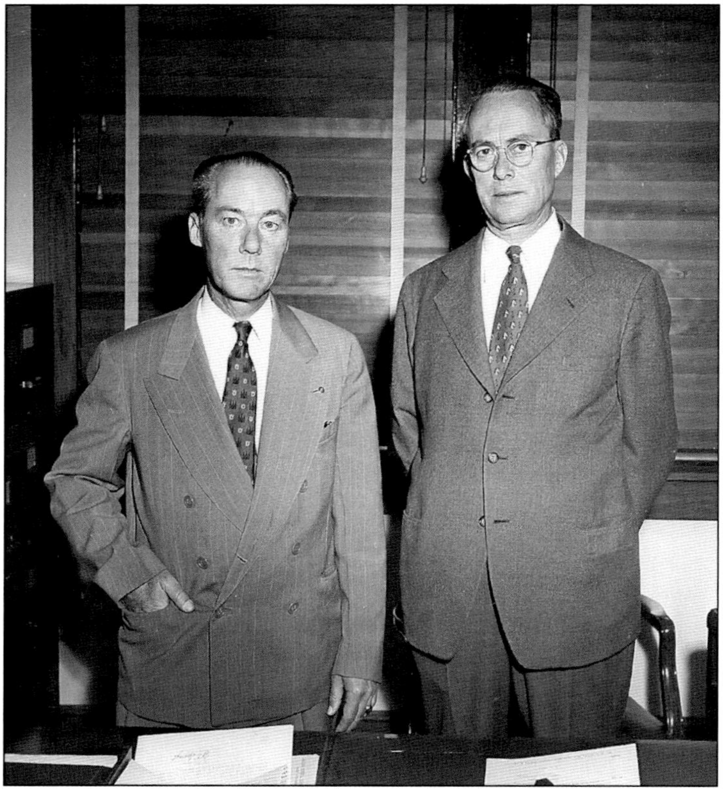

Another family that supported GWC and left its mark across the campus was the Dover family. Cleveland County textile leaders Charles I. Dover (left) and John R. Dover Jr. supported the school generously. Their names can be seen today on the John R. Dover Library, Dover Chapel, and the Charles I. Dover Campus Center (known to 25 years of alumni as CID and now as DCC).

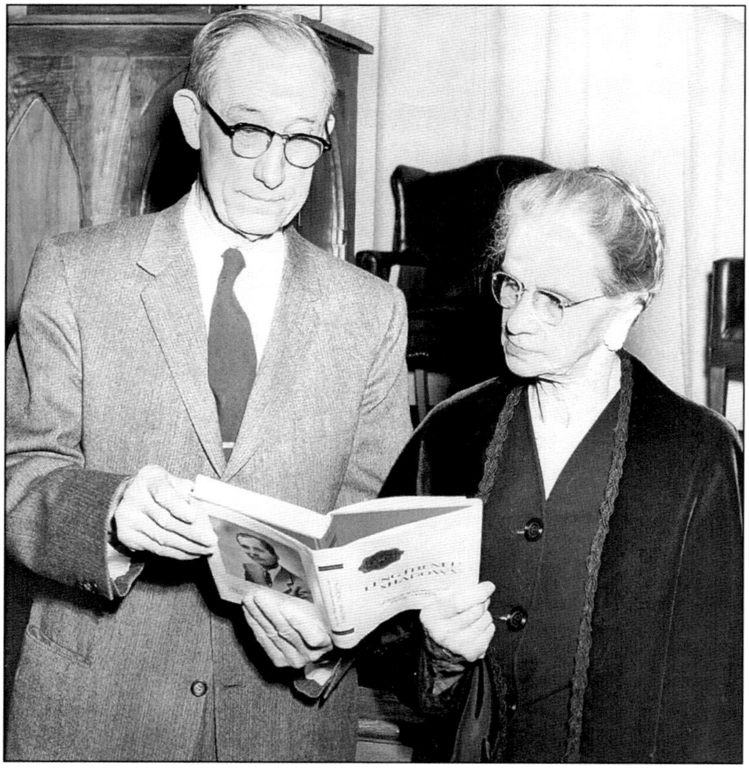

Another John Roberts photo shows Dr. Elliott at the home of Mrs. Huggins. One can see the newly released history of Gardner-Webb with author Francis Dedmond's photo on the back. The title, *Lengthened Shadows*, was borrowed from Emerson to suggest that Gardner-Webb is the lengthened shadows of many people who worked, gave, and sacrificed to build a college.

By the late 1950s, GWC was playing its home football games at the Shelby High Stadium on West Sumter Street in Shelby. The old metal fence is seen behind the 3rd base stands. Dr. Elliott crowns Irva Smith as homecoming queen.

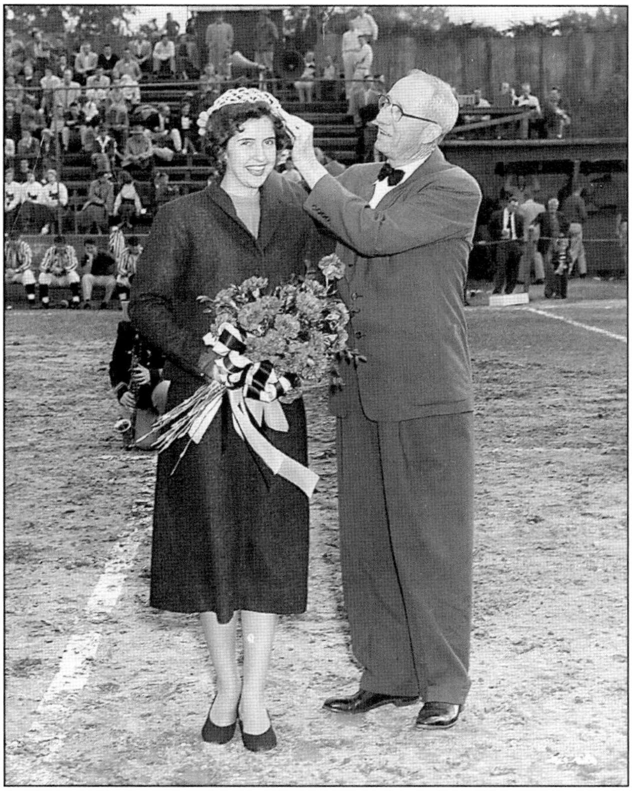

Gardner-Webb made news when Martha Mason completed her two-year degree at GWC before going on to Wake Forest. Ms. Mason was and is in an iron lung due to polio. Recently, Gardner-Webb awarded Ms. Mason an honorary doctorate. Pictured with her are Congressman Basil Whitener and her mother.

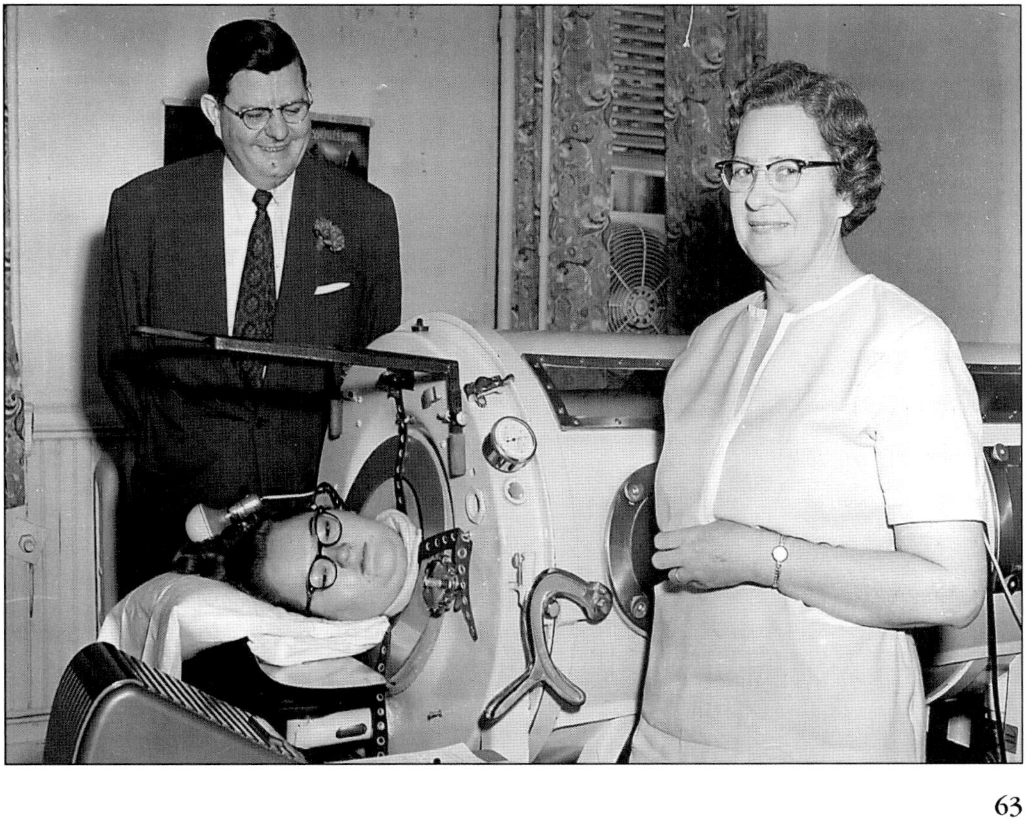

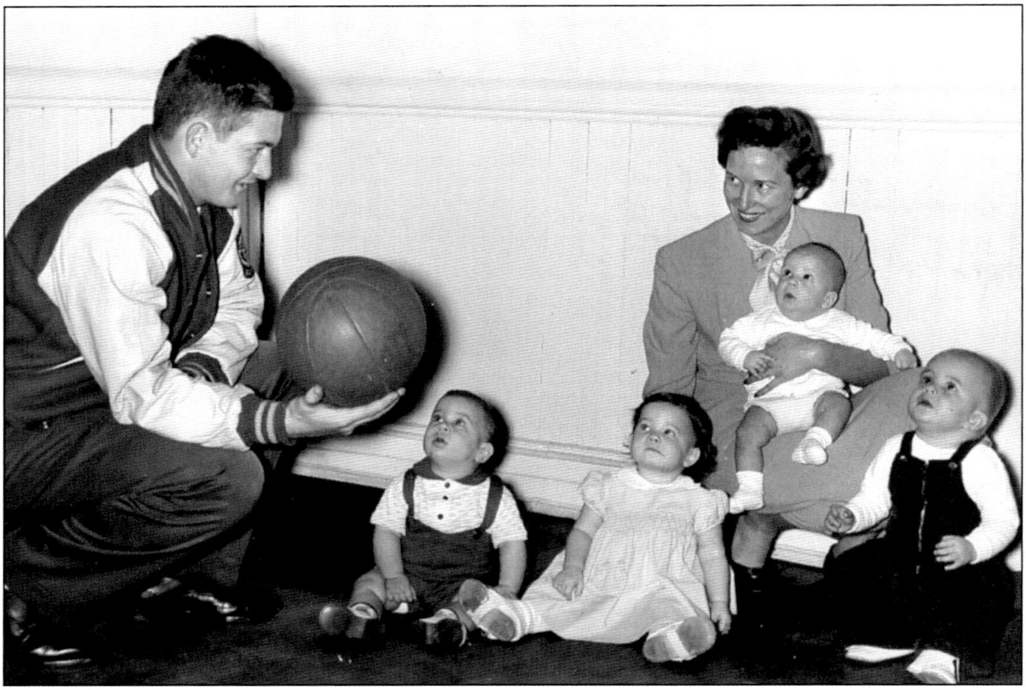

This August 1954 photo shows Coach Norman Harris and instructor Saranan Morgan recruiting for the future. The children are as follows, from left to right: Mark Roberts, son of John and Helen Roberts; Anne Harris, daughter of Norman and Jane Harris; Arthur Moseley, son of M.A. and Emily Moseley; and Chris Dyer, son of Robert and Mary Dyer.

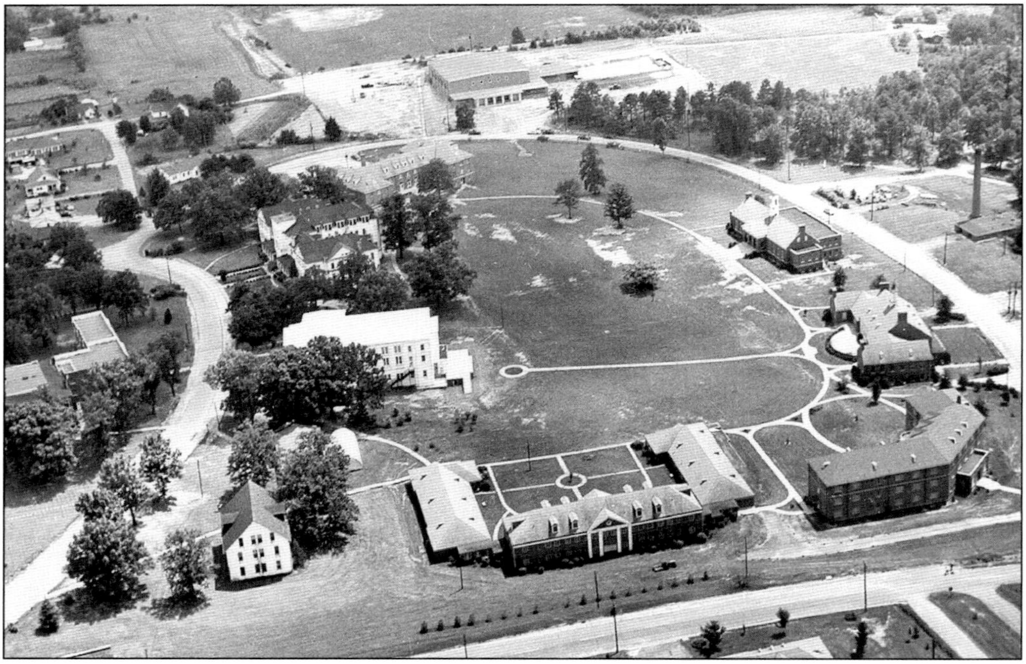

This view of the campus shows the newly completed Stroup Dormitory at the right. Huggins-Curtis can be seen at the upper left. The building burned in the summer after the photo was made.

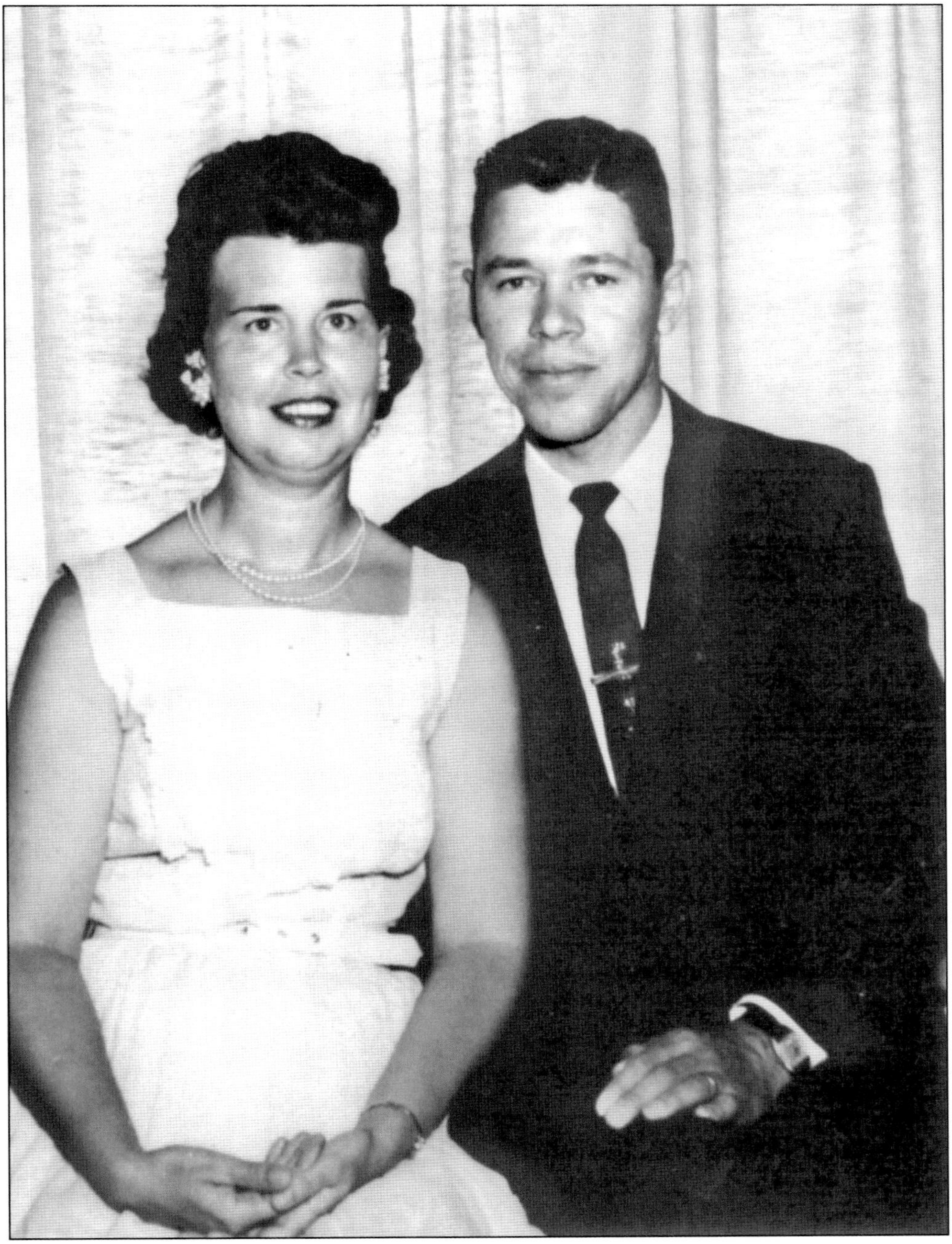

John Roberts and his wife, Helen, pose for this 1950s picture. John is an excellent example of someone who has been involved with Gardner-Webb most of his life. The Shelby native graduated from GWC in 1949, winning the citizenship award that year. Today he sponsors the award. After going to Furman University and then earning a master's degree, John returned to GWC in 1954 to work for six years in public relations. During his journalism career in North and South Carolina, he was active in the alumni association and served as president. When the rules were changed to allow for out-of-state trustees, John became a GWU trustee. In 2005, he served on the presidential search committee. If you want to explore GWU's history, just call John.

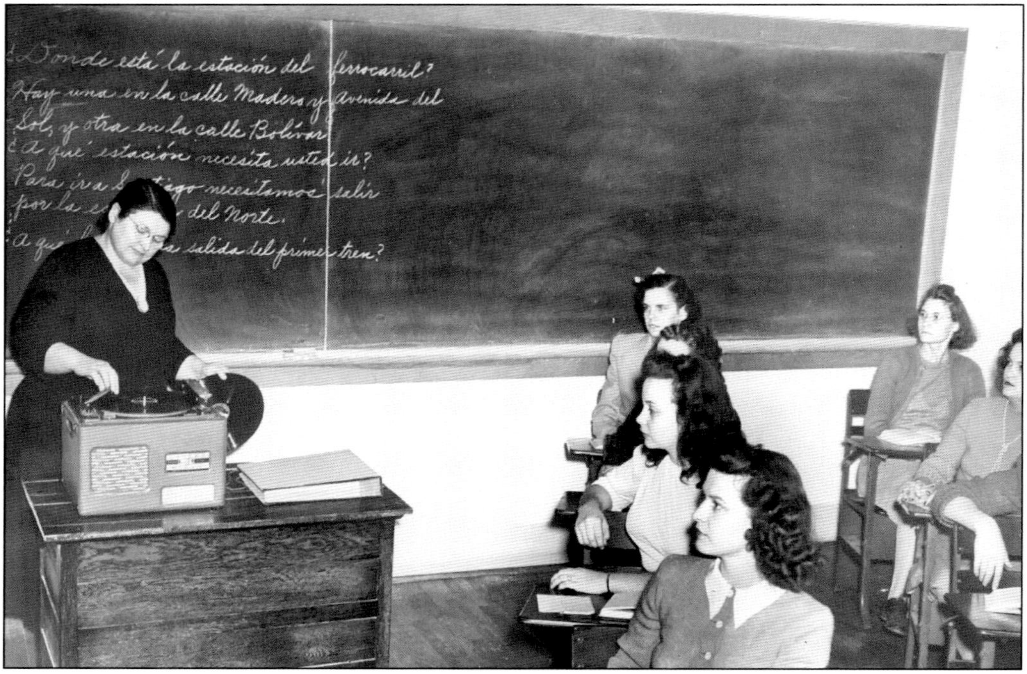

Language labs were things of the future at GWC when the 1950s students studied Spanish with Prof. Elma Pollack. Current students may have trouble remembering record players.

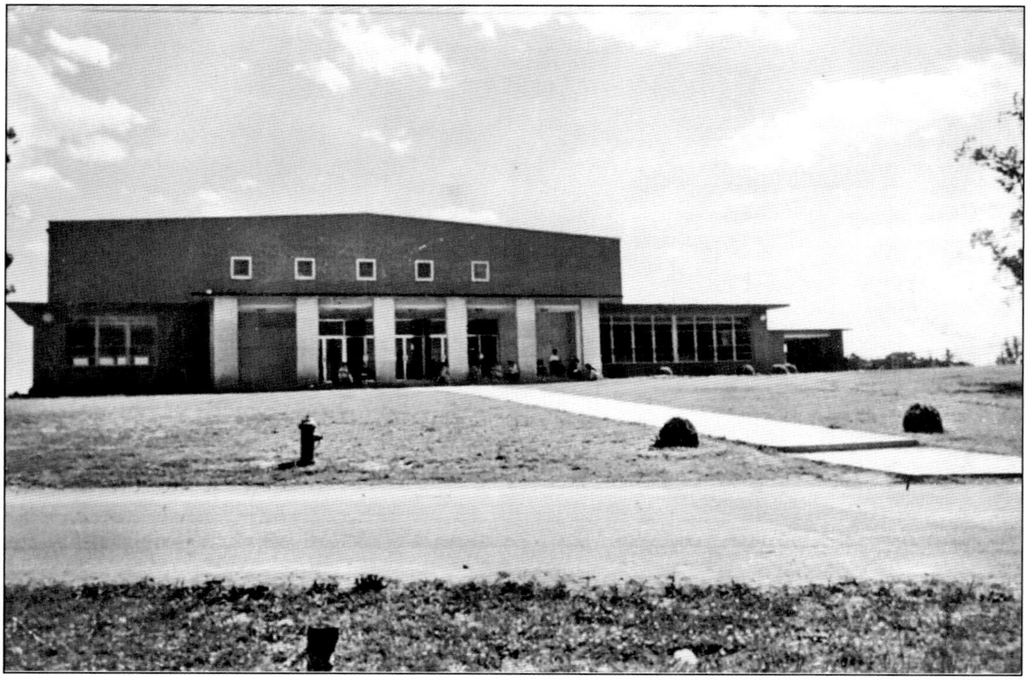

When the Old Rock Gym was torn down in 1952, GWC was left without a gym for five years. In 1957, a modern new gym was made possible by the Bost family of Shelby.

In the fall of 1958, GWC graduate Robert Blackburn (right) returned to assist Coach Norman Harris. Basically, they coached all the men's teams and taught all of the men's physical education classes. Coach Blackburn left in 1962 and returned in 1969 as Dr. Blackburn. He then built the physical education program at the four-year school.

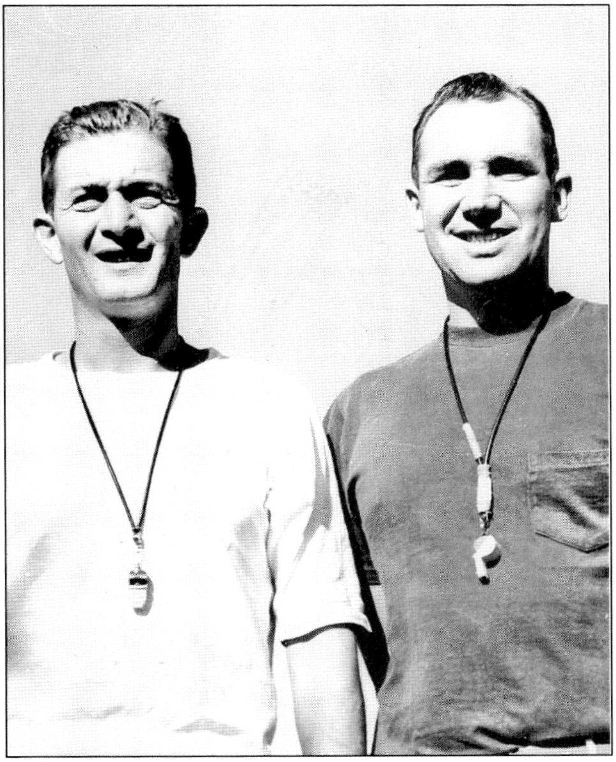

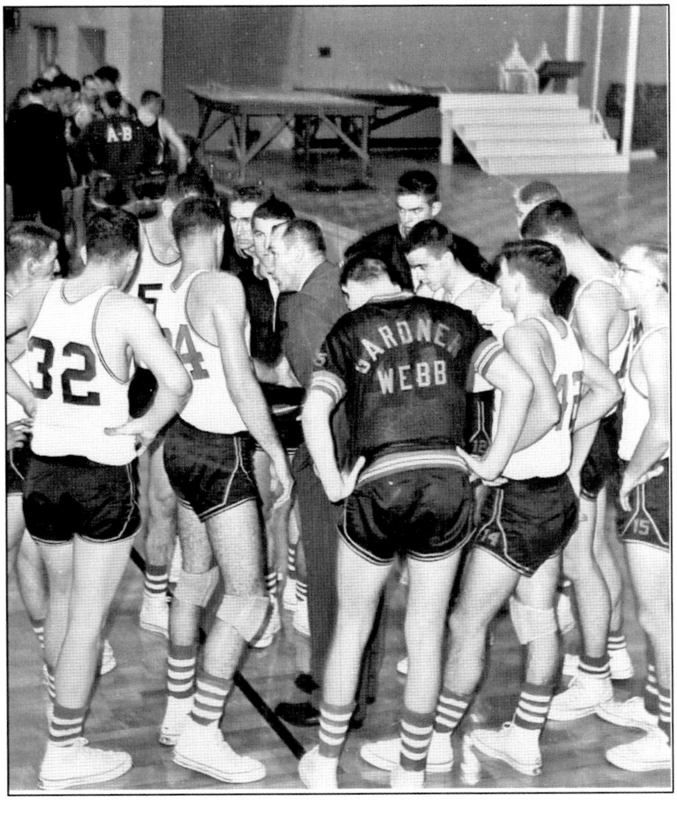

Coach Blackburn talks with the basketball team during a timeout. The team benches were at the end of the court. The Bost Gym stage is behind the benches.

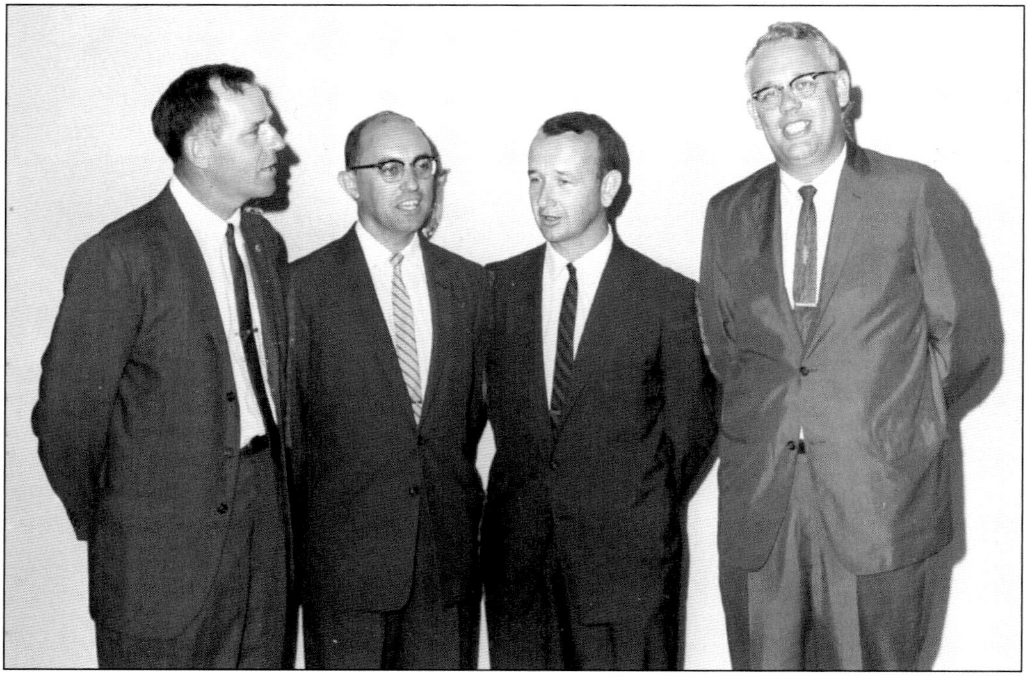

We are told by a reliable source (Cothenia Jolley) that these four faculty members sang at a faculty meeting. If you were a GWC student in the late 1950s or the 1960s, you probably took courses with one of these men. From left to right we see Hubert Dixon (math), Thirlen Osborne (English), Alan Burris (history), and Lansford Jolley (social sciences). Lansford and Thirlen can be seen regularly at the post office or the Snack Shop today.

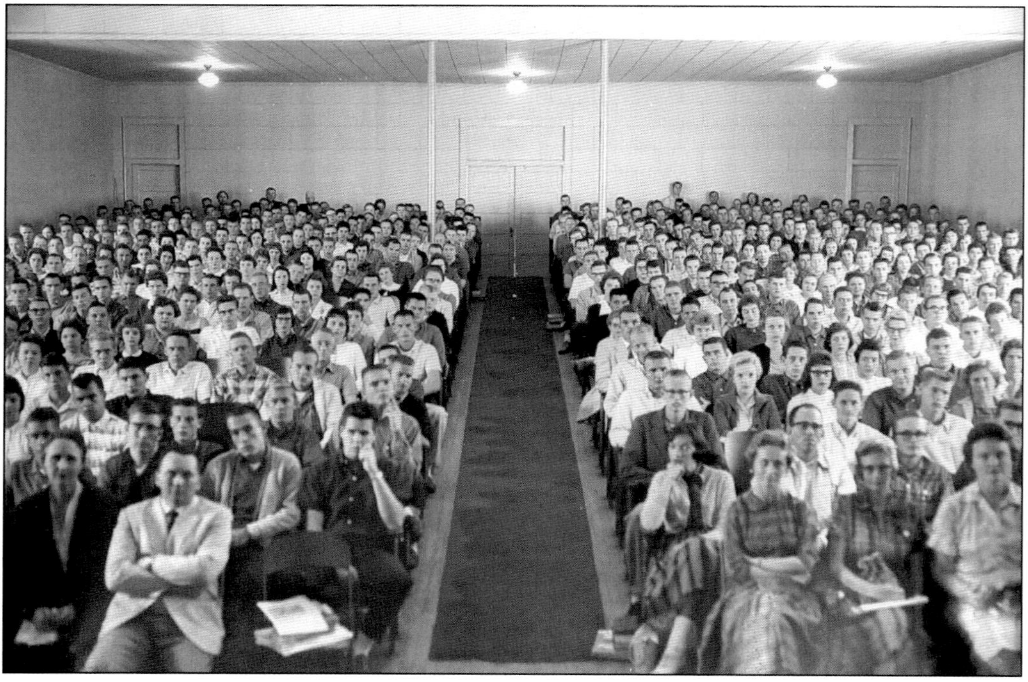

This is the way speakers saw chapel in Hamrick Auditorium. Some faculty sat on the front row. Abbie Miller and Jim Henson are on the left, and Doris Jones is at the far right.

In the February 1960 *Quarterly*, John Roberts (who would soon leave to become editor of *Charity and Children)* pointed out key events of the 1950s. The following are some of his comments:

"In 1951 the Western Carolinas Junior College Athletic Conference was organized, and GWC won the first football championship."

"In 1954 the college launched an effort to raise $1.75 million for new buildings. Dr. Elliott suffered a heart attack and had to take an extended leave."

"Joe Godwin, Doris Jones, and Seth Washburn joined the faculty in 1956."

"In 1957 the college celebrated its golden anniversary year with the publication of Francis Dedmond's *Lengthened Shadows*."

"Martha Mason, in her iron lung, held the school's scholastic lead and earned her diploma.

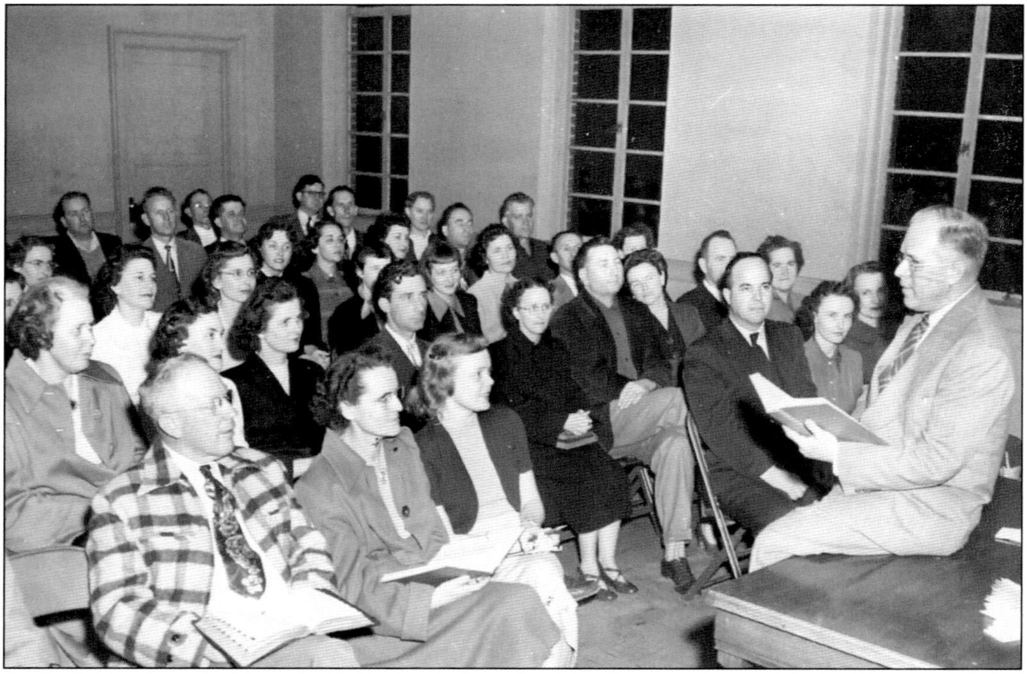

Dr. Stephen Morrisett is seen leading a Bible study. In the dark suit on the front row is the Reverend T. Max Linnens, who in 1958 became the pastor of Boiling Springs Baptist Church. Reverend Linnens led the church to its current location in 1969 and remained pastor until his retirement.

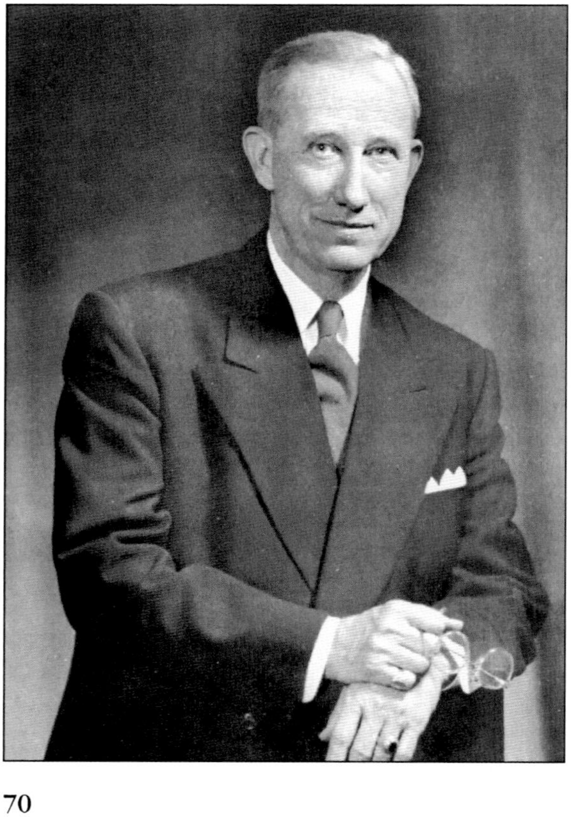

Truly, 1961 was a landmark year at Gardner-Webb. Dr. Elliott announced his retirement, and the search committee selected Dr. E. Eugene Poston as his successor. Dr. Poston was from Shelby and was a GWC graduate. He had returned to GWC in 1959 to teach religion, sociology, and Greek. Dr. Elliott died in his office in April, leaving a truly saddened college community.

Four

GARDNER-WEBB COLLEGE

The Transition to Senior College Status: 1961 to 1985

The college planned a large event for the inauguration of Dr. Eugene Poston as president. The week of events was capped by a formal ceremony, which was attended by North Carolina governor Terry Sanford.

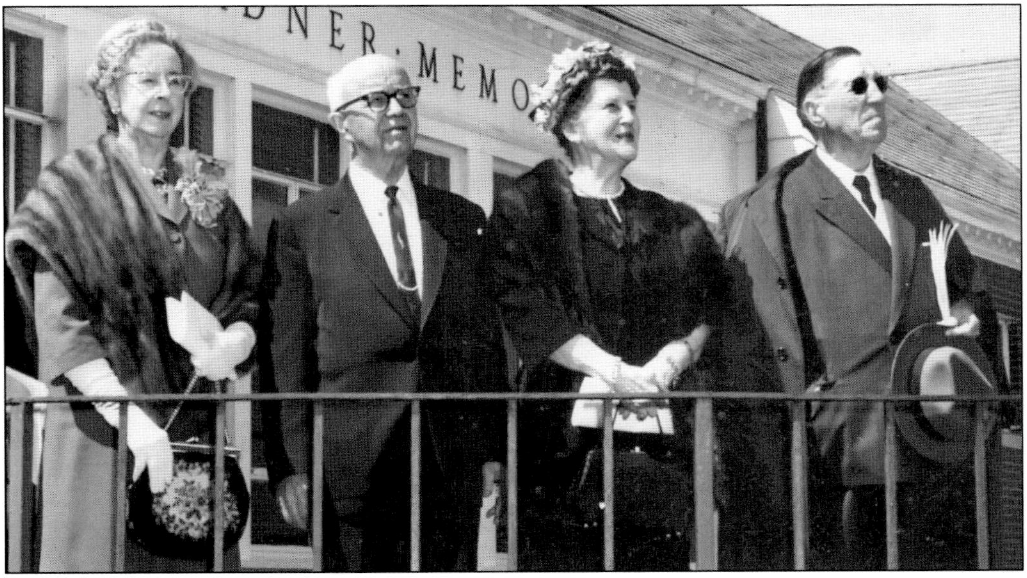

On Dr. Poston's inauguration day, many Gardner-Webb supporters were in attendance. These four people standing on the porch of the O. Max Gardner Memorial were all key supporters of the college. From left to right are Mrs. Rush Stroup, trustee and benefactor; Rev. J.L. Jenkins, who served as president in the 1930s; Mrs. O. Max Gardner; and Dr. Zeno Wall, who had served as pastor of First Baptist Church of Shelby for over 20 years and as one of the college presidents in the 1930s.

Snapshots of Inaugural Even April 11 - 16

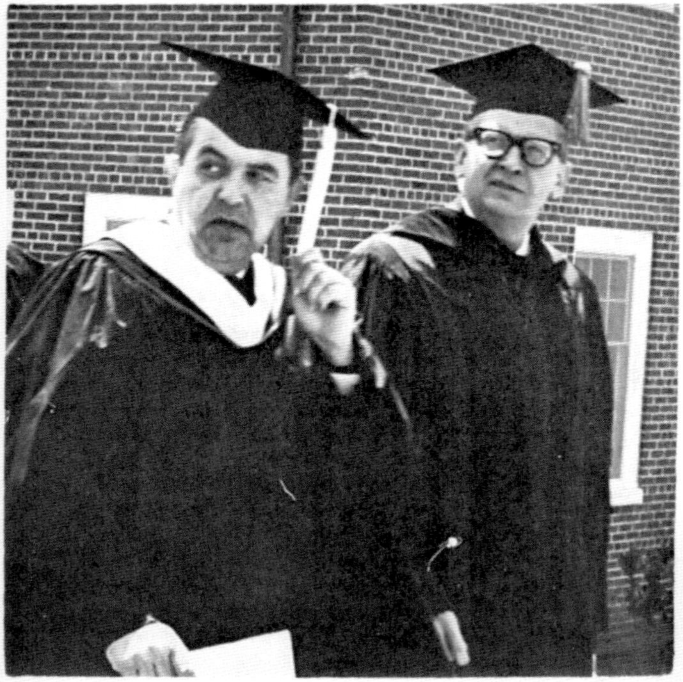

Prof. Dedmond and the Governor lead one segment of the procession

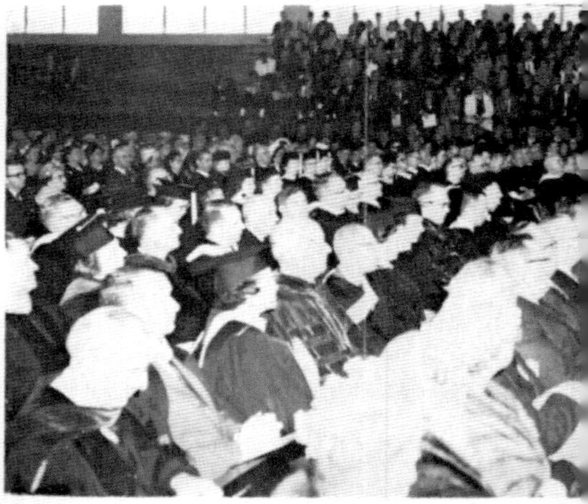

Official delegates from more than 50 colleges were

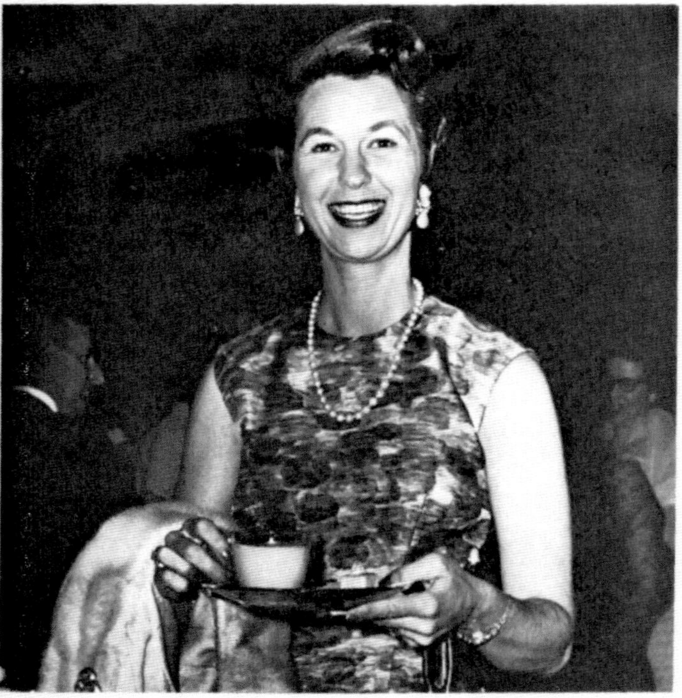

Mrs. O. Max Gardner, Jr., at the President's Reception April 15.

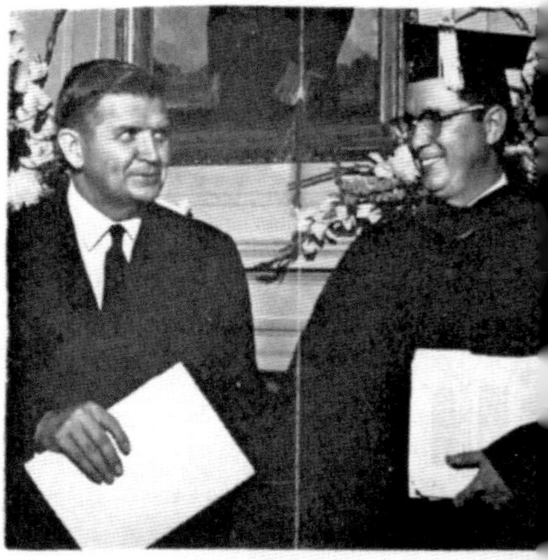

Dr. and Mrs. Poston chat with t

dance

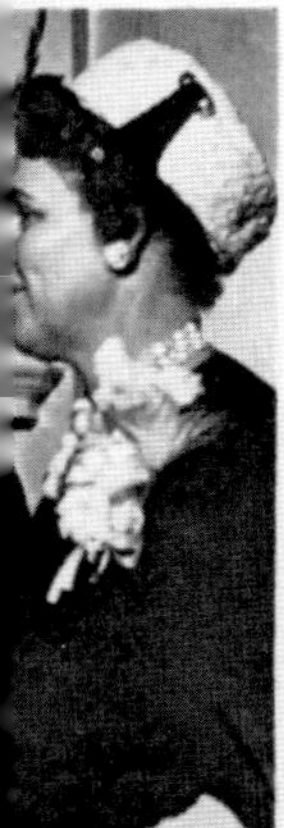

rnor

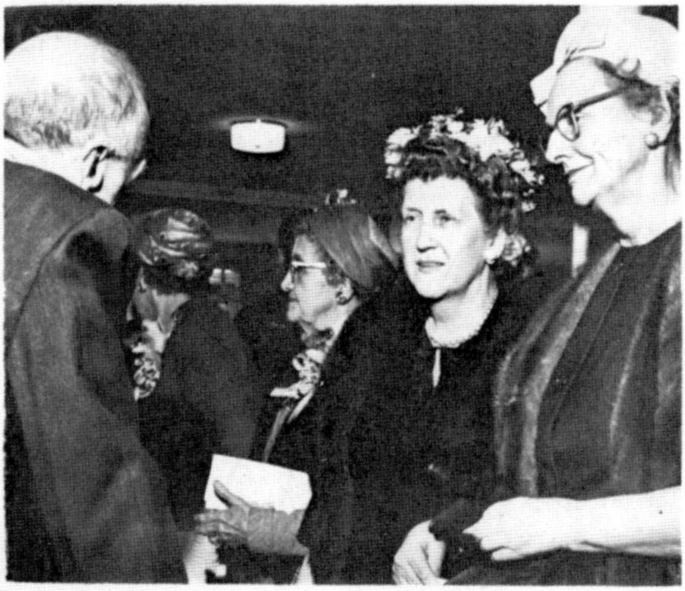

Mrs. O. Max Gardner, Sr., at the Inaugural Luncheon
At right is Miss Charline Stamey, another trustee.

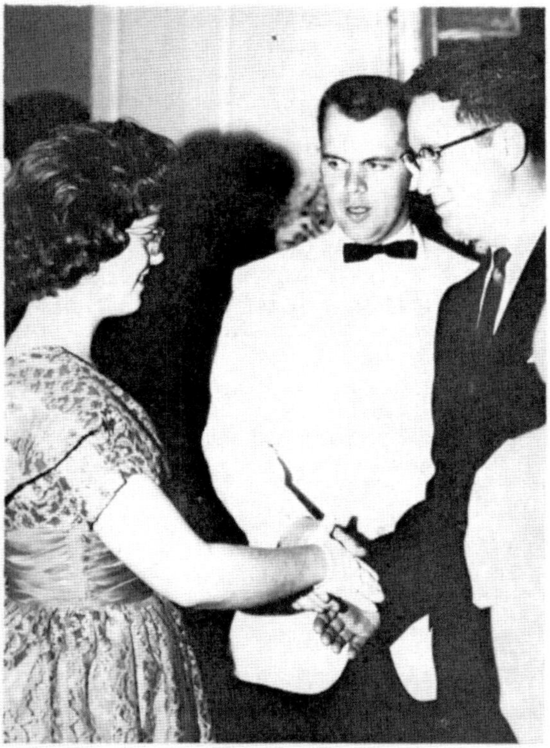

Buddy Freeman, student government president, introduces Miss Edith Davis to Dr. Poston at Student Reception April 14.

April 11 through April 16, 1962, served as inaugural week at Gardner-Webb. North Carolina governor Terry Sanford led a parade of dignitaries at the event.

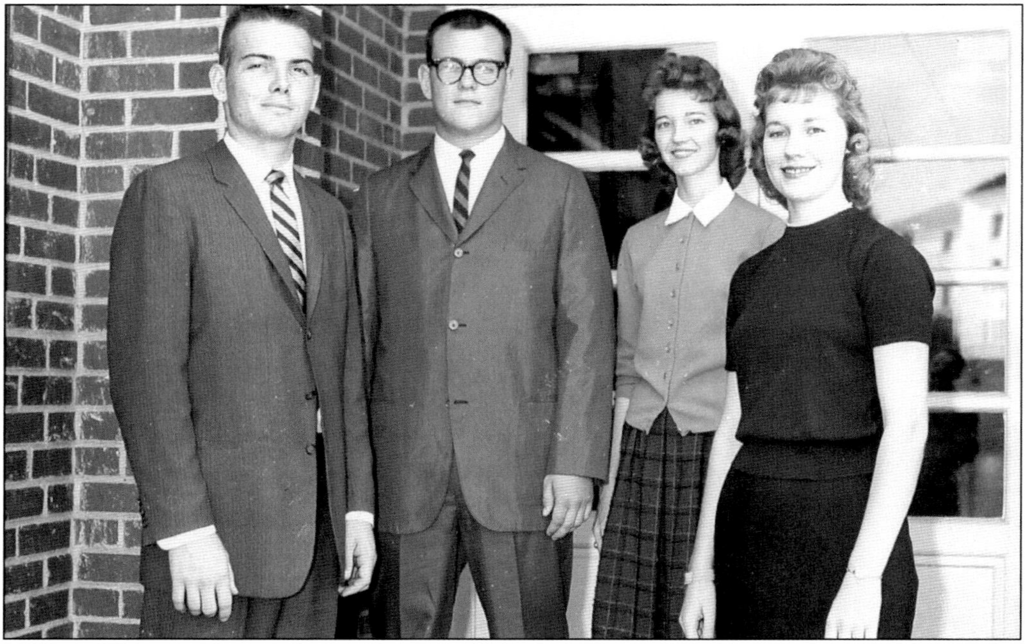

The four pictures on these two pages show Gardner-Webb as it was in the early 1960s, as leadership passed to a new president. From left to right are student leaders Buddy Lee, Sam Craven, Monea White, and Betty Stott, who served as sophomore class officers in 1960 and 1961.

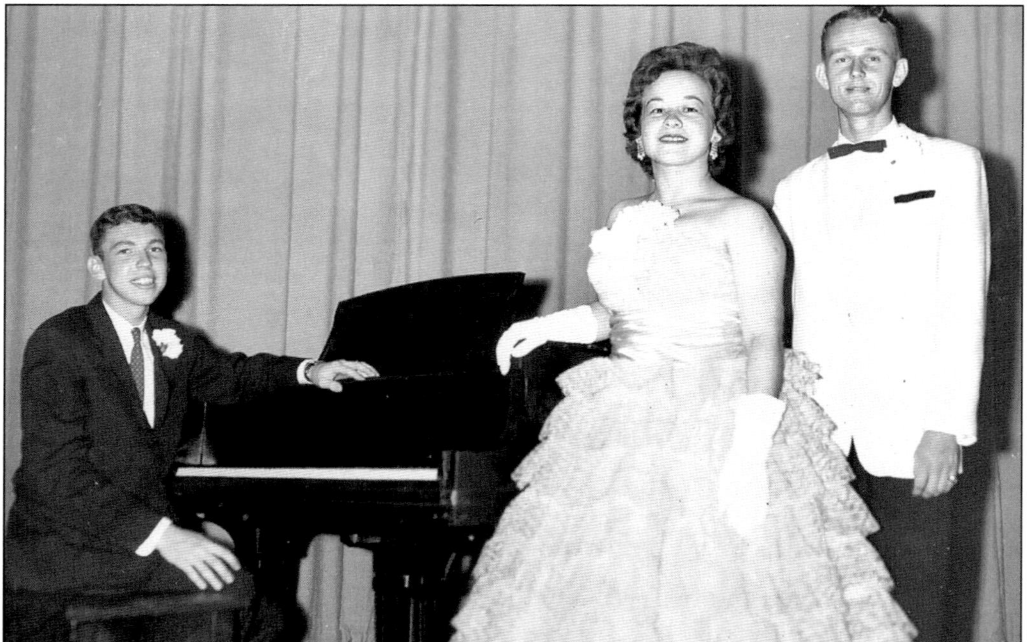

Larry Hicks (left) sits at the piano. Larry was the student organist for chapel. Larry, who still lives in the area, was organist at Central Methodist Church in Shelby. Stanley Webb, with several 1961 classmates, transferred to Carson-Newman and then attended seminary. Today he serves as pastor of a local church. The young lady is Jane Wilson.

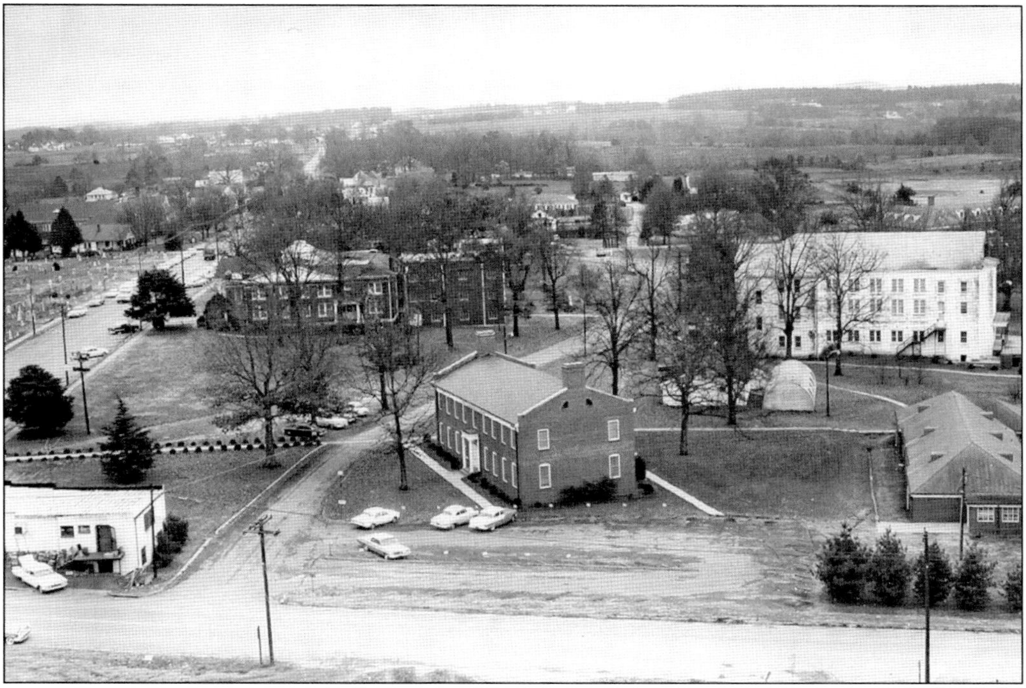

When Dr. Poston became president, the main corner of campus looked as this photo shows. G.T. McSwain's occupies the corner. The new Webb Administration Building was half the size of the current hall. The Boiling Springs Baptist Church still stands on South Main Street.

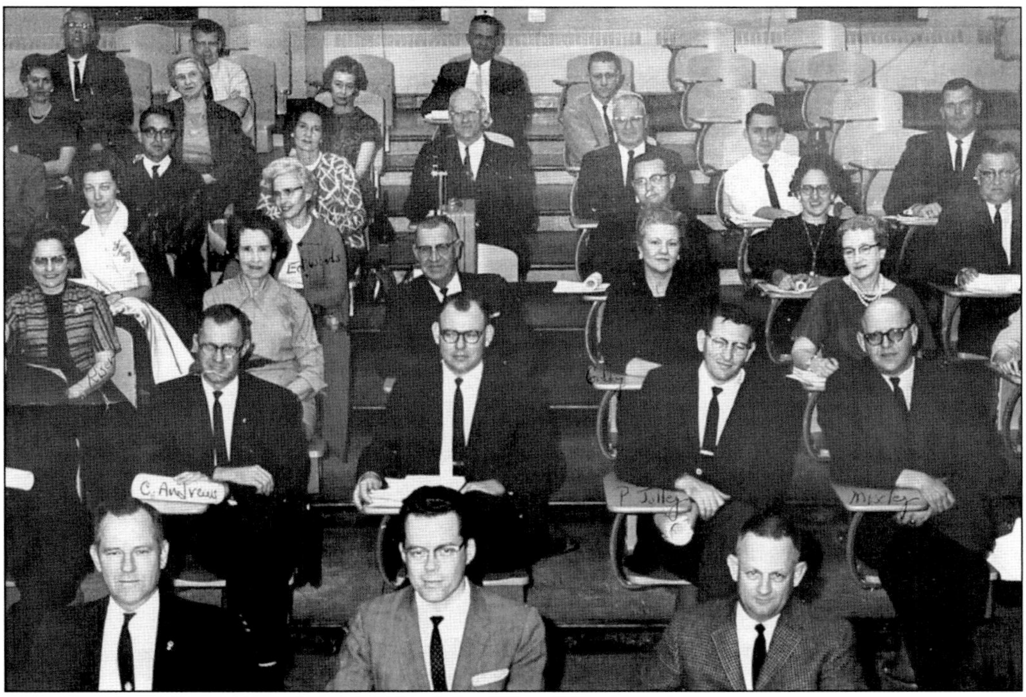

Faculty meetings were held in the new Withrow Science Hall. This *c.* 1963 photo shows the growing faculty. Veterans like Hubert Dixon and M.A. Mosley remained, while new faculty such as Drs. Robert Lamb and Paul Jolley can be seen.

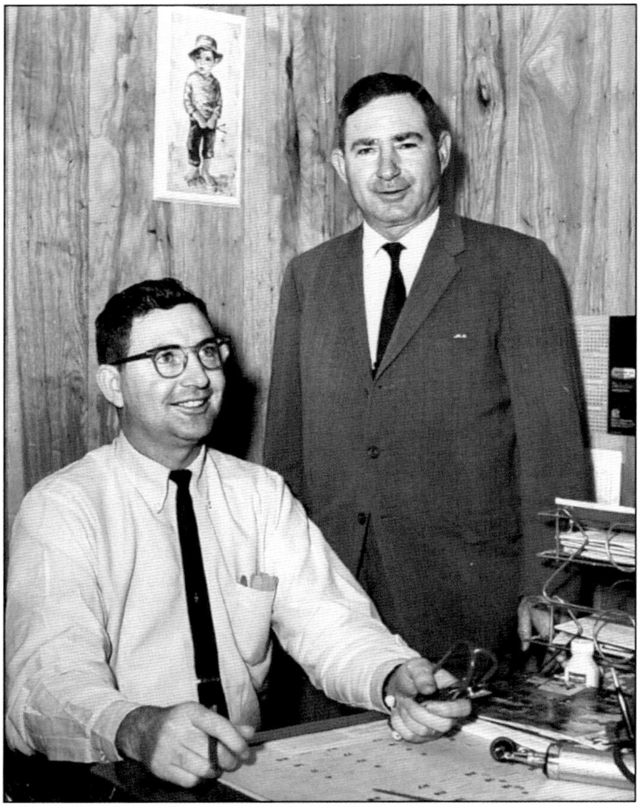

The union between community and college is best exemplified by the Washburn family. Seth and Dorothy worked at the college. Gene and Wyan Washburn were local physicians for years. To avoid the last name confusion, they were known as Dr. Gene and Dr. Wyan while serving college students as patients. They also served in various roles, including trustee. Dr. Gene Washburn serves in 2005 as vice-chair of the GWU trustees.

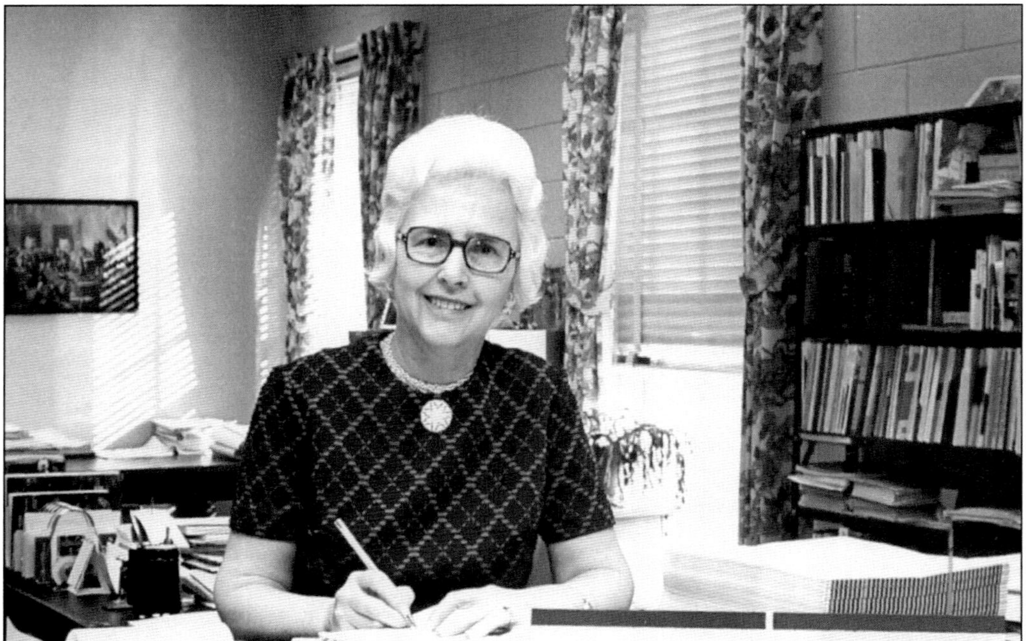

The doctors' sister, Dorothy Washburn Hamrick Edwards, served the college from 1949 through the 1980s. Students of the era have memories of the mild-mannered woman in the registrar's office.

Another local family that has supported the college while running a business is the O.P. Hamrick family. Maxwell "Maxie" Hamrick operated an insurance agency that his family still operates today. He told stories of hearing men meet at his father's house in the 1930s to discuss whether to close the college. Daughter Teresa, a GWC graduate, married Professor Huggins's grandson, and they still live in Boiling Springs.

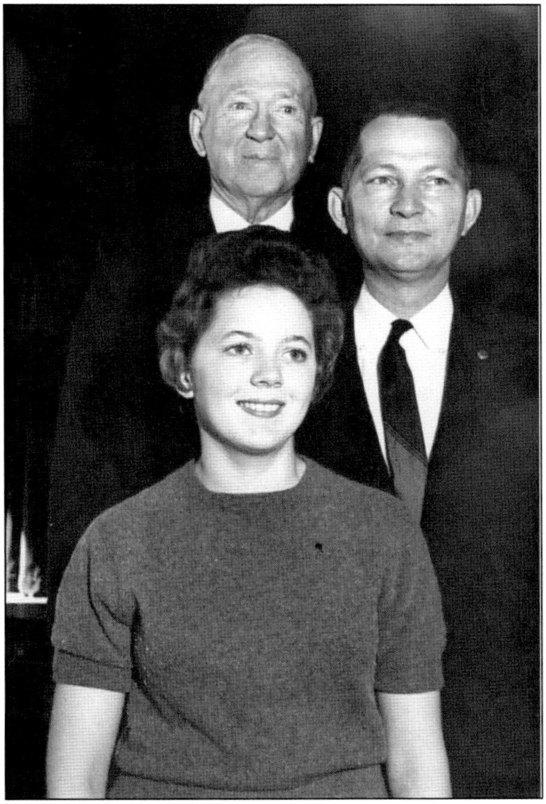

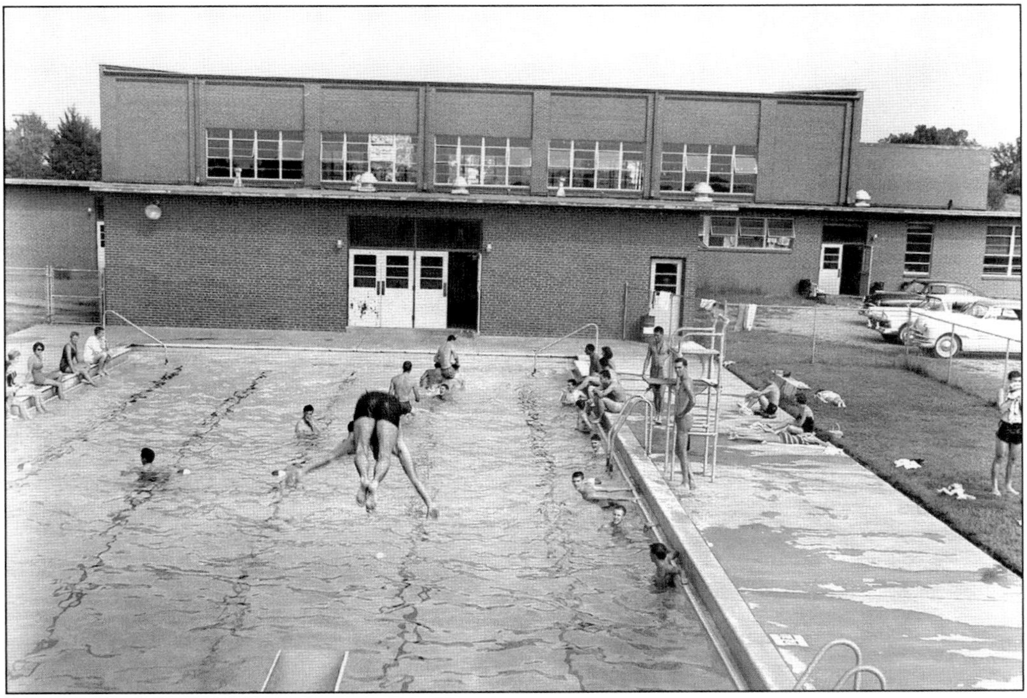

Students from the 1960s will remember the original swimming pool beside Bost gym. The cover would be built later, but for years it was open air.

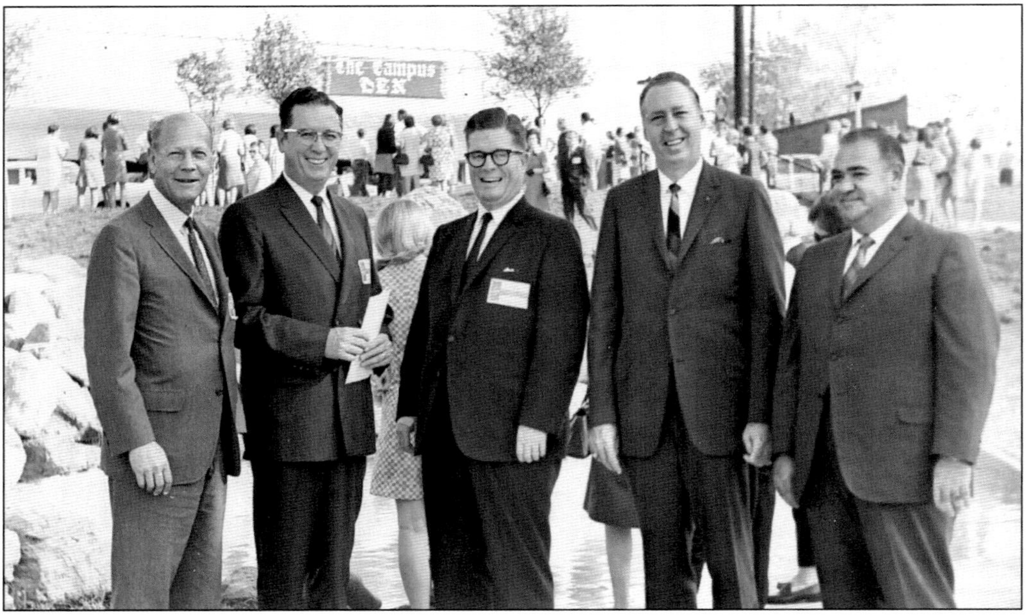

After the college acquired the McSwain property on the corner, the store came down and a pool with artificial rocks was built. This photo shows some key community leaders with Boiling Springs businesses across the street. From left to right are J.L. Suttle Jr. of Shelby; Dr. Poston; unidentified; Lloyd Bost, who served several terms as chair of the trustees; and Boiling Springs businessman Jim Beason.

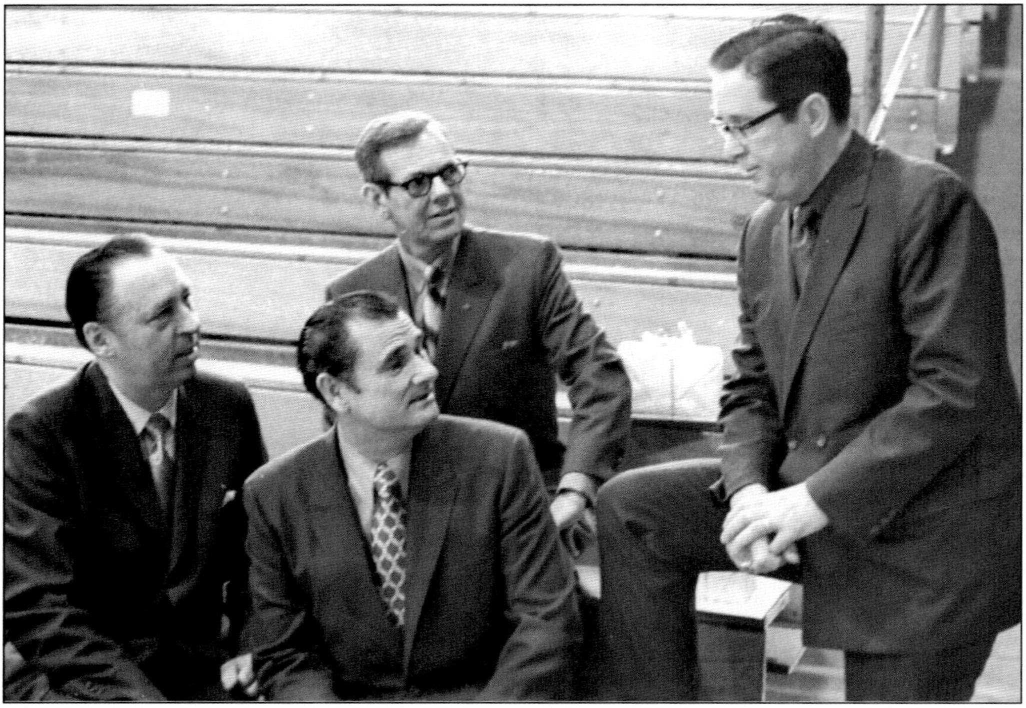

Dr. Poston brought regional figures to the board of trustees. Here Dr. Poston talks with Lloyd Bost (left), Charlotte TV entertainer Arthur Smith (front), and Carolina Freight executive John "Buck" Fraley (rear).

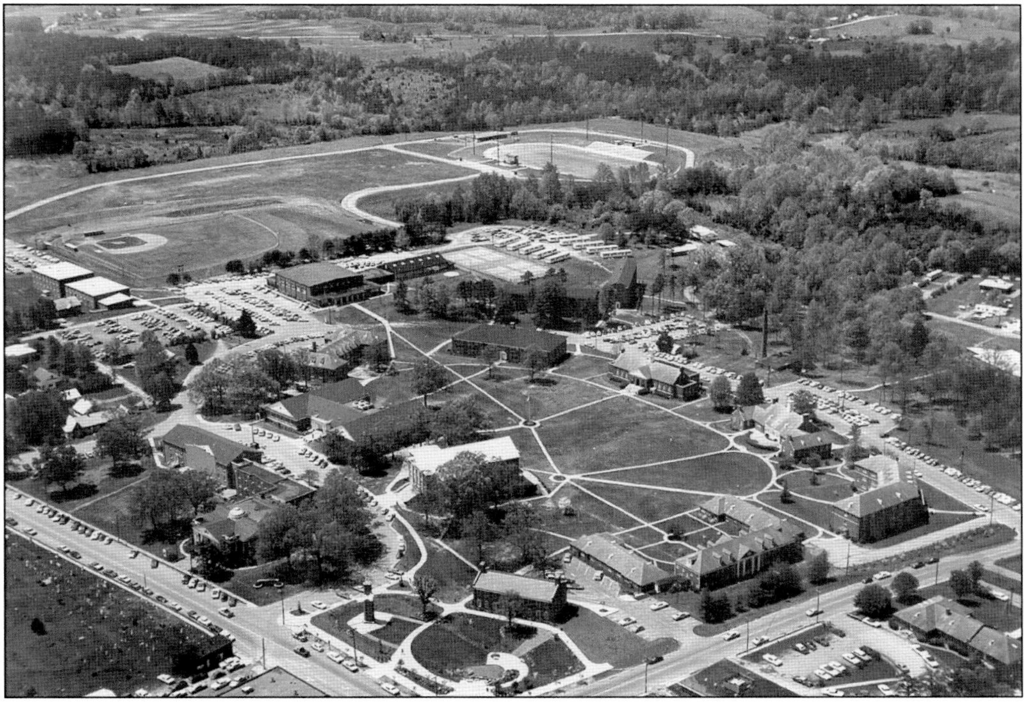

This view of campus in the late 1960s shows the pool and tower of light at the front. The Charles I. Dover Campus Center has filled the void left by the Huggins-Curtis fire.

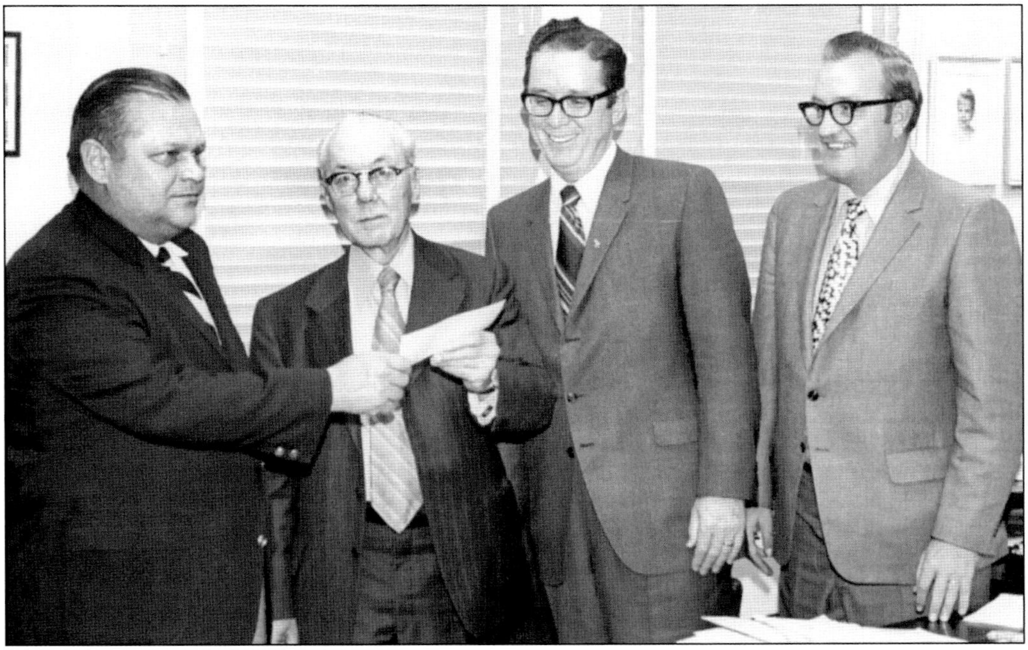

In this picture, Poston is joined by longtime supporter Charles I. Dover and two men who played key roles in the 1960s and 1970s. Shelby businessman R. Patrick Spangler (left) would lead the trustees on several occasions. Thomas J. McGraw served as academic dean and vice-president before later becoming the chief clerk of the United States District Court for the Western District of North Carolina.

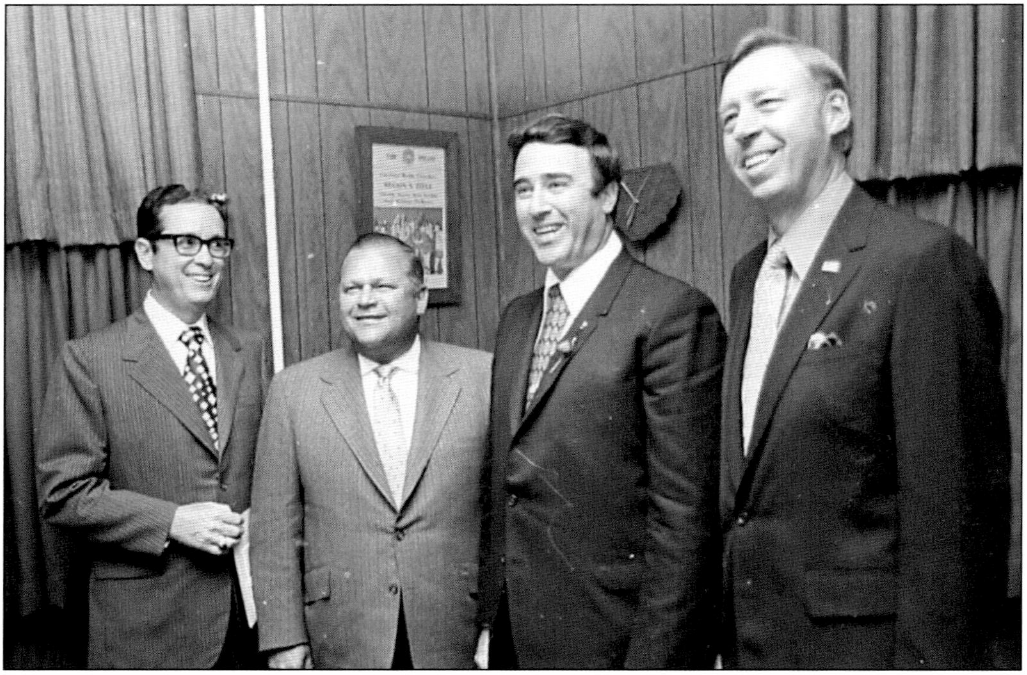

Seen in this photo, from left to right, are Dr. Poston, Pat Spangler, Robert Scott, and Lloyd Bost. Trustee Spangler was active in politics and brought people such as North Carolina governor Bob Scott to campus.

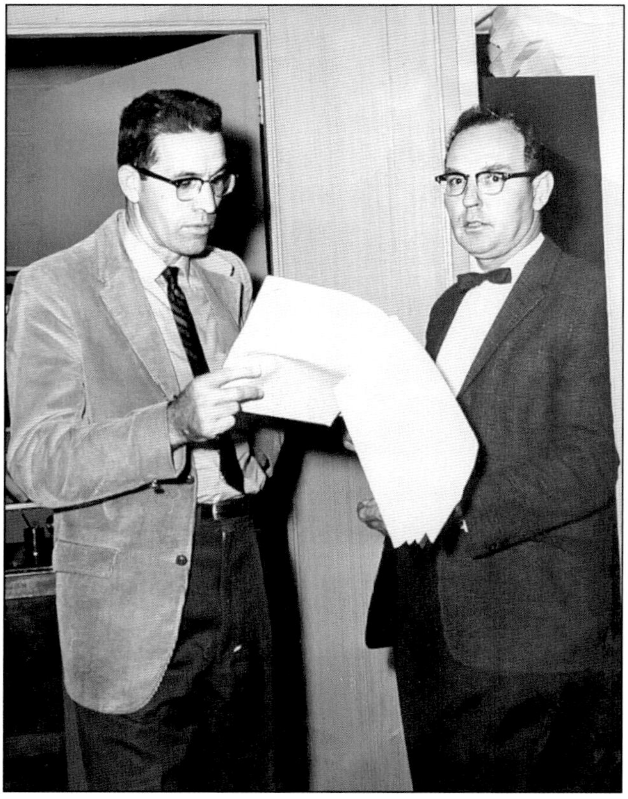

Garland Allen (left) and Robert Abrams came to Gardner-Webb shortly after Dr. Poston became president. Dr. Allen taught history and religion for over two decades. His golf teams won two national NAIA titles. Bob Abrams served as director of admissions and later as registrar. Both men are retired and live in Boiling Springs.

Dr. Poston recruited Wallace Carpenter from R-S Central High to develop a data-processing program. In 1965, Keith Griggs joined him, and the two developed a data-processing department. Both taught at GWU for over 30 years.

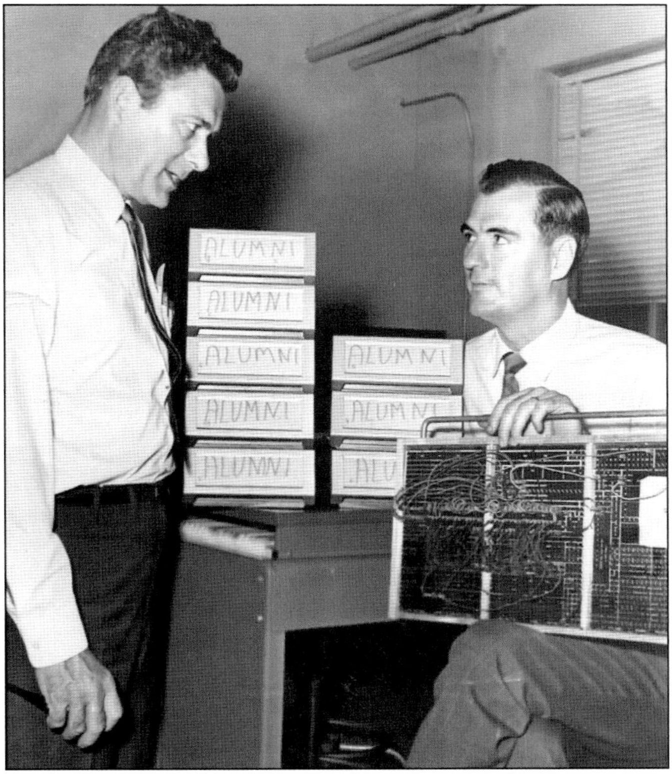

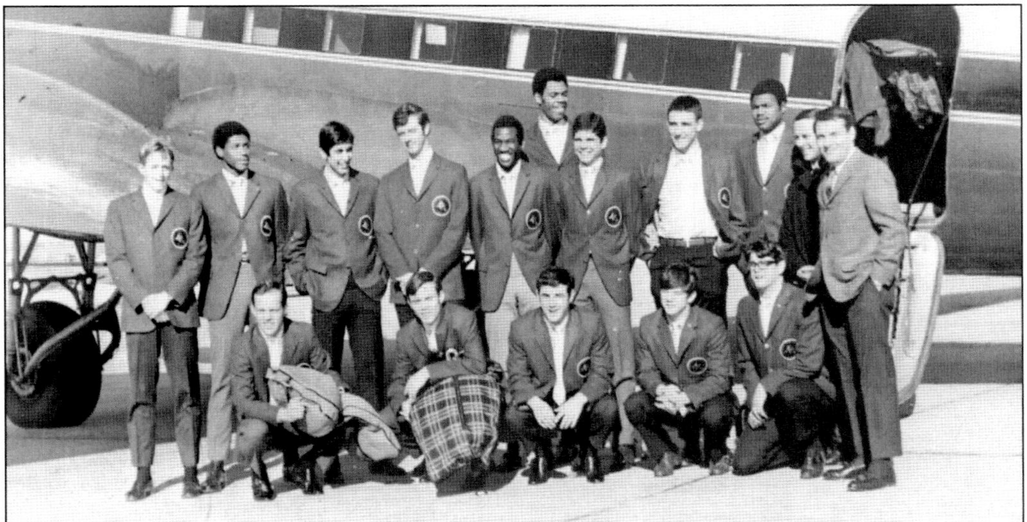

After Coach Eddie Holbrook came to Gardner-Webb in 1964, the college gained national recognition through its basketball program. By the late 1960s, with the coming of Artis Gilmore, the Bulldogs made the National Junior College tournament in Hutchinson, Kansas. Pictured here, from left to right, are (front row) Steve Kubeck, Jack McGill, Alan Ladd, David Crisp, and Larry Thomas; (back row) Kevin Cartwell, ABA star George Adams, Tony Spagnola, Willie Rogers, Joe Brookins, ABA and NBA standout Artis Gilmore, Gerry Vallaincourt (later WBT's Gerry V.), Meriedith Scruggs, Ernie Fleming, Coach Holbrook, and assistant coach Ron Hooper.

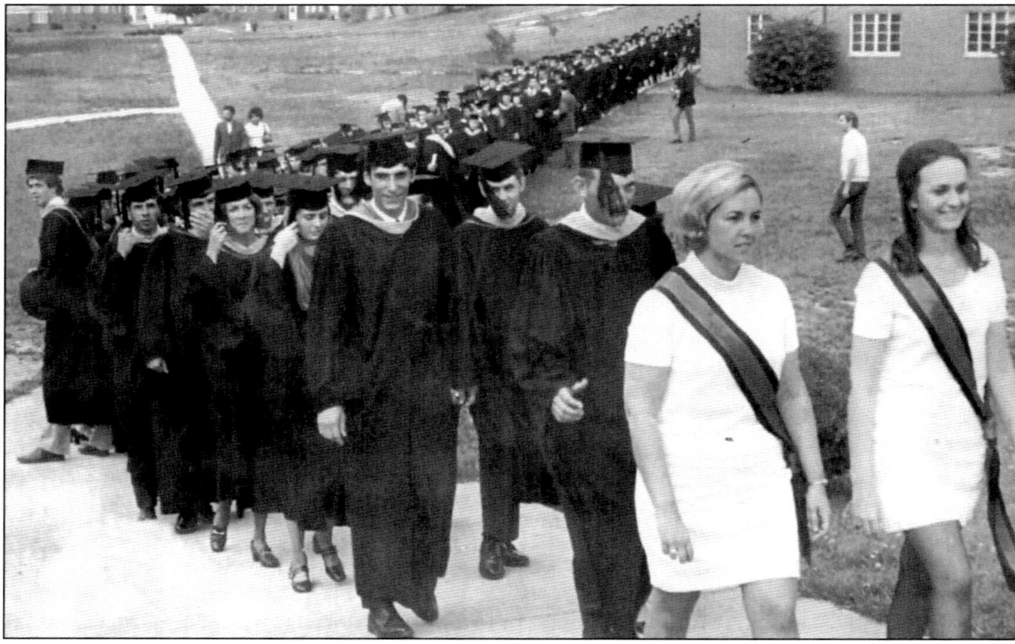

In 1971, the four-year institution graduated its first class. Marshal Lynn Moss (left) leads the class toward Bost Gym for the ceremony. Based on the luck of the alphabet, J.J. Abernathy received the first diploma.

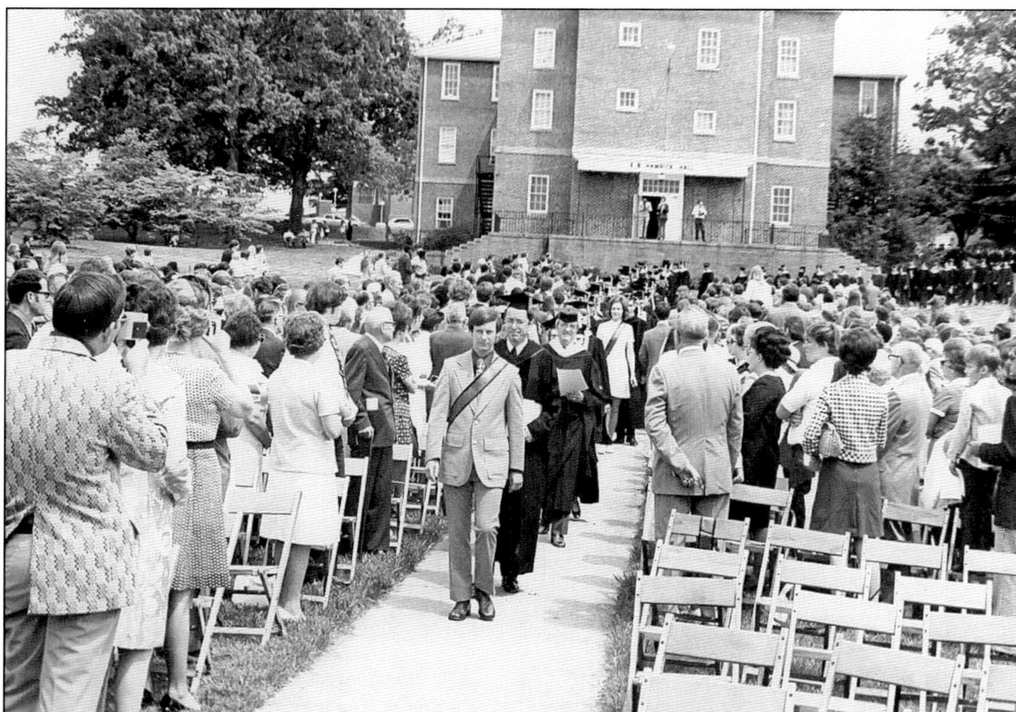

Graduation soon outgrew Bost Gym. Dr. Poston and Mr. McGraw are seen following the marshal to the porch of OMG for the ceremony.

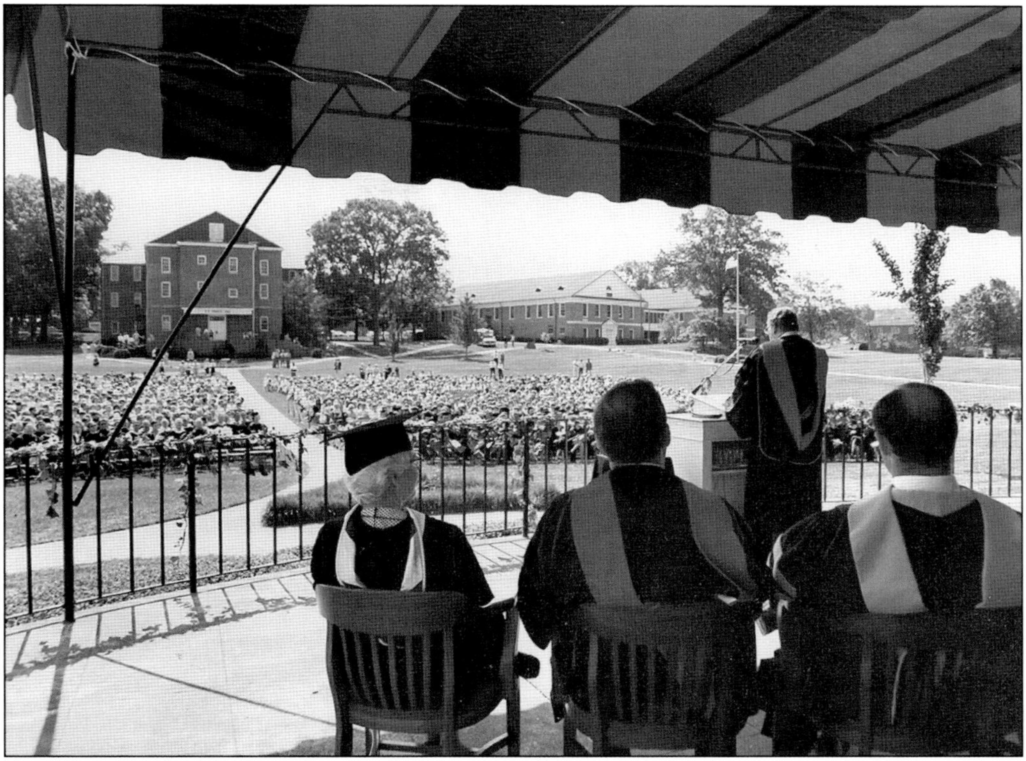

One can see a panoramic view of the quad filled with graduates, faculty, families, and friends.

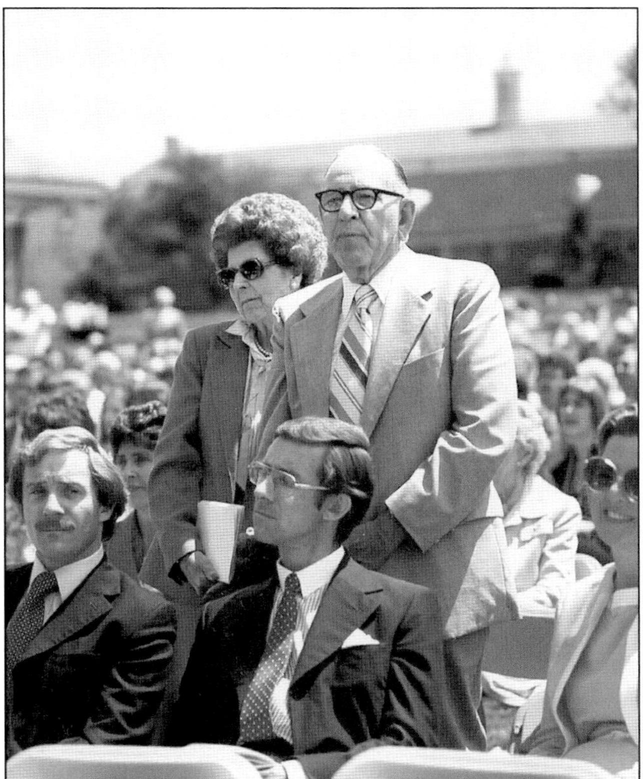

Shelby businessman J. Ray Lutz and wife, Lillian, are recognized during a graduation ceremony.

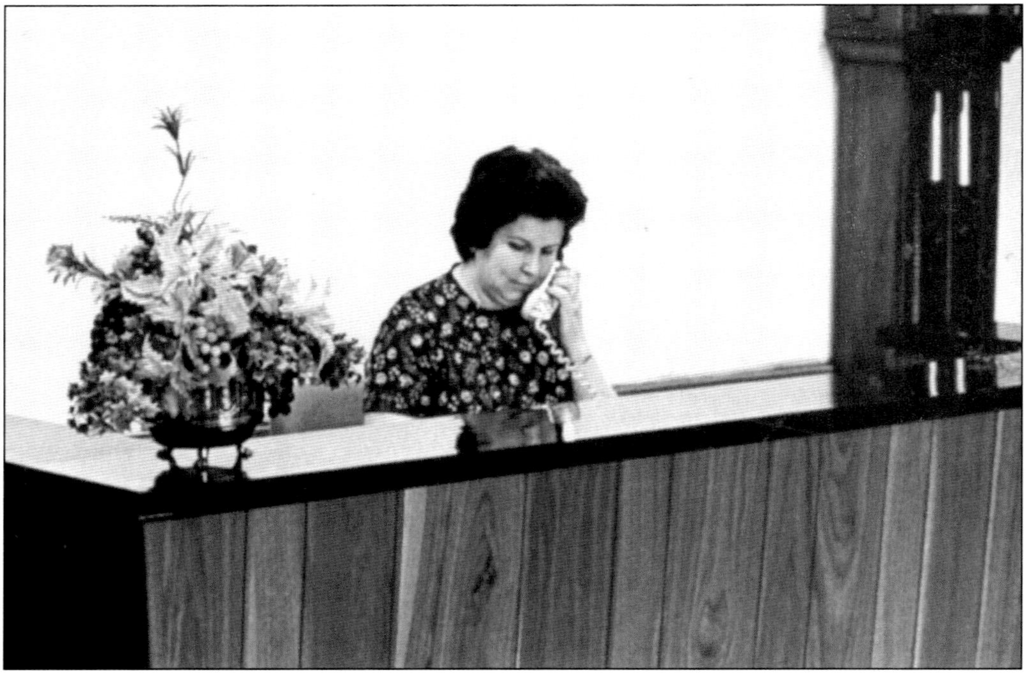

Shirley Washburn was a fixture at the switchboard in Webb Hall. All incoming calls passed through here. To get a live WATS (Wide-Area Telephone Service) line for long distance, one had to get on a list.

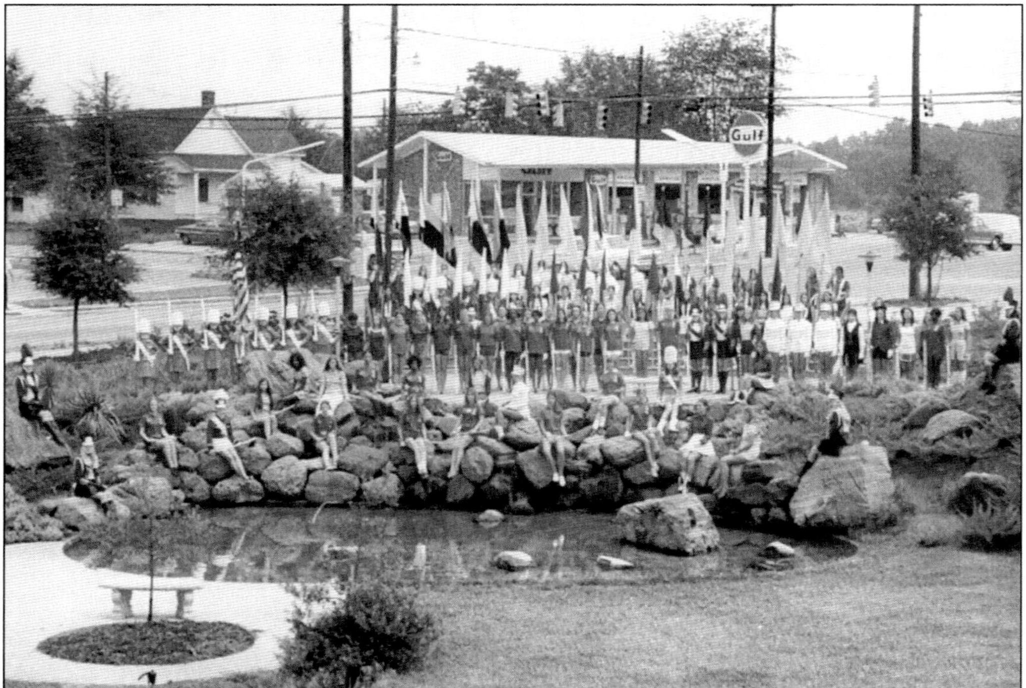

A band poses on the rocks around the pond. The newly built Gulf station is in the background. Thousands of gallons of gas were pumped into the growing fleet of Gardner-Webb automobiles. The station closed in February 2005.

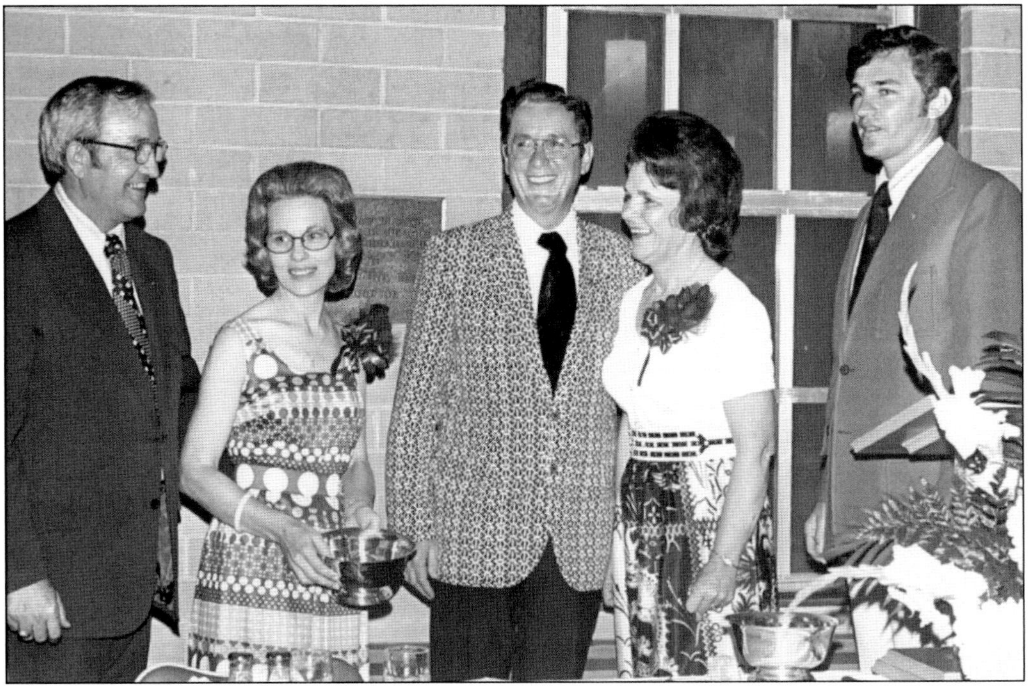

From left to right are Tom McGraw, Betty McGraw, Dr. Poston, Dot Poston, and alumni director Jerry Walker. Mrs. Poston and Mrs. McGraw were joint recipients of the Alumnus of the Year award.

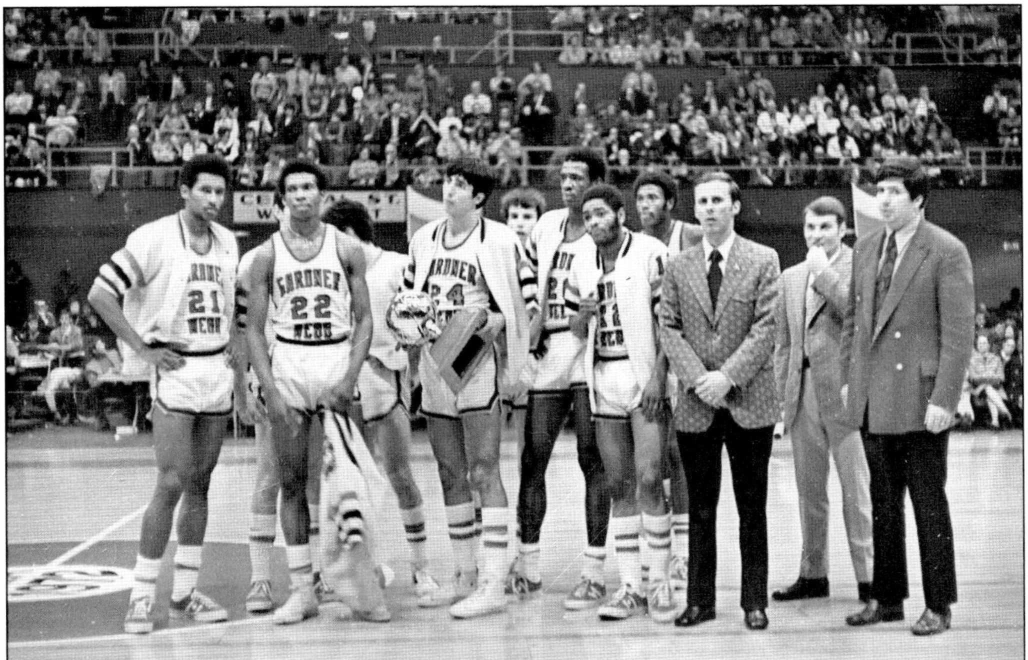

In the early days as a four-year institution, the Bulldogs were members of the NAIA. In 1972, the basketball team went to the 32-team national finals in Kansas City and finished fourth in the nation. Coach Holbrook stands in front of the team.

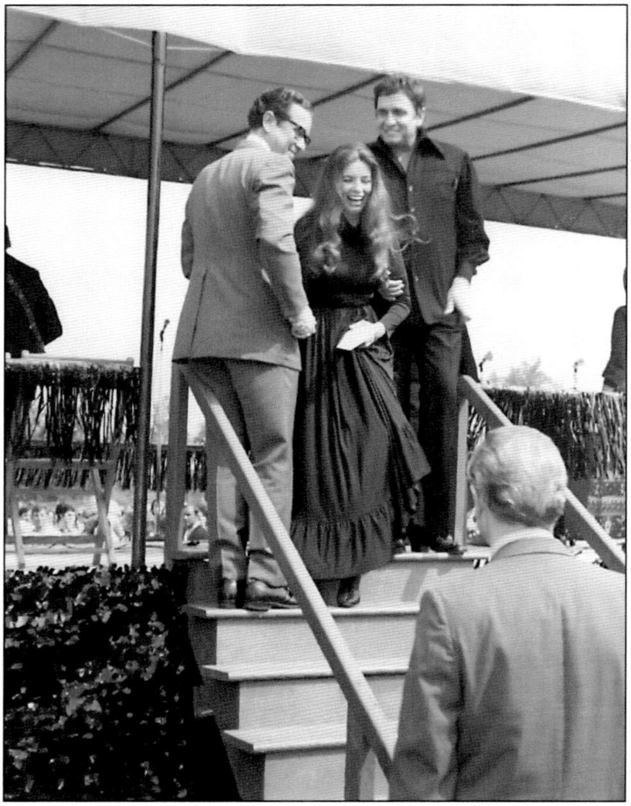

Through the connections of trustee Arthur Smith, Gardner-Webb offered an honorary doctorate to singer Johnny Cash. Cash brought his singers and family to Gardner-Webb. There was a morning concert in Spangler Stadium and an academic ceremony in the afternoon. The photo shows Dr. Poston with June Carter Cash and her husband, Johnny, on the Spangler Stadium platform.

Early in Dr. Poston's presidency, Grace Lee came to Gardner-Webb to establish an associate degree program in nursing. Dr. Shirley Toney (pictured here) inherited the program and has developed it so that it now also offers a bachelor's of science in nursing and a master's degree.

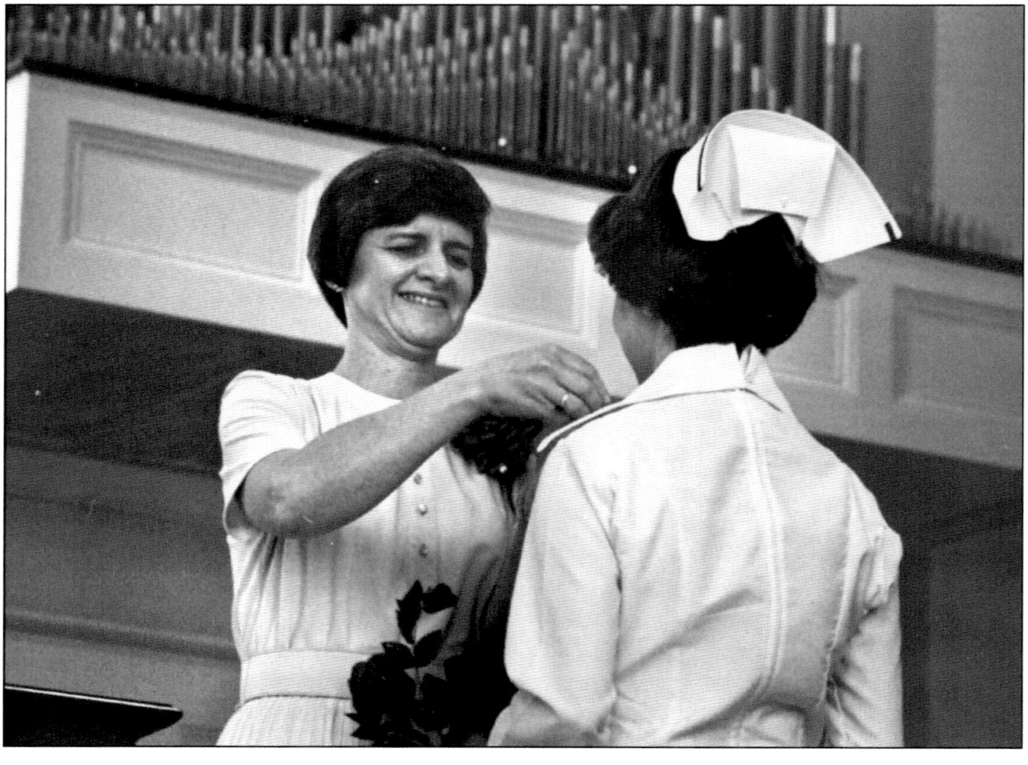

Coach Eddie Holbrook shows his ability to enlighten officials. Holbrook's intensity produced quality teams.

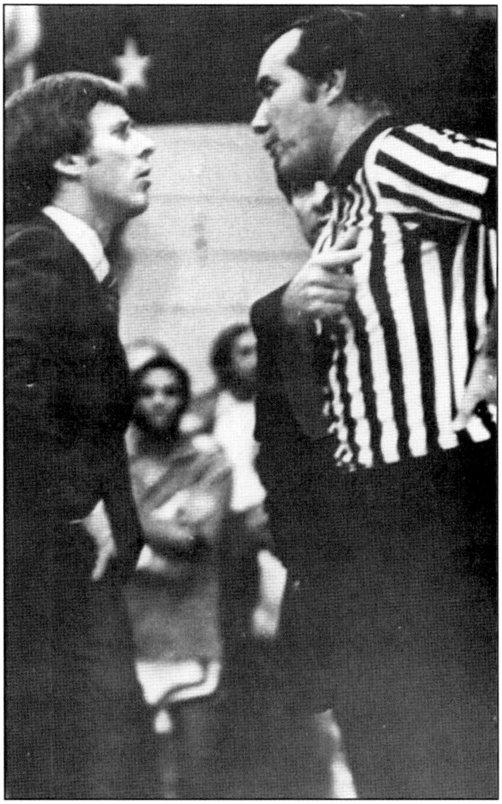

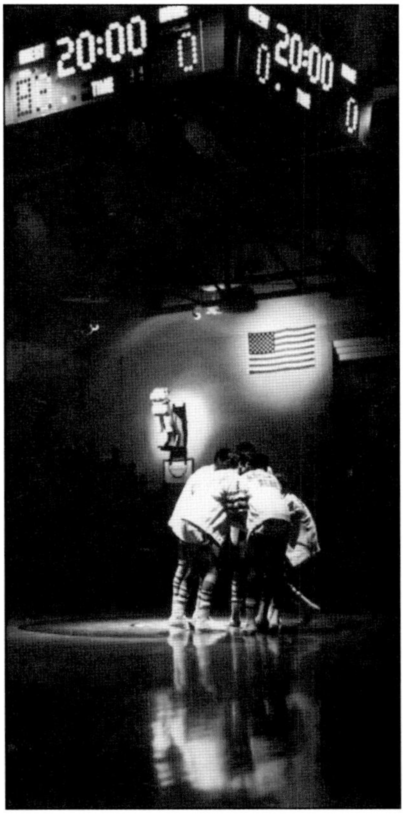

This image in Bost Gym should be familiar to students of the 1970s. When the lights dimmed and the red carpet was rolled out, the spotlighted players were greeted with deafening cheers. The Bulldogs once went five years without losing in Bost.

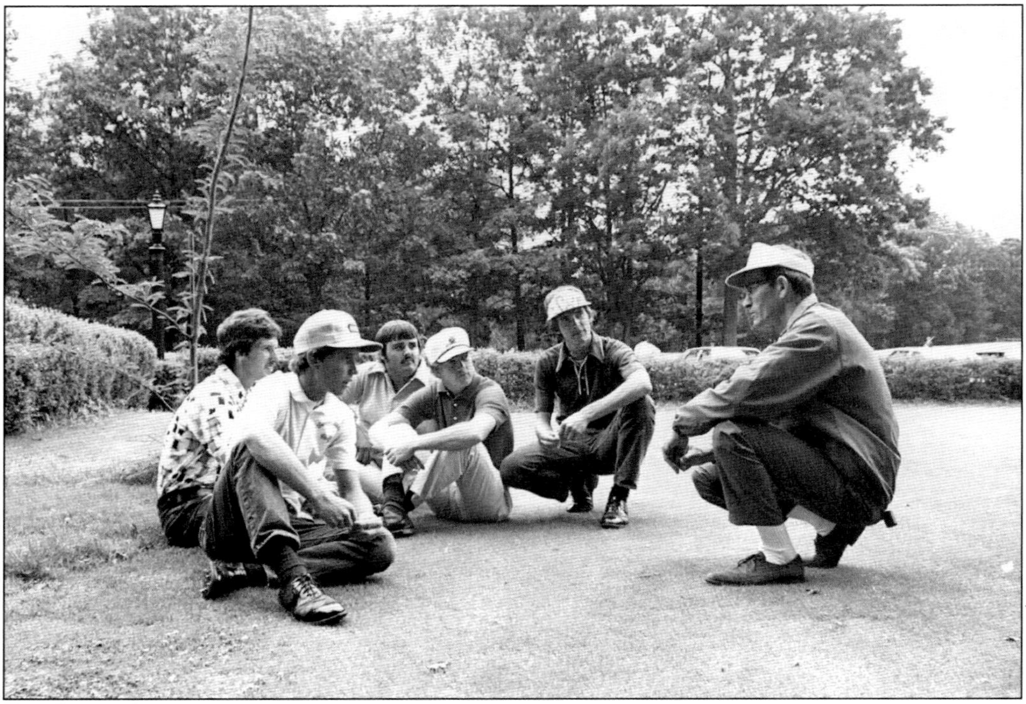

Dr. Garland Allen talks with his golfers. Coach Allen led the team to the top at Gardner-Webb.

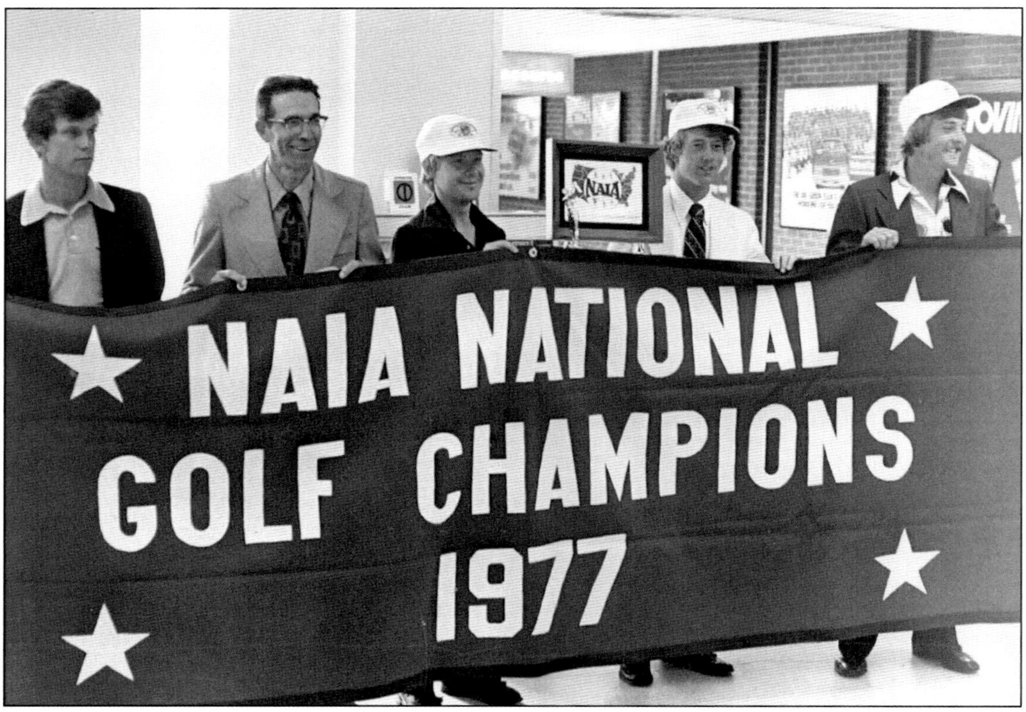

Coach Allen and his golfers hold the championship banner from the 1977 NAIA National Championship. This was their second consecutive championship.

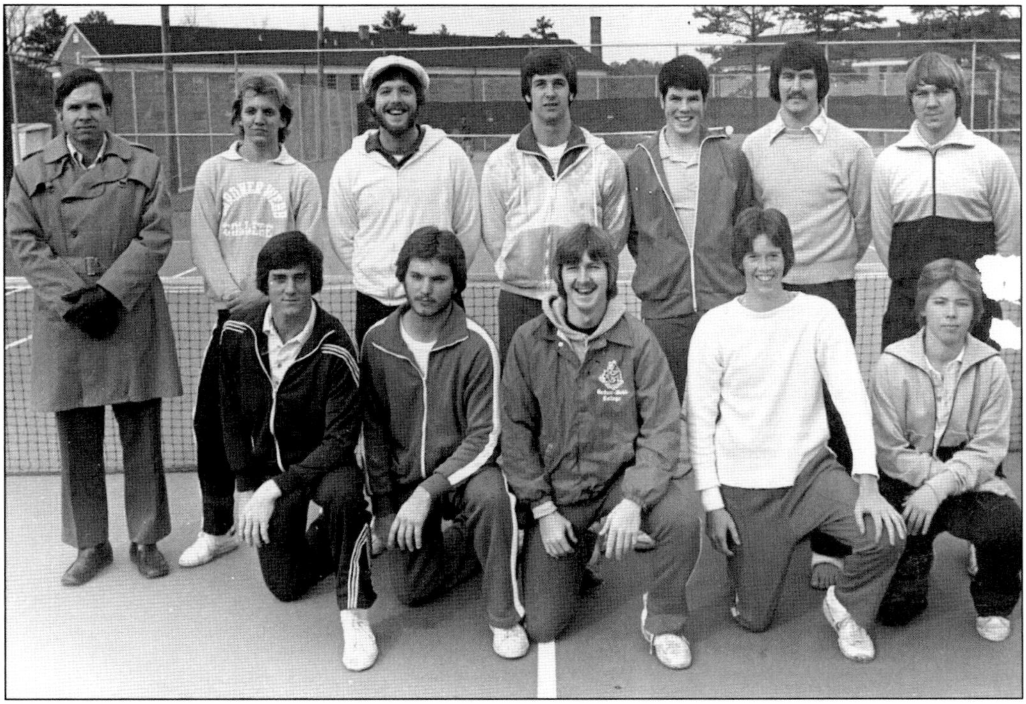

Gardner-Webb's men's tennis team was coached for years by English professor Jim Taylor. Dr. Taylor retired early due to illness. He is fondly remembered by students and athletes alike.

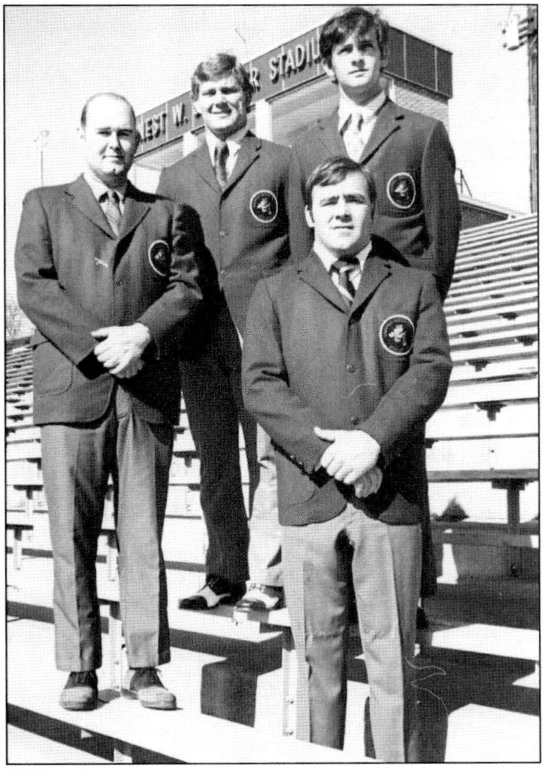

Coach George Litton (left) followed Norman Harris to lead the football team as the school moved to four-year status. His team played in the Poultry Bowl in Gainesville, Georgia. Today Mr. Litton is chair of the Cleveland County School Board.

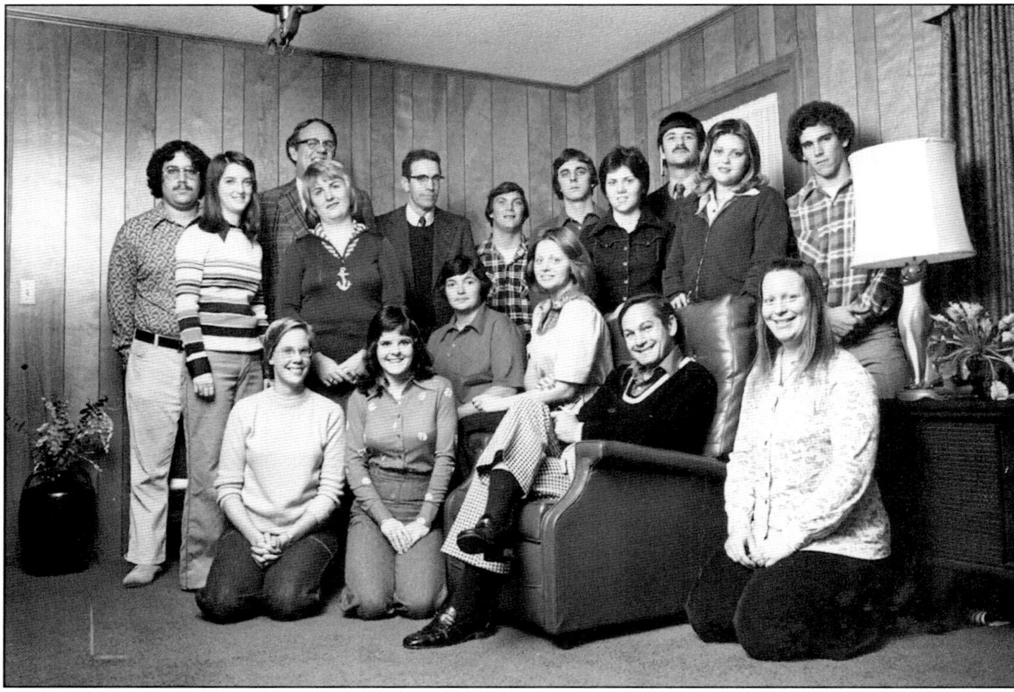

This *c.* 1975 picture shows the social science club with professors. Lansford Jolley and Garland Allen are at the back left, and Dr. Tony Eastman is sitting in the chair. Karen Andrews, daughter of Dr. Charles Andrews and current town manager of Rutherfordton, North Carolina, is kneeling at the right.

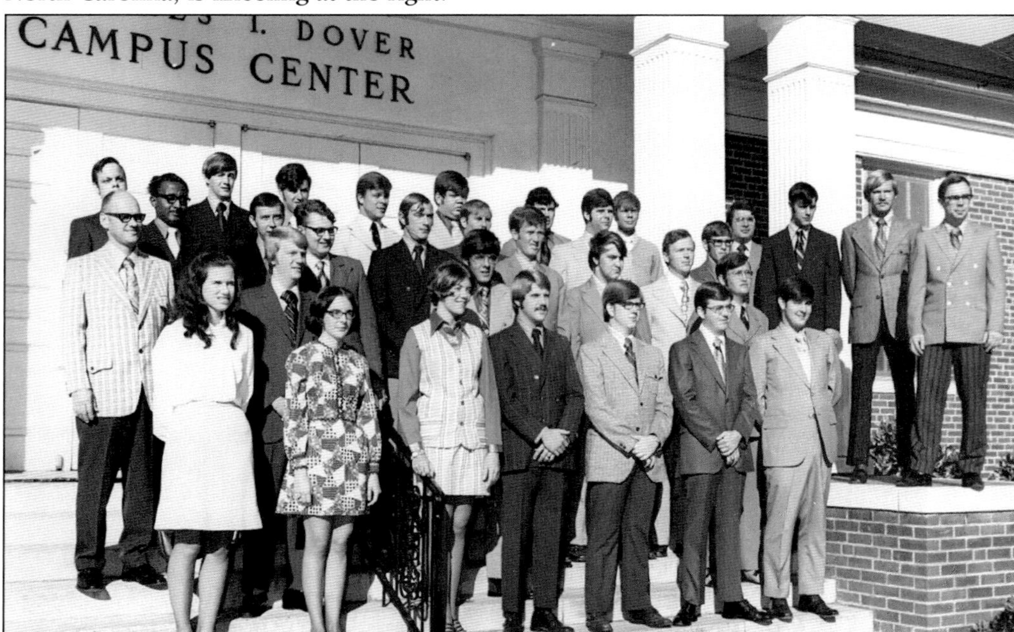

Business became a popular major when the four-year program began. Business students were part of organizations that gave them business experience and connections. A group of students pose with Prof. Joe Allen (left).

In 1976, Dr. Poston was succeeded by Dr. Craven E. Williams, who would direct the school for 10 years. Here Dr. Williams poses at the Dixon Gate with Mrs. Katie Ruth Dixon. The gate is named in memory of her husband, Prof. Herbert Dixon, who passed away in 1976.

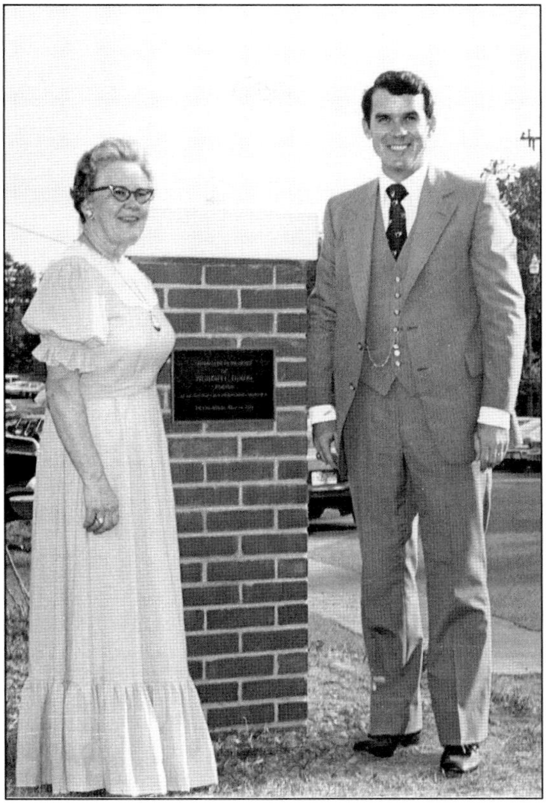

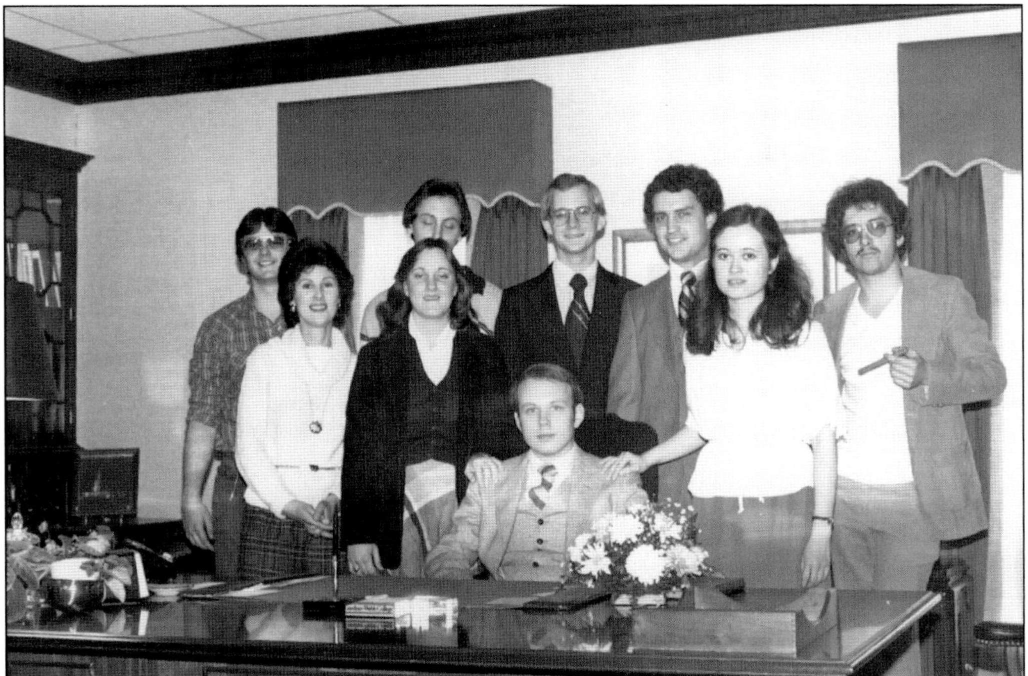

GWC student Evans Whitaker (seated) poses with a group of friends in the president's office. Evans, who aspired to be a college president, has obtained that goal at Anderson College.

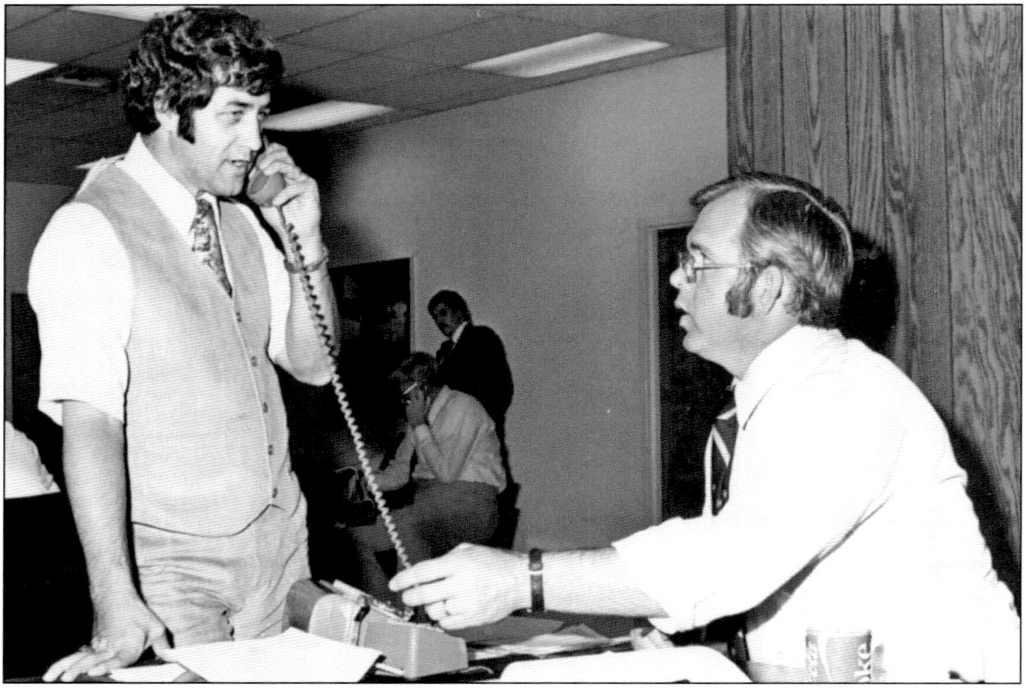

Gardner-Webb has often been a training ground for college administrators. Jerry McGee (left) is president of Wingate University, and Charles "Buddy" Freeman is a vice president at North Greenville College.

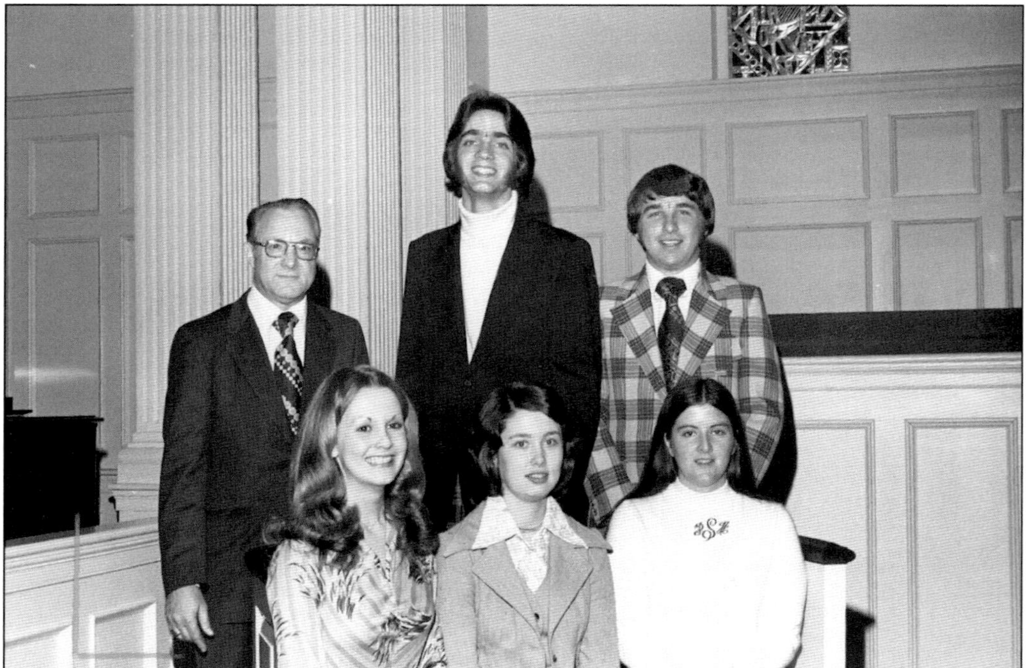

Prof. Robert Trexler poses in Dover Chapel with a group of students. The one with the outstanding jacket is Keith Dixon, who is now the director of missions for the Greater Cleveland Baptist Association.

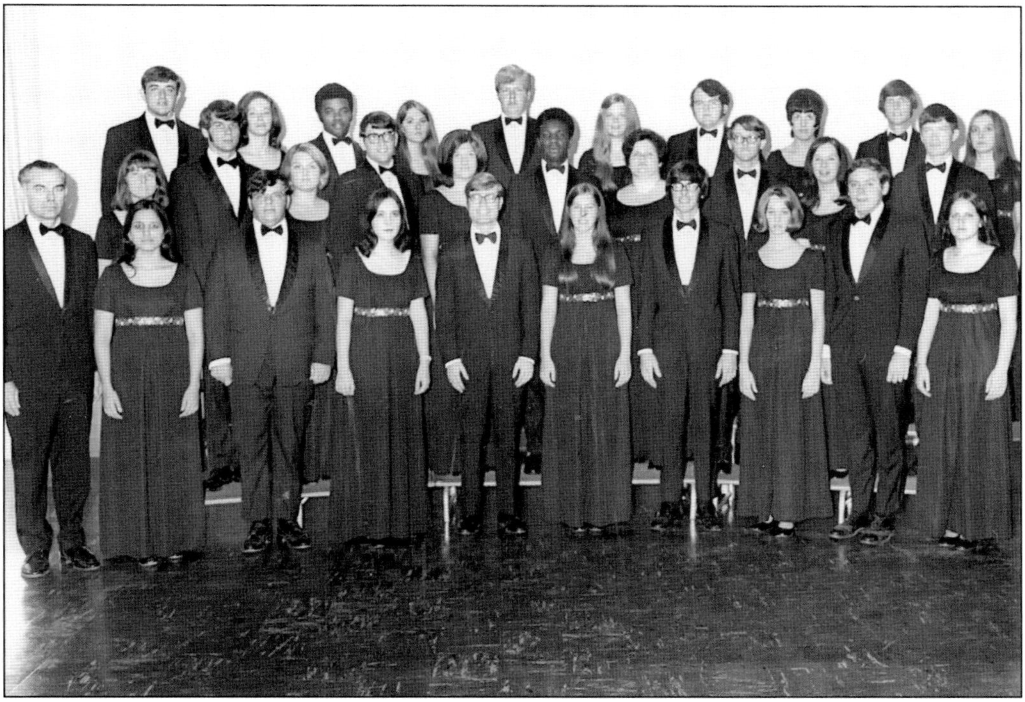

The Gardner-Webb music department takes pride in its performance. Dr. George Cribb (far left) taught at Gardner-Webb for 23 years.

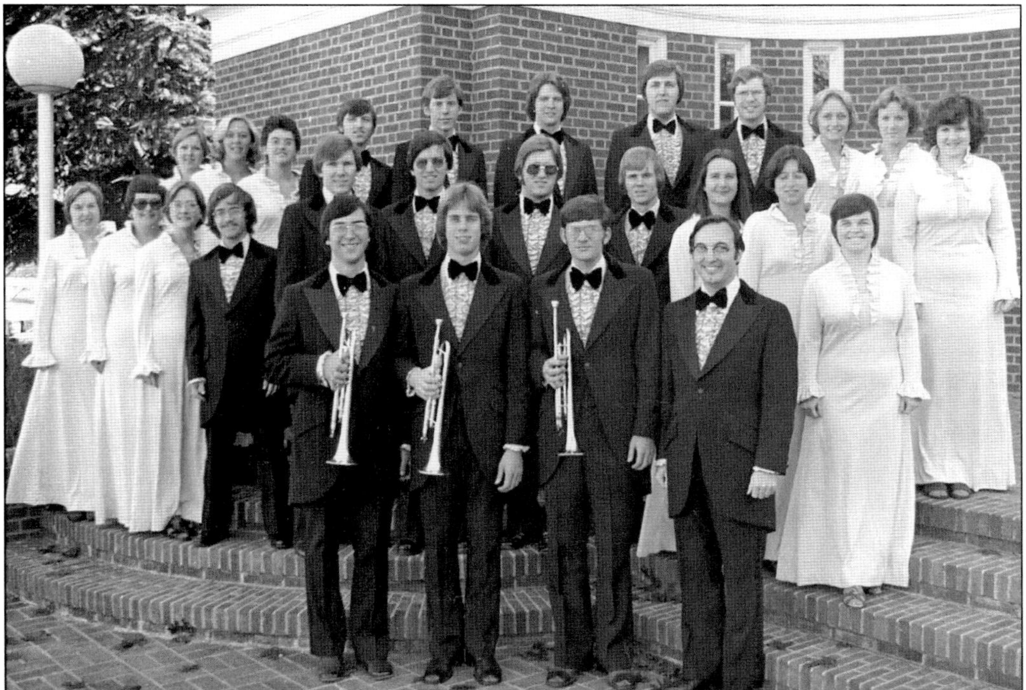

Dr. Cribb's colleague during his years at Gardner-Webb was Dr. Phil Perrin. Dr. Perrin not only produced excellent choirs, he also climbed the highest mountains on six continents. Dr. Perrin recently retired, and he and his wife are doing mission work in Africa.

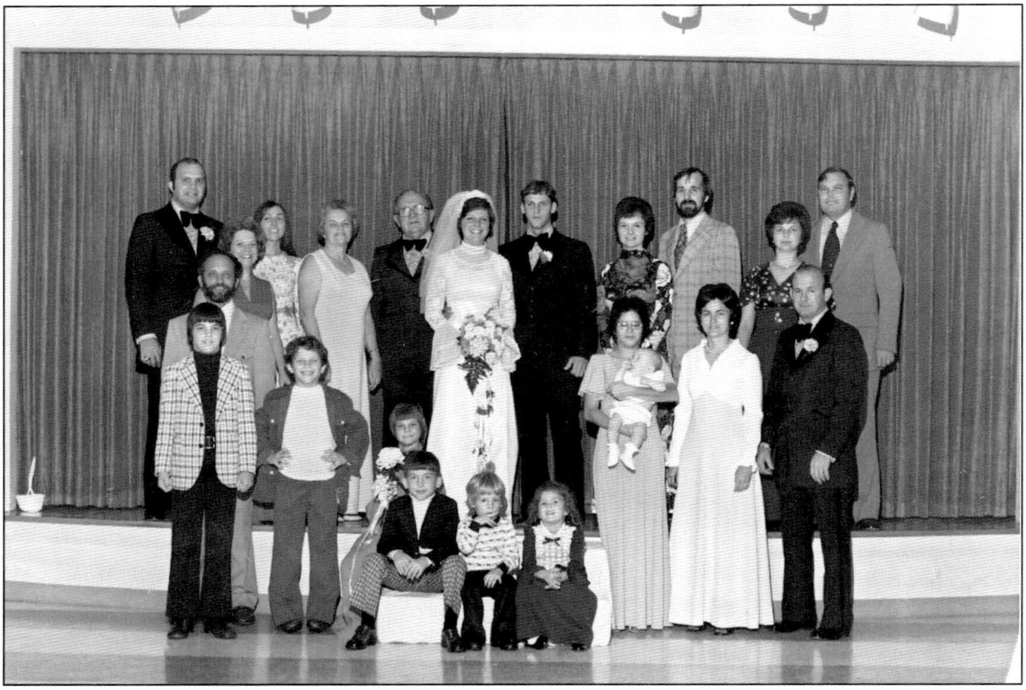

Gardner-Webb is often a family affair. This 1977 wedding photo of Fred Edwards and Gin-g Hedrick is filled with Gardner-Webb graduates. Fred and Gin-g are GWC graduates. On Gin-g's right are her parents, Carl and Rachel Hedrick. Rachel is the daughter of Prof. J.D. Huggins. The Hedrick children attended Gardner-Webb.

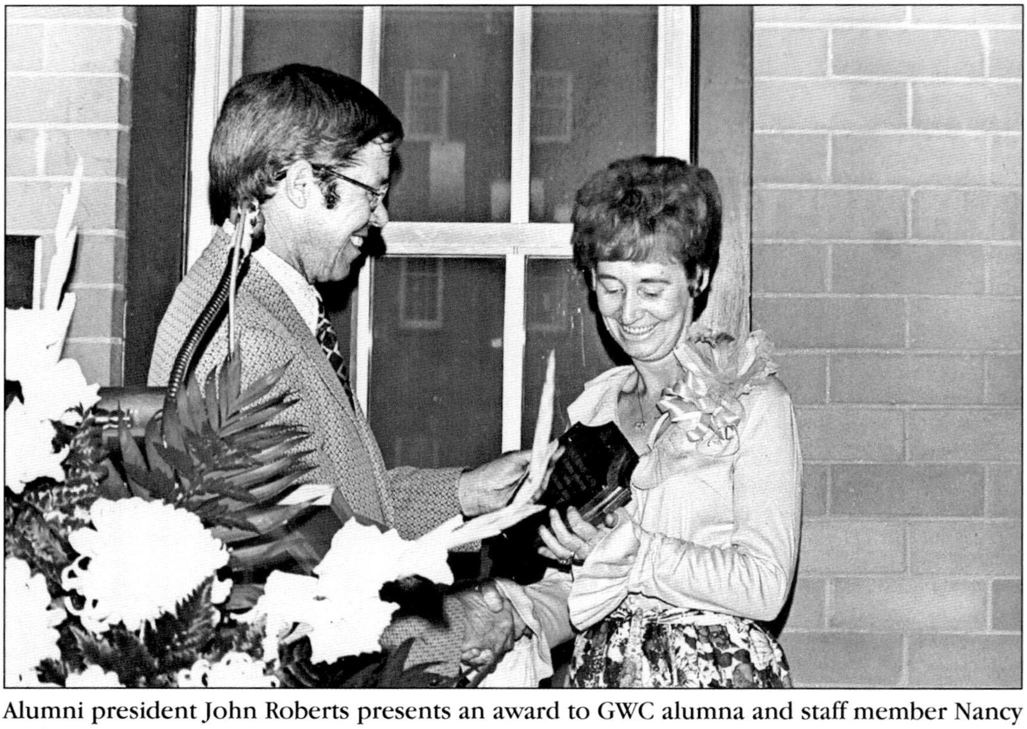

Alumni president John Roberts presents an award to GWC alumna and staff member Nancy Anthony Poston.

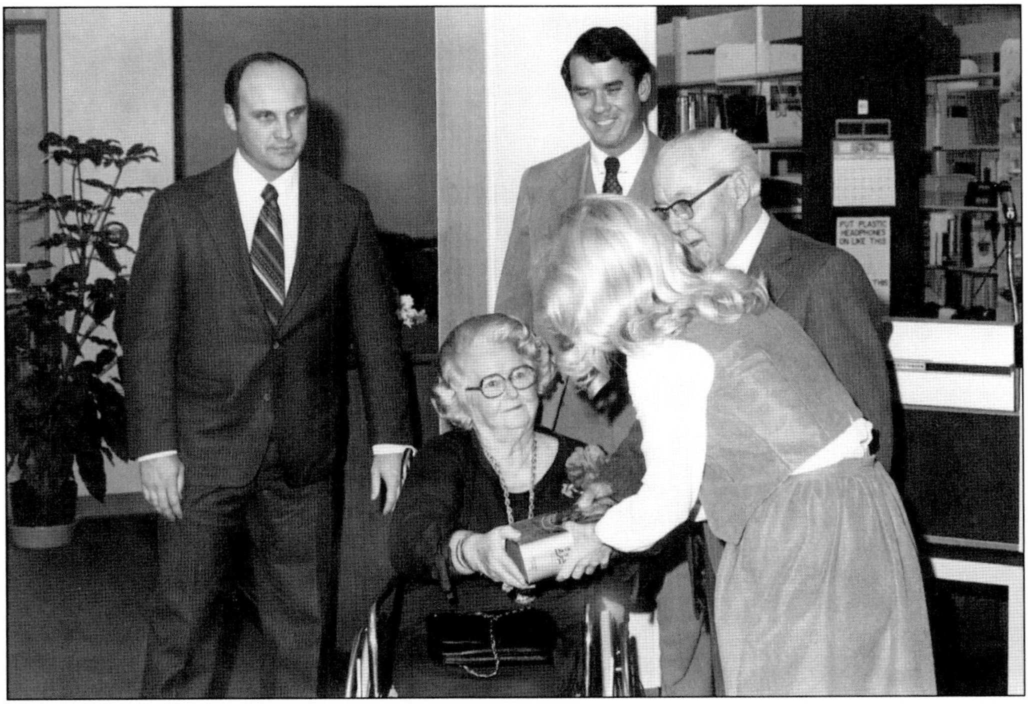

The lady seated is Kathleen Nolan Dover, wife of Charles I. Dover (at right). Gardner-Webb's theater in the Lutz Yelton Convocation Center is named in honor of Mrs. Dover. Dr. Robert Knott (left) was GWC's academic dean then, and is now president of Catawba College.

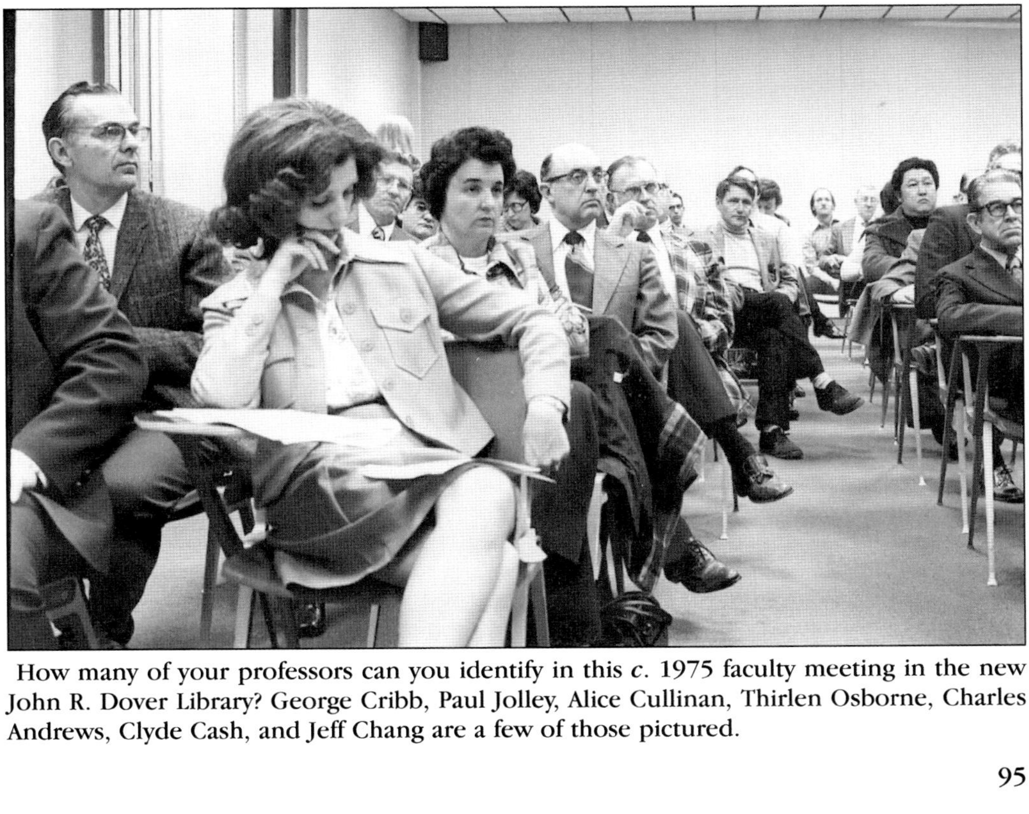

How many of your professors can you identify in this *c.* 1975 faculty meeting in the new John R. Dover Library? George Cribb, Paul Jolley, Alice Cullinan, Thirlen Osborne, Charles Andrews, Clyde Cash, and Jeff Chang are a few of those pictured.

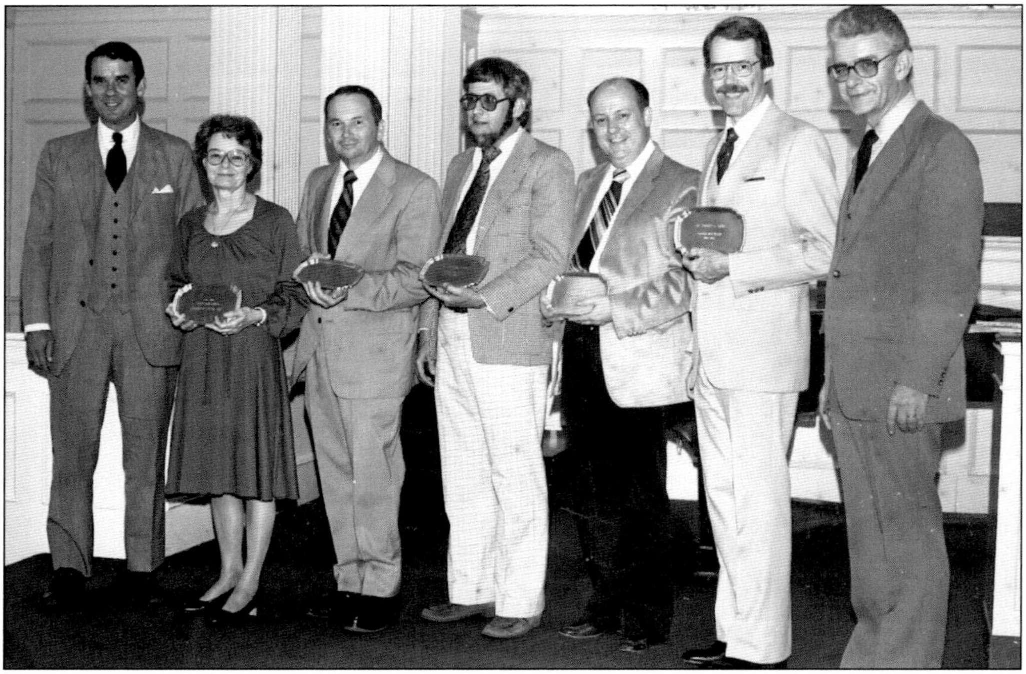

Dr. Williams is pictured with six people who are receiving awards for service at Gardner-Webb. From left to right are Joy Sandifer, Jim Henson, Bill Stowe, Bob Morgan, Robert Lamb, and John Drayer.

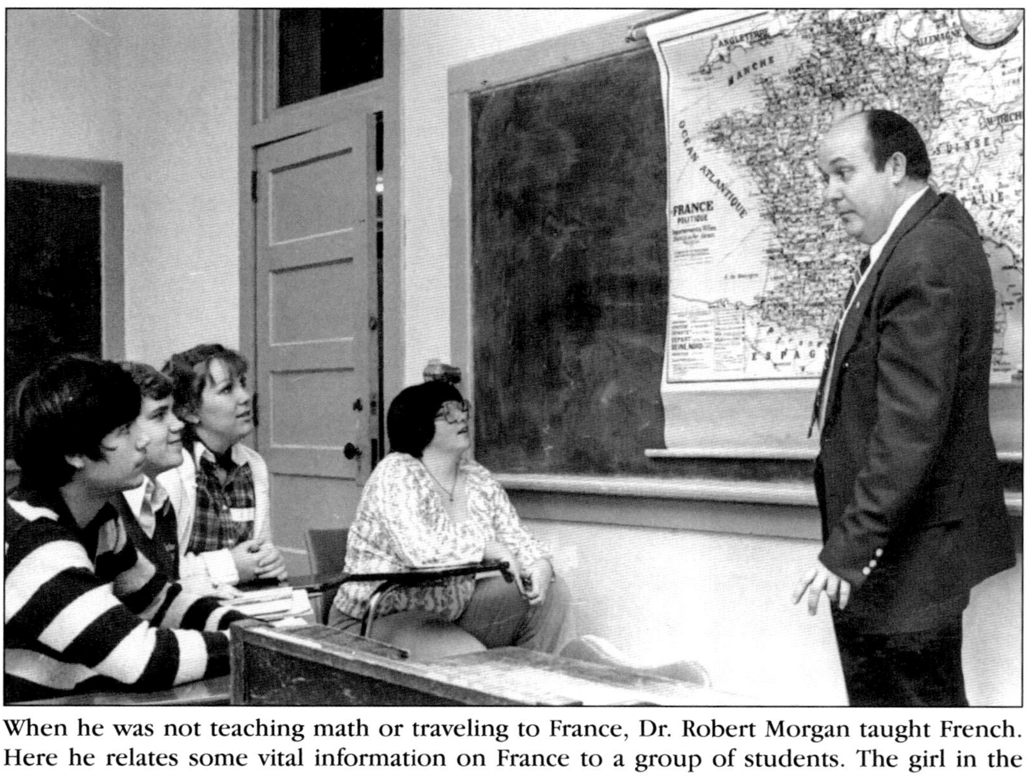

When he was not teaching math or traveling to France, Dr. Robert Morgan taught French. Here he relates some vital information on France to a group of students. The girl in the middle is Ruth Ann Brunson.

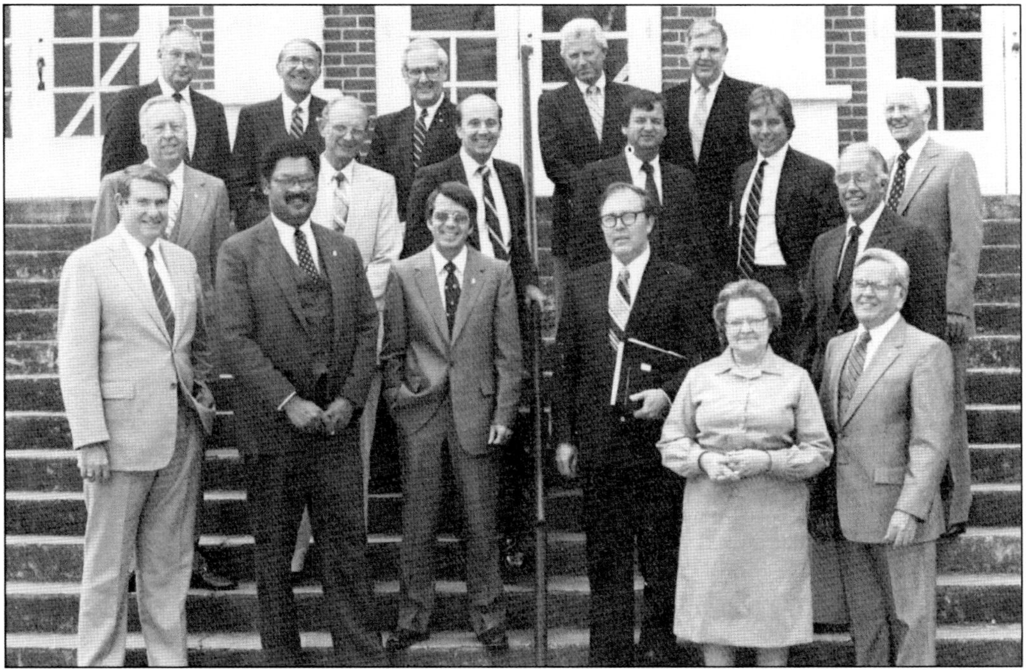

The GWU Board of Trustees did not regularly have a group picture made. This 1983 group did make the GWC annual. They are, from left to right, as follows: (first row) Olna Daves and Kyle Graybeard; (second row) Maylon Little, Tom Philson, Jimmy Jacumin, Charles Hicks, and John McCulloch; (third row) Lloyd Bost, Joe Medford, Lee Proctor Jr., Don Kincaid, Ed Broyhill, and George Blanton Jr.; (fourth row) Hobart Smith, Bernard Parker, Guy Walker Jr., Ron Hawkins, and Ralph Bentley.

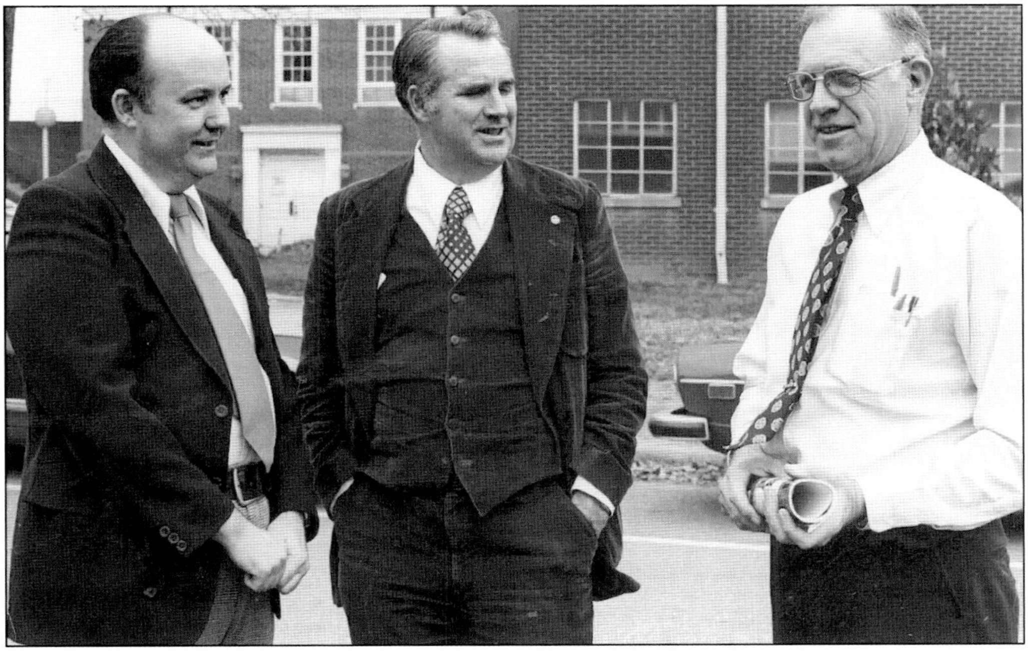

These three men represent over 80 years at Gardner-Webb in the foreign language department. From left to right are Bob Morgan, Alan Setzer, and Charles Andrews.

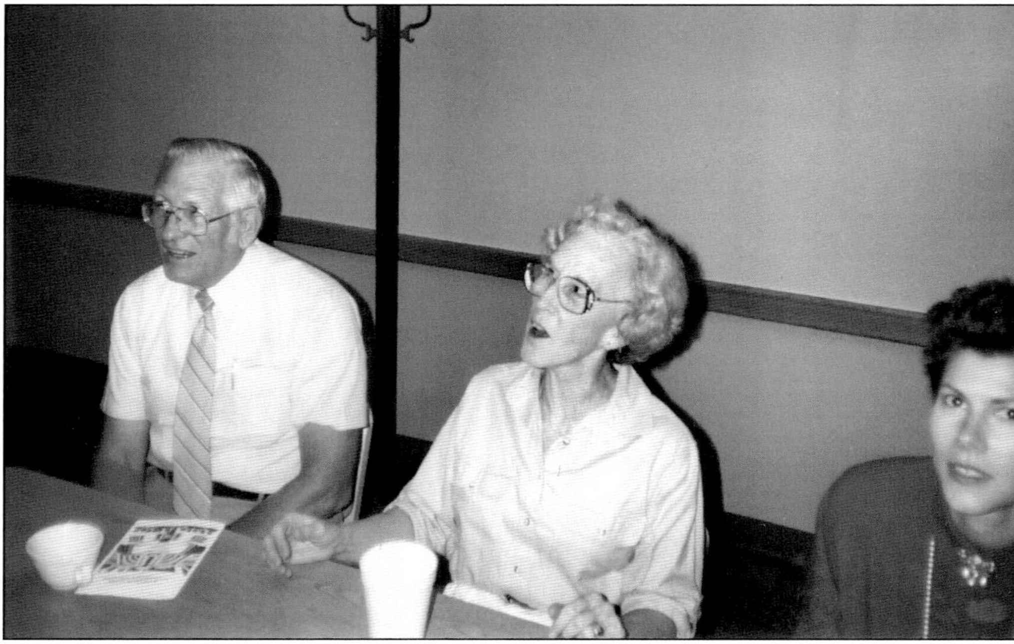

If you wondered where a large number of faculty were at 10 o'clock each morning during the last 35 years, you may not have heard of the famous (or infamous) ten-o'clock coffee group. Pictured here from left to right are Dr. Paul Jolley, Dr. Barbara Burkett, and Barbara Stansbury. This may be a rare photo, since Dr. Burkett avoided the camera and is absent from most annuals.

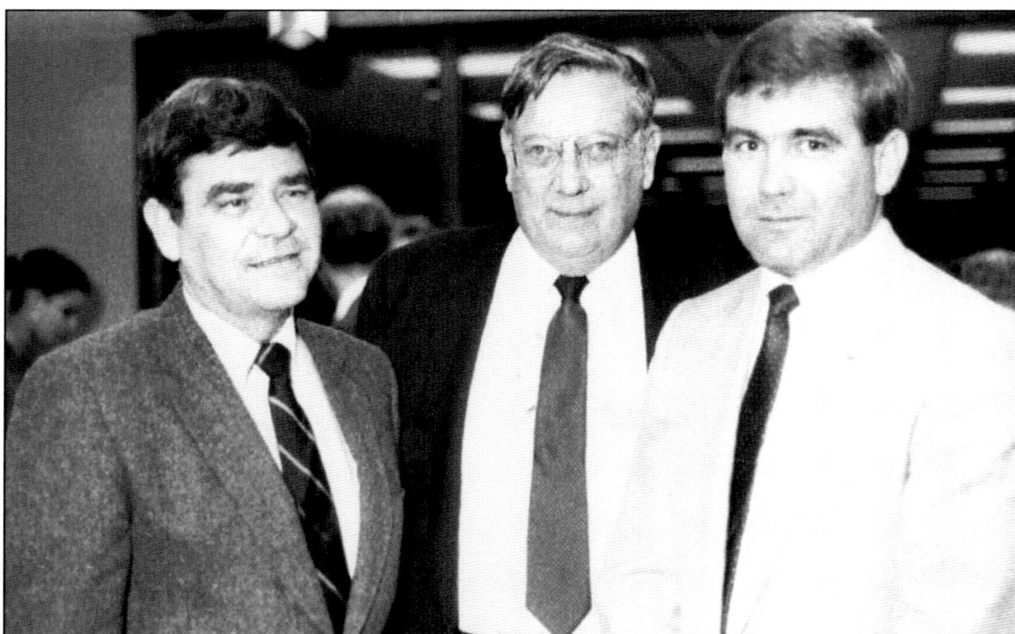

Alumni of the 1980s should remember this trio. Pictured from left to right are Chuck Mosley, who was the voice of the Bulldogs on the radio; Hank Garrity, who served as vice president for development and athletic director; and Woody Fish, who coached football at GWU for 13 years.

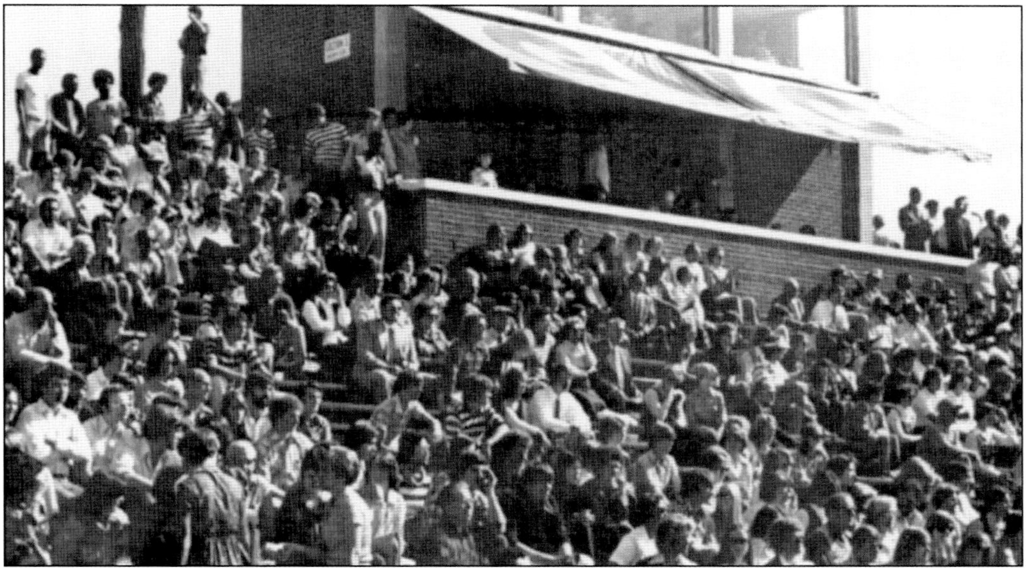

For years, the home side at Spangler Stadium faced the sun, but the students endured. The awning covered the president's box, and the press box was expanded to three levels over time. Today, with the modern new home facility, visitors have inherited the sunny side.

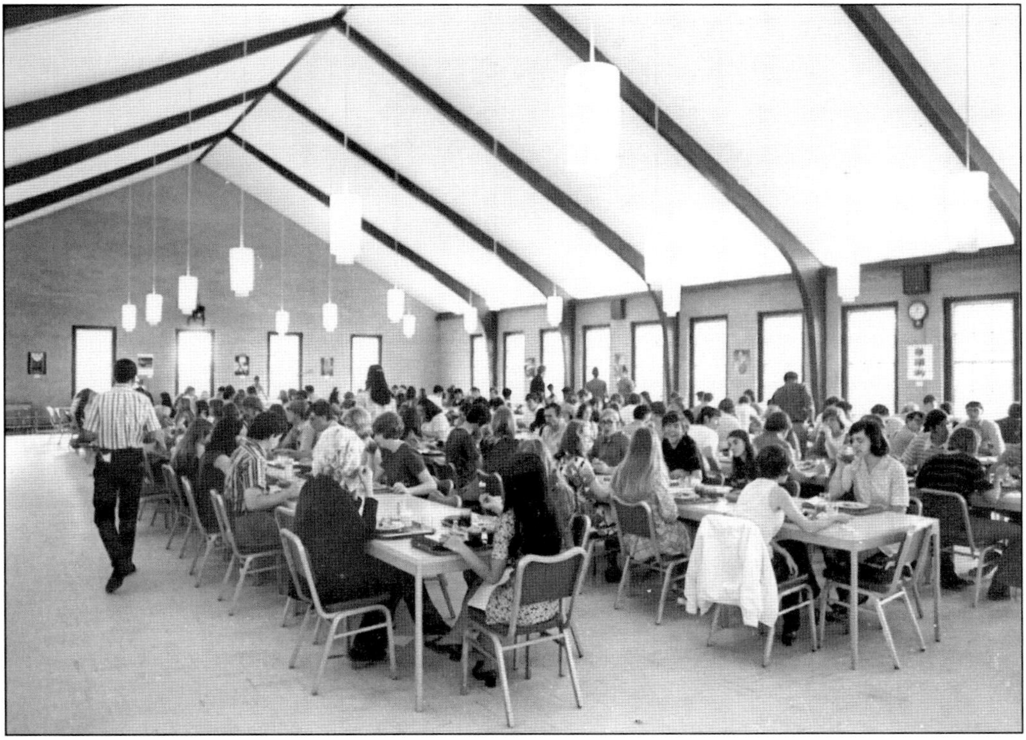

The cafeteria in Dover, as it was in the 1970s, should bring back memories for many. This is before the long salad bar now available.

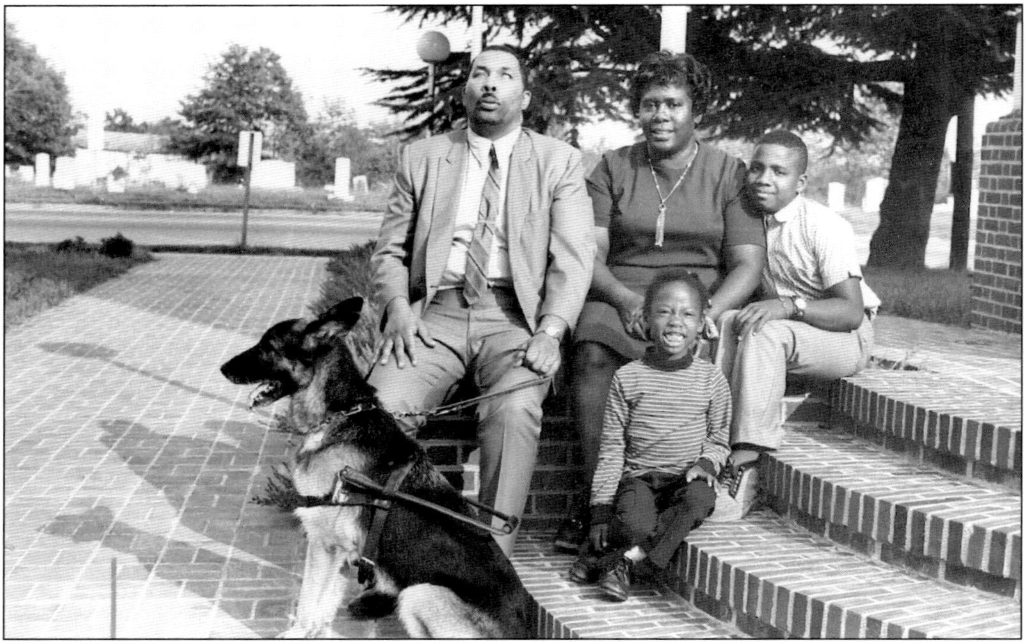

If you are an alumnus from the 1970s and 1980s, you will recognize one of the favorite religion professors of that era. Dr. Logan Carson; his wife, Glenwood; his daughter, Tricia, an alumnus; and his son are pictured here. Students never could understand how Dr. Carson knew when they tried to sneak out of class. The faculty did not know either.

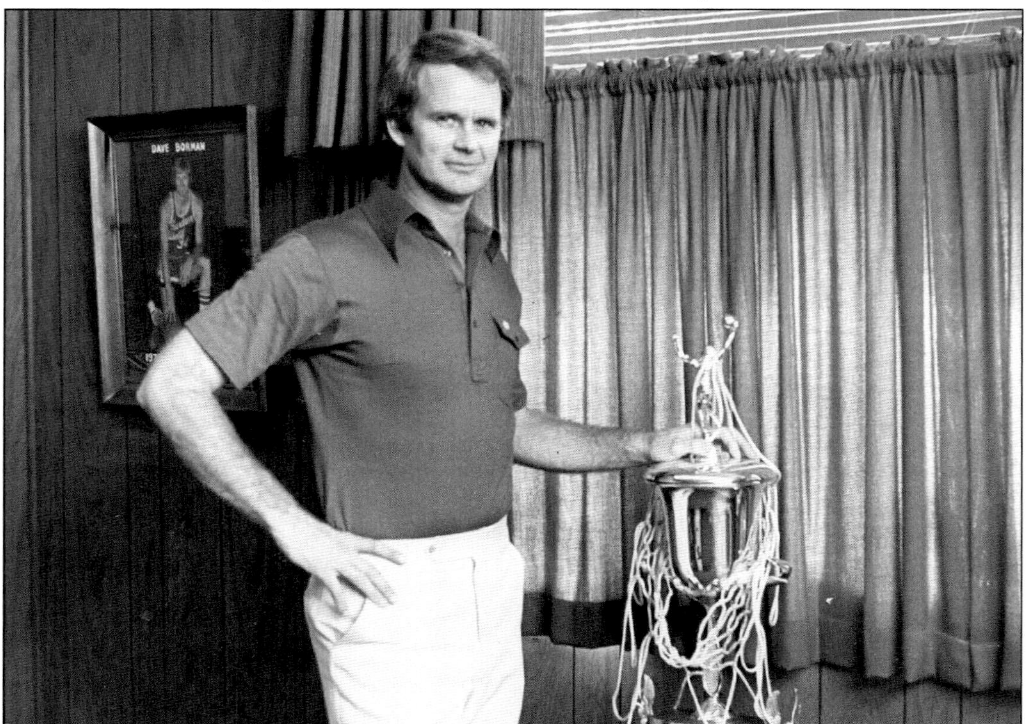

Coach Jim Wiles came from Anderson College to coach basketball when Eddie Holbrook departed for Furman.

Five

GARDNER-WEBB UNIVERSITY

The Emergence of the University: 1986 to 2005

In 1986, Dr. Christopher White arrived from Elon College to assume the presidency of GWC. The college had had over 25 years to mature as a senior institution. In the next decade, GWC would experience growth in virtually all areas and become a regional university.

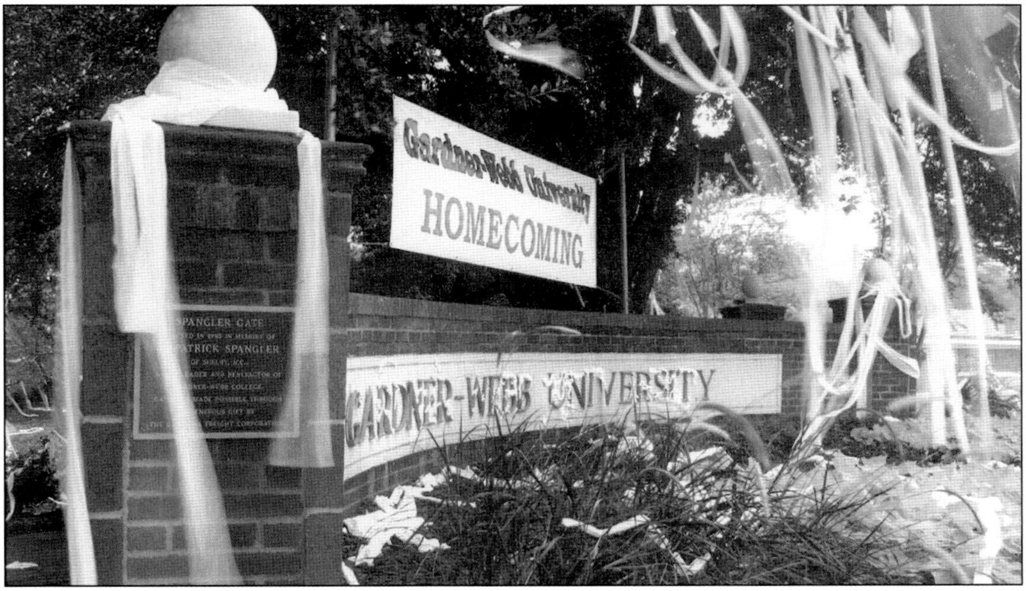

People arriving at GWU from Shelby see the Spangler gate at the front of the campus. Signs, such as the homecoming one here, welcome groups to the campus. Alumni of the last two or three decades will notice another "sign" of homecoming—the toilet tissue decorations. Twenty years ago, the college staff tried to prevent the decorating. One year, two students were arrested for littering the town—Dr. Eastman had to come to their defense. Finally, it became accepted that this tradition was okay.

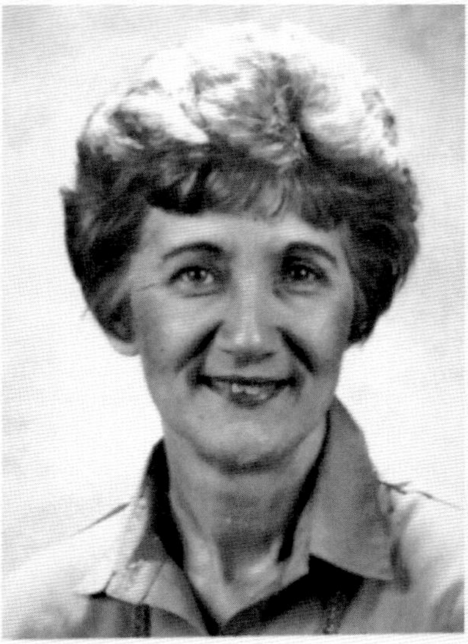

Kitty Eeds
Sec., President

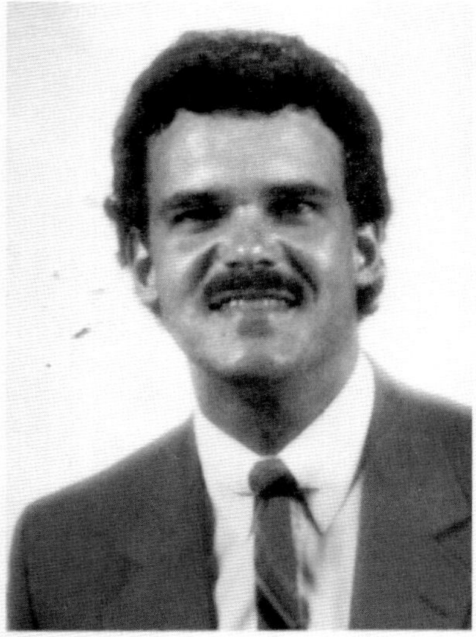

Ray Hardee
Admissions Counselor

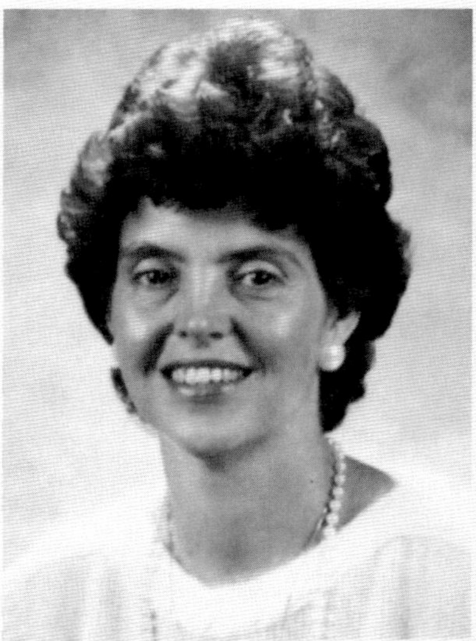

Kathryn Hamrick
Dir., Public Info.

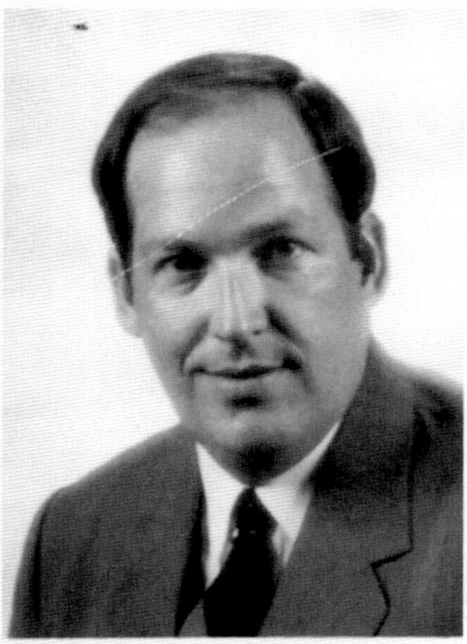

Randy Kilby
Dir. of Admissions

Many memorable people at Gardner Webb were staff members that guided us as they did their jobs. Kitty Eeds was the friendly, efficient assistant to the president in the 1980s and 1990s. Kathryn Hamrick served as director of public information. Ray Hardee and Randy Kilby are GWC graduates. Ray recruited hundreds of students with his friendly style (and bad jokes). Ray is a pastor in Belmont, North Carolina, today. Storytelling Randy Kilby recruited before Ray arrived. Randy left to work at Georgetown College and later became president of Fruitland Bible College. The college was saddened when Randy died of a heart attack at an early age.

Homecoming 1987 saw the James Gang (led by quarterback Jesse James) beat Lenoir-Rhyne 56-5. Cara Barker, pictured here with escort Brent Winslow, was selected homecoming queen.

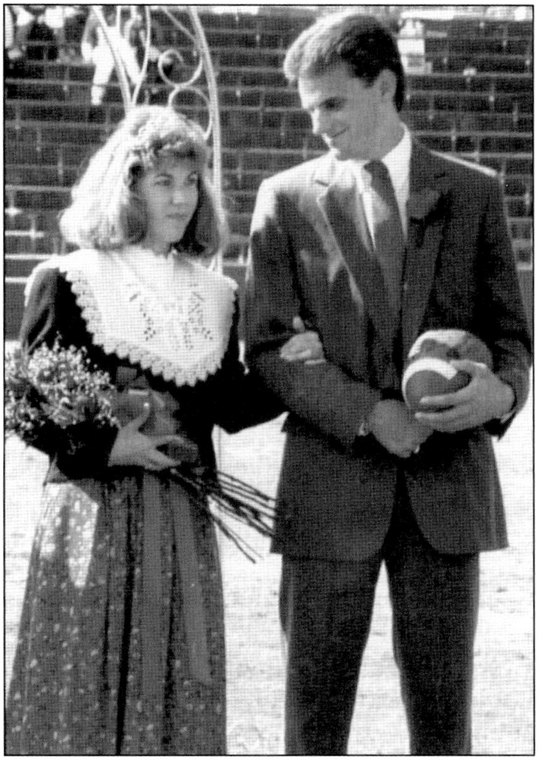

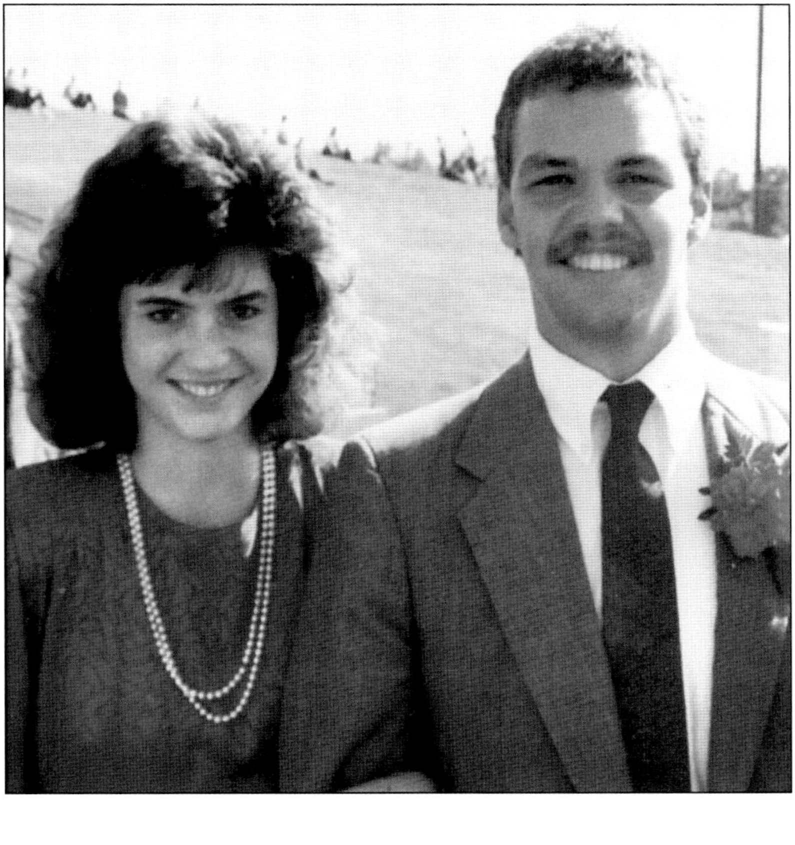

Beth Lamb, 1987 junior class attendant (Mrs. Noel Manning today), is escorted by Rich Hardee.

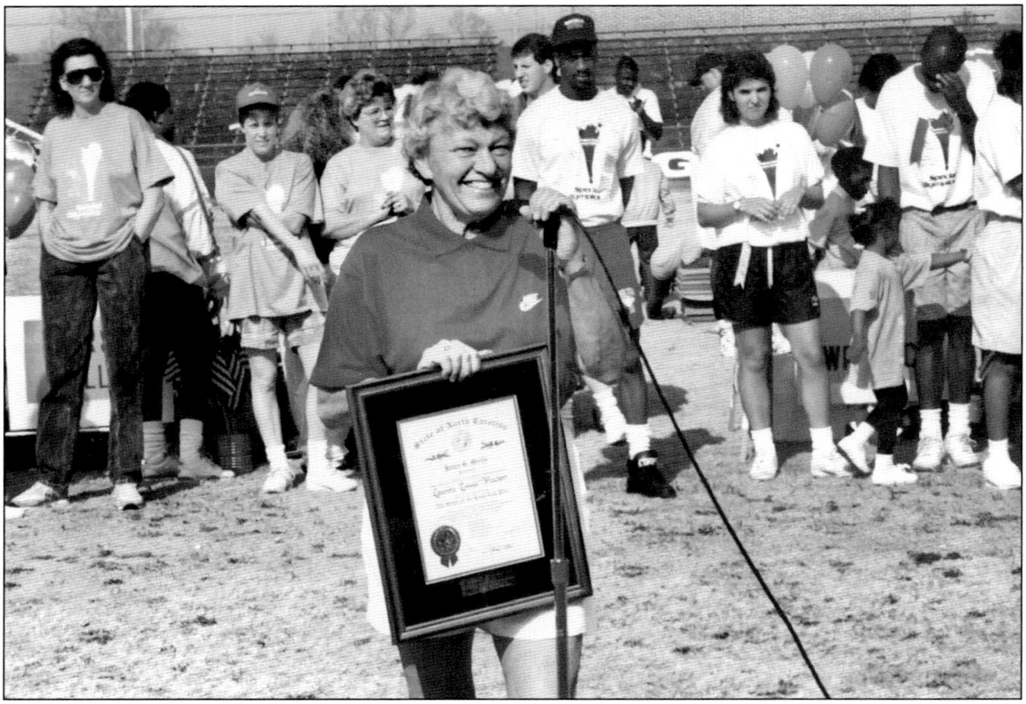

For years, students studied with Dr. Lonnie Proctor, but many others knew her for her dedicated work with the Special Olympics. Dr. Proctor still has the yellow Volkswagen and is active in senior games.

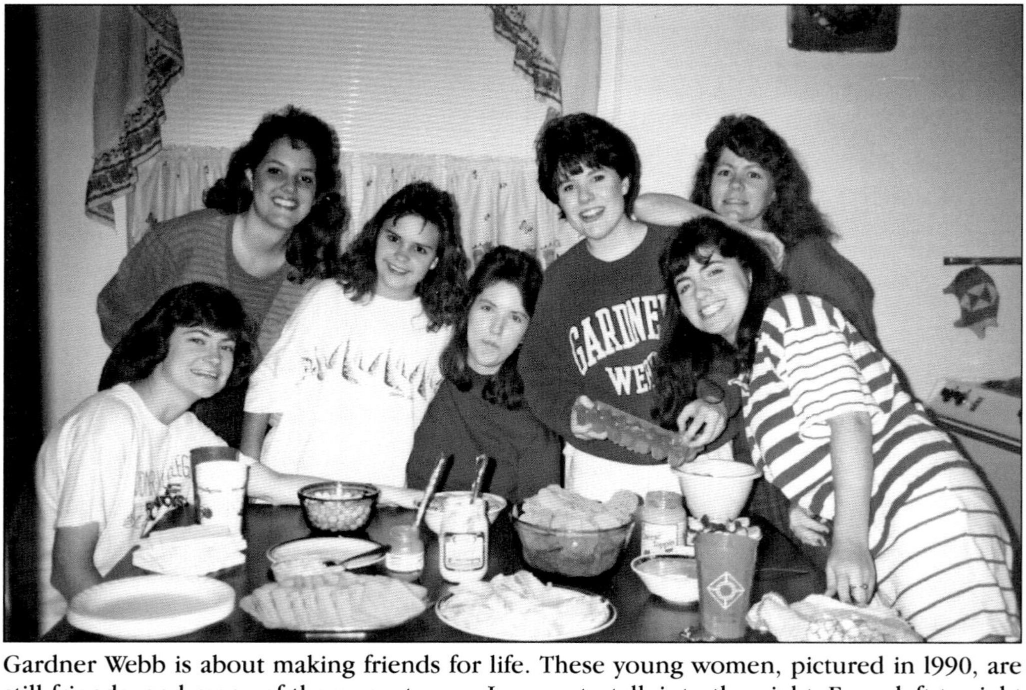

Gardner Webb is about making friends for life. These young women, pictured in 1990, are still friends, and many of them meet every January to talk into the night. From left to right we see Nancy Reid, Kim Freeman, Michele Philemon, Christie Hambright, Chrissy Vaughn, Pat Davis, and Donna Pritchard.

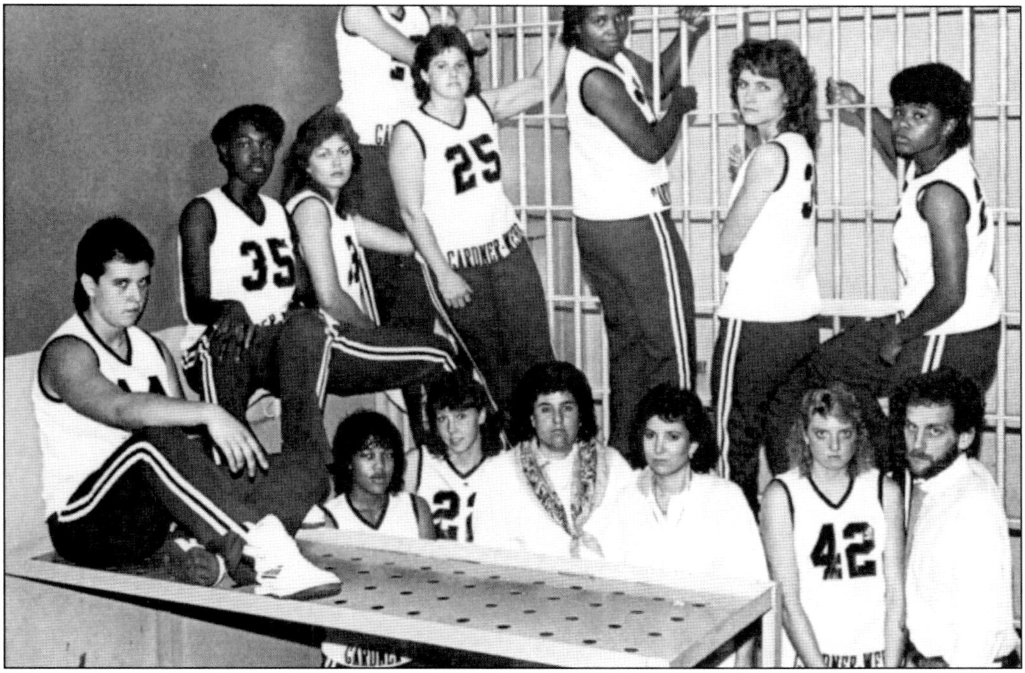

The 1987–1988 women's basketball team poses at the Cleveland County Jail. Coach Jeff Tubbs led the team for the last time before he moved back to the classroom and then to the administration. Pictured from left to right are the following: (front row) Roxanne Ferguson, Cheryl Wright, Angie Black, Beth Hambright, Donna Hendrix, and Dr. Tubbs; (middle row) Lisa Sabbarth, Lana Chambers, Mechelle Hamilton, Amy Dellinger, Gloria Campbell, Tanya Taylor, and Kim Haywood; (back row) Benita Tilley.

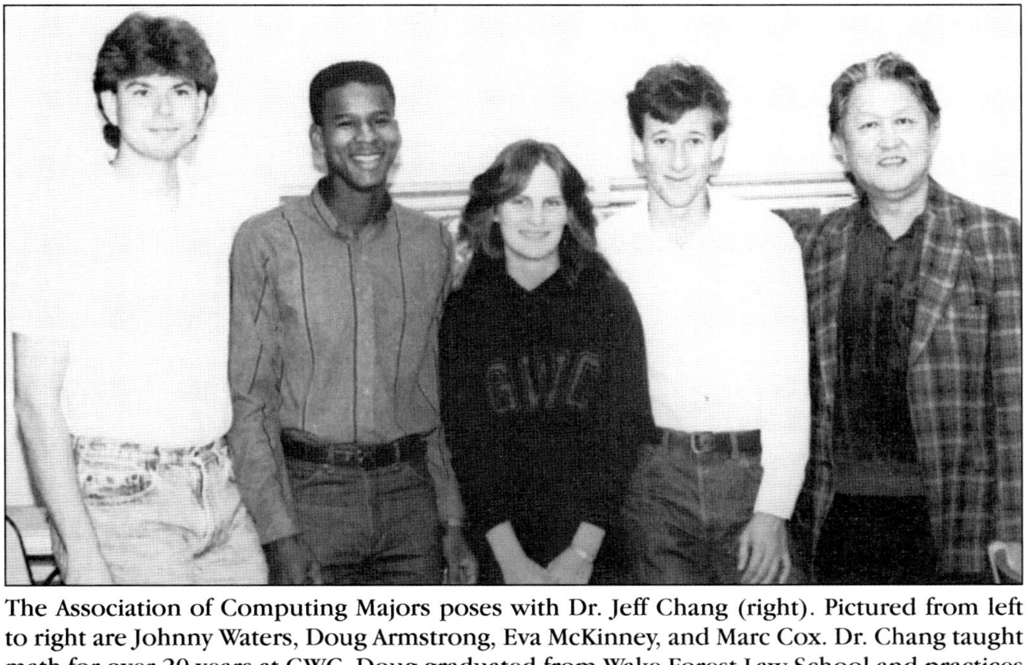

The Association of Computing Majors poses with Dr. Jeff Chang (right). Pictured from left to right are Johnny Waters, Doug Armstrong, Eva McKinney, and Marc Cox. Dr. Chang taught math for over 20 years at GWC. Doug graduated from Wake Forest Law School and practices law in Cincinnati.

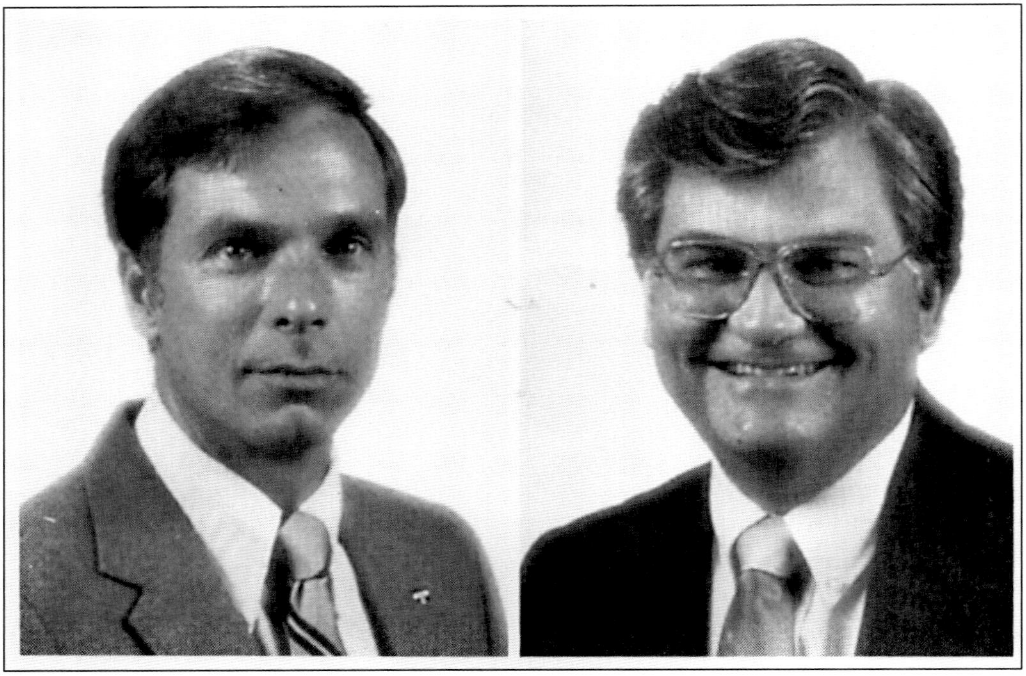

Gardner-Webb has had a large number of faculty members who have spent their careers teaching with the college. Dr. Sherman Parrish taught chemistry for over 30 years. Dr. Tom Jones has spent 20 years teaching biology. He also leads the university's honors program.

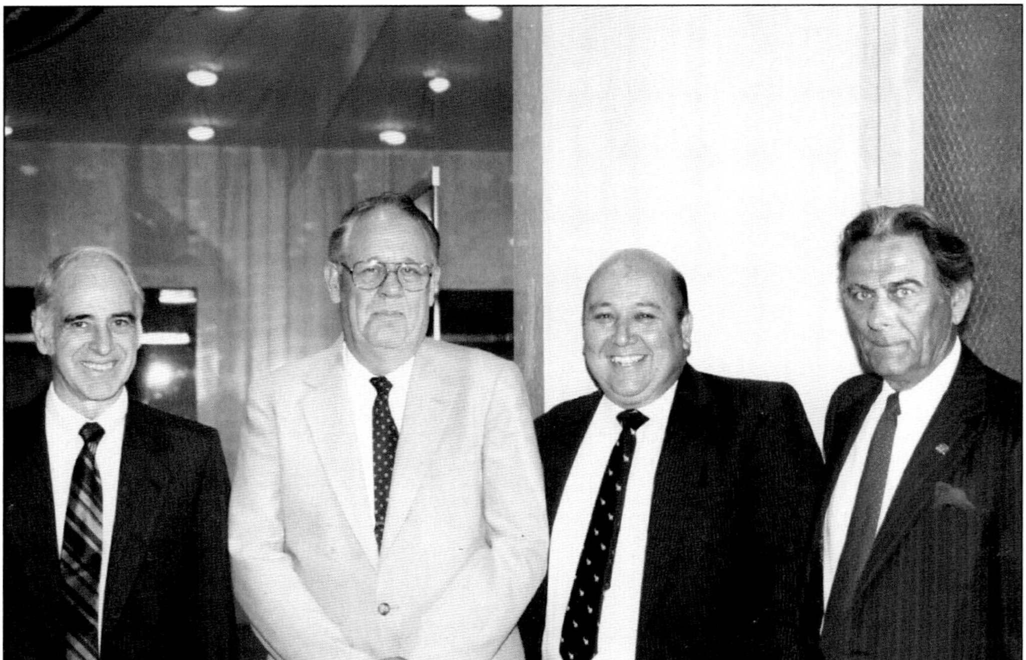

Several professors in the 1980s found fun and relaxation during spring break in New York City. At the Wellington Hotel on Seventh Avenue we see, from left to right, Ernest Blankenship, Lansford Jolley, Barry Hambright, and Wallace Carpenter.

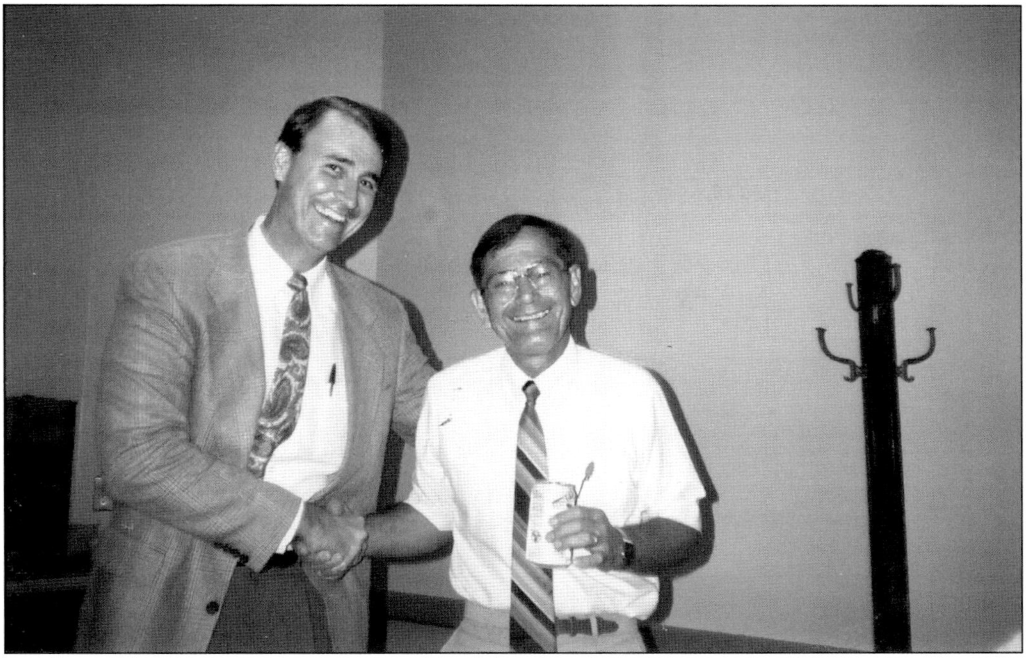

Students of Dr. Tony Eastman may be surprised to see him socializing with a preacher. Rev. Buddy Corbin (left) was pastor of the Boiling Springs Baptist Church for several years. Today Buddy serves in Asheville and is active in the Baptist State Convention.

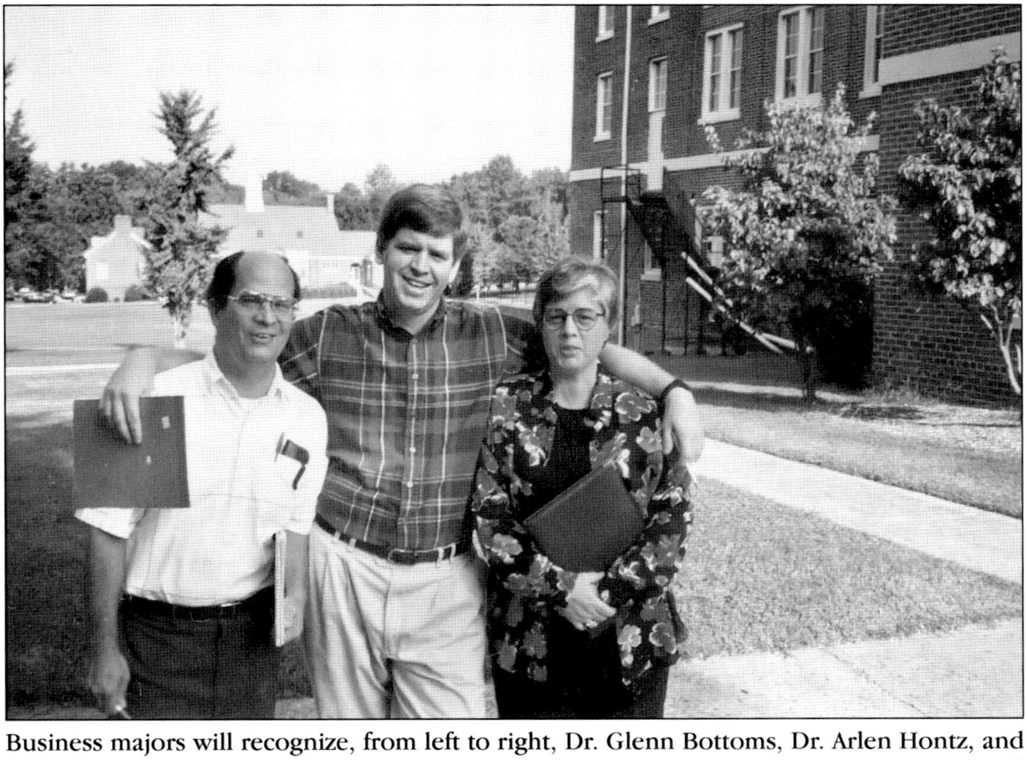

Business majors will recognize, from left to right, Dr. Glenn Bottoms, Dr. Arlen Hontz, and Dr. Sue Camp. Dean Hontz led the Broyhill School as it grew in prestige. Dr. Bottoms and Dr. Camp have combined for over 50 years at GWU.

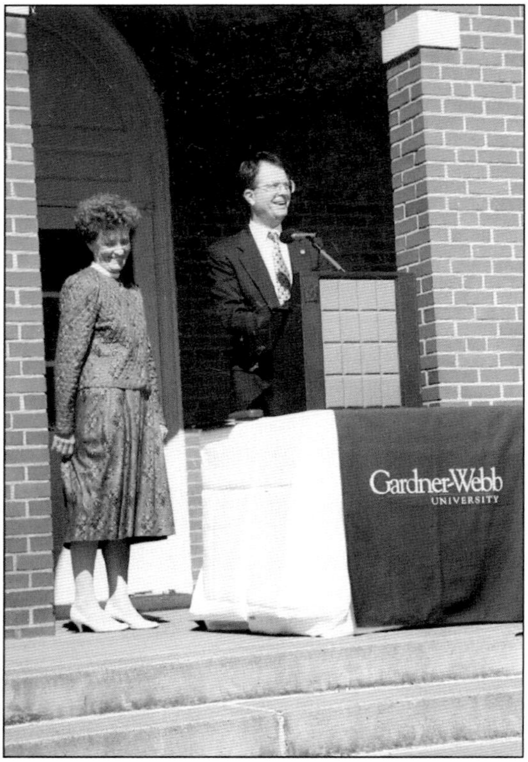

Dr. M. Christopher White led the college to university status during his 16 years as president. Here, he announces the appointment of Dr. Delores Hunt as dean of the college of education.

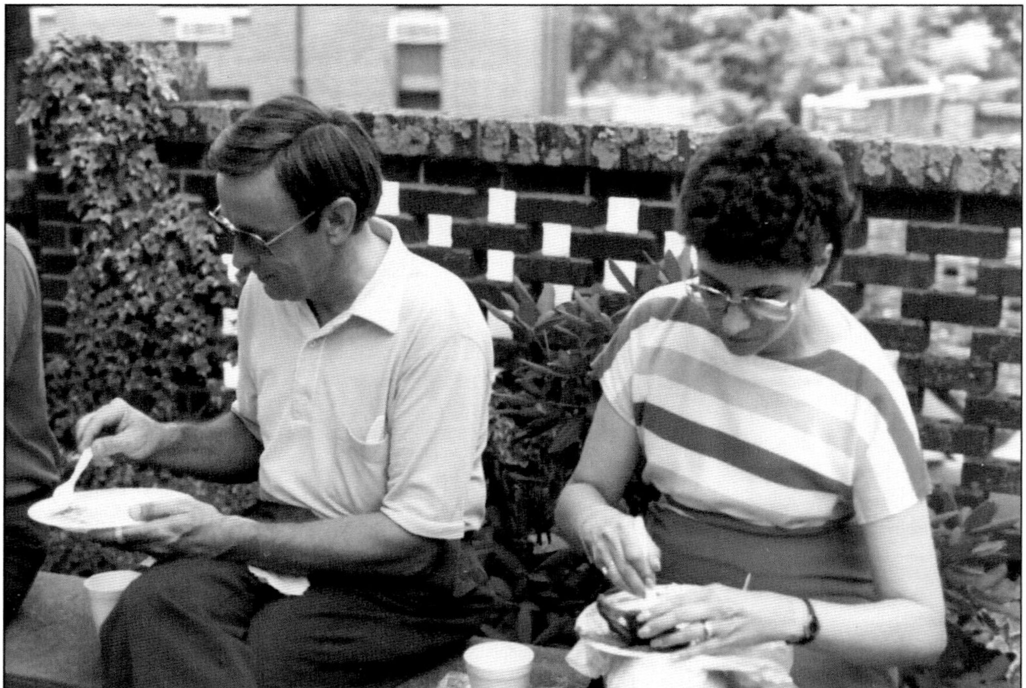

Students from the 1960s to the 1990s will remember Melvin Lutz as teacher or administrator. Joann Lutz worked in the business office and in the development office during those years. The Lutzes have retired and live in Boiling Springs.

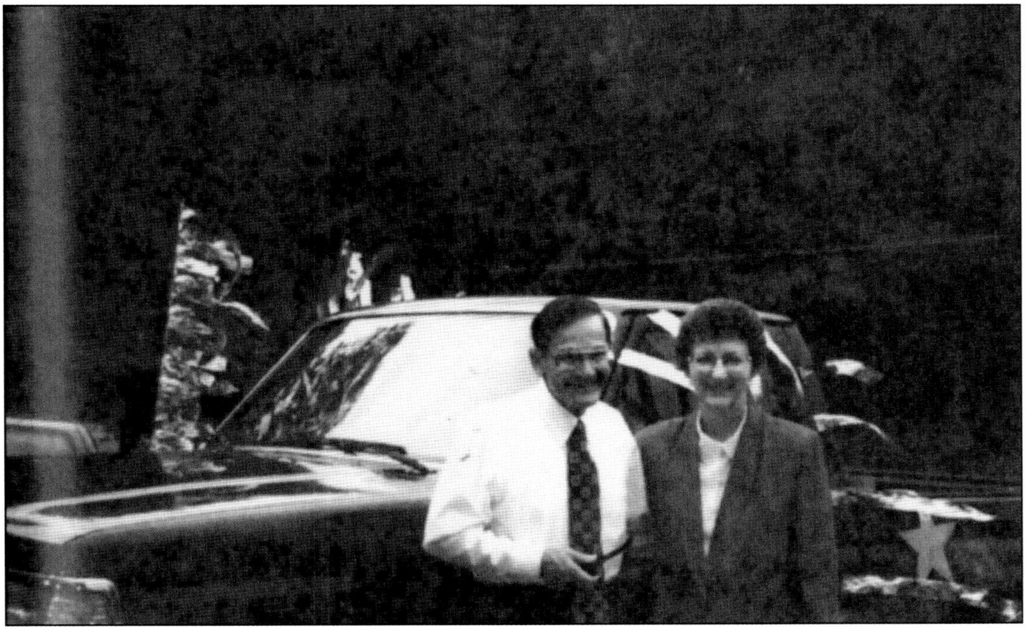

Posed beside the senior class's homecoming float, Joetha Eastman joins her husband in his role as senior-class advisor. Mrs. Eastman still works in the physical education department. Dr. Eastman has not learned the meaning of "retirement."

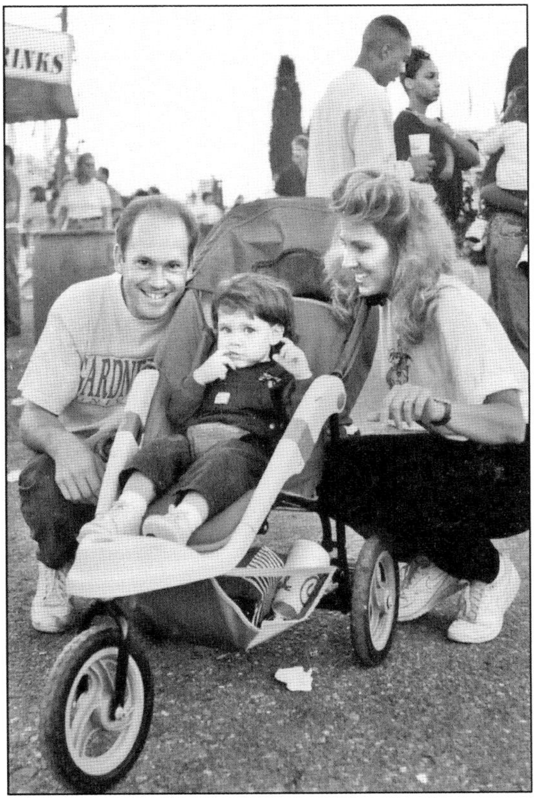

These two GWC grads both made *A*s in Dr. Hambright's United States government class. Teresa Cannon rejected the advice of Dr. Hambright to marry a businessman and has been happily married to Tracy Jessup for years. The happy parents pose with their son, Christian. Tracy is minister to the university.

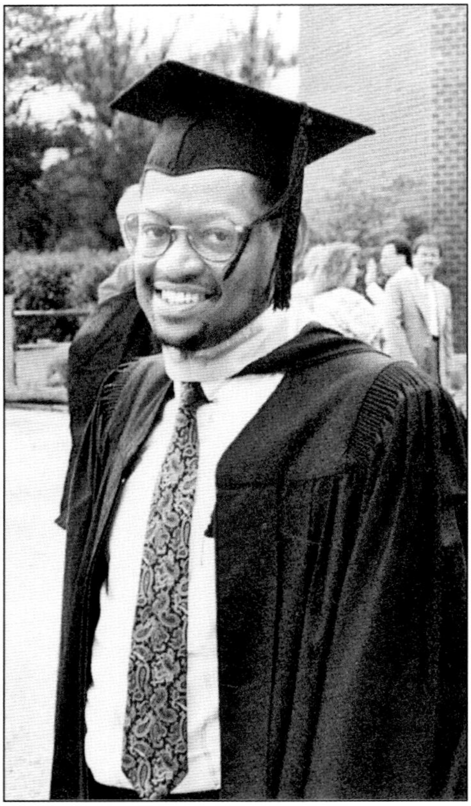

Jerome Scott was hired from Cleveland Community College to work in the GOAL program. Soon he was promoted to dean of students and then vice president. When he died suddenly while at a trustee retreat, his funeral was held in LYCC to handle the crowd of friends.

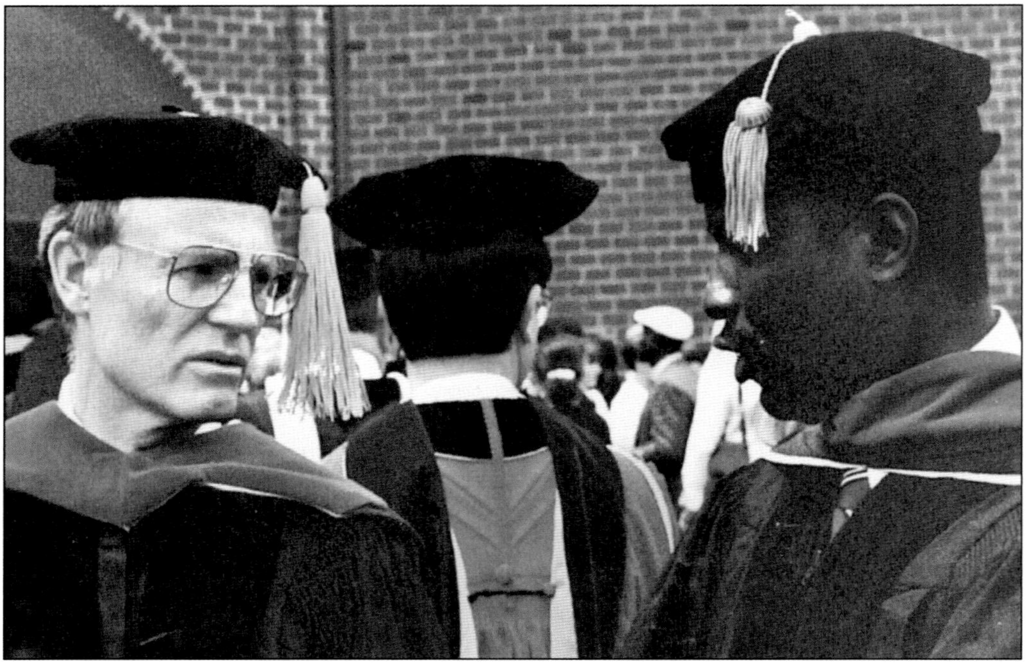

Graduation is the end of an era every year. The university sends several hundred graduates out into "the real world." Academic dean Dr. Gil Blackburn and Dr. Anthony Negbenebor reflect on the year just completed.

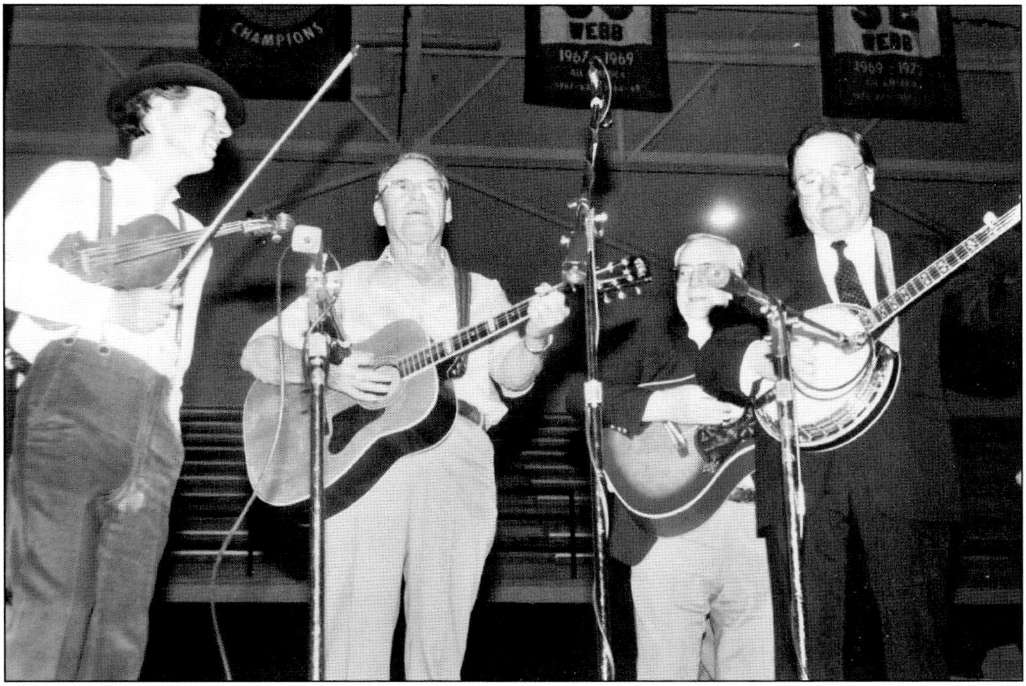

Gardner-Webb recognized musician Earl Scruggs with an honorary doctorate in September 1986. Earl grew up near GWC before he left for Nashville. At this event, Earl (right) plays with, from left to right, unidentified, his brother Horace, and television personality Doug Mayes.

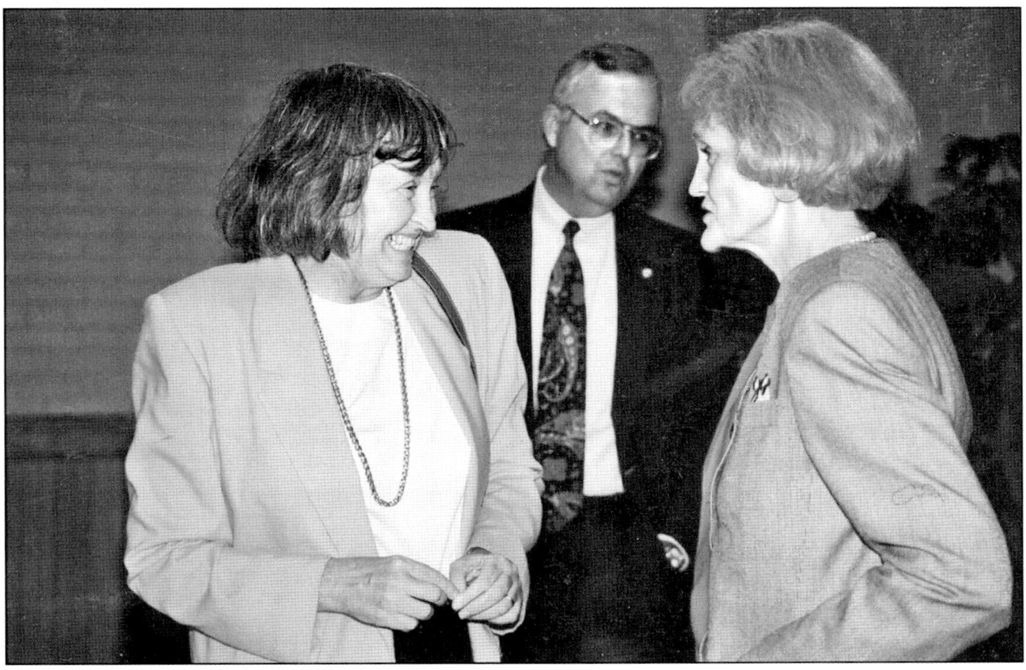

English professor Dr. Joyce Brown (left) did the background work to bring Earl Scruggs to GWC. As she talks with education professor Dr. Doris Banner, Vice President Ralph "Scoot" Dixon can be seen in the background.

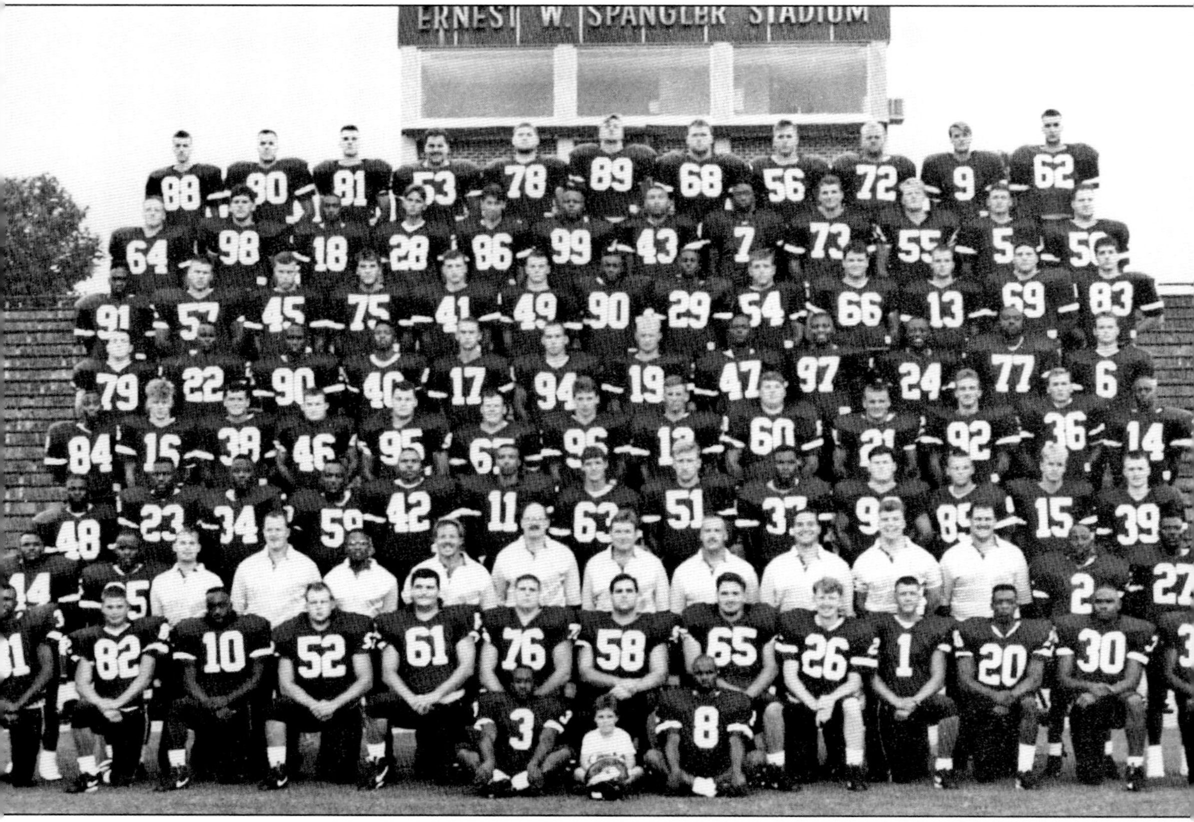

In 1992, Coach Fish's GWC team played in the NAIA National Championship game. The game was held at Spangler Stadium, and GWC lost a close game late in the fourth quarter. The current football team, led by Coach Steve Patton, is working toward a return to a championship game in the NCAA's Division I-AA

Coach Woody Fish sometimes made promises that were hard to keep. In 1992, he told the GWC football team that if they beat Carson-Newman in Jefferson City, they could shave his head. Here is the result.

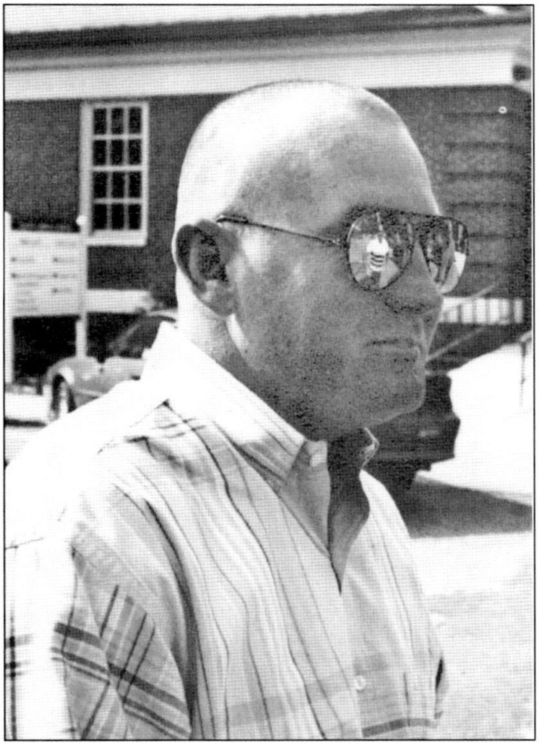

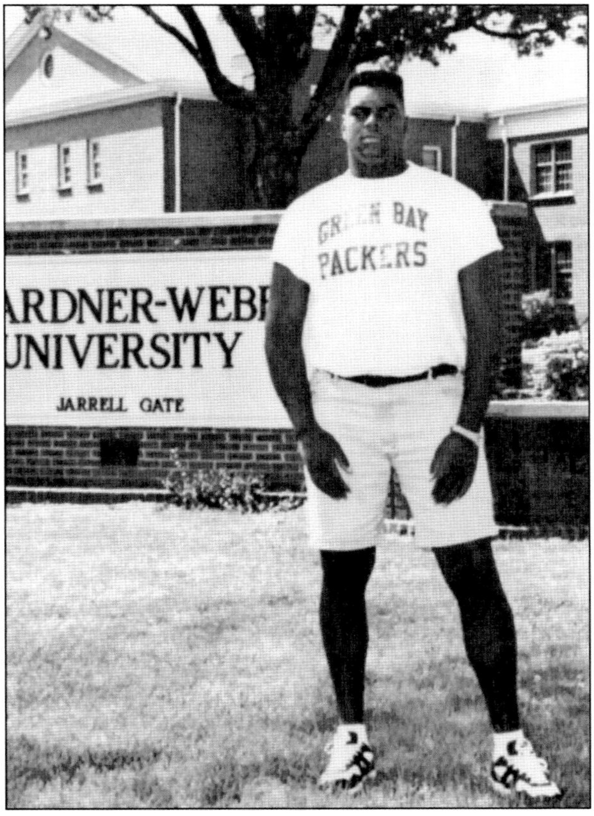

Probably Gardner-Webb's most famous football player is Gabe Wilkins. In 1994, he was chosen in the NFC draft by the Green Bay Packers. Gabe played on the Packers' winning Super Bowl XXXI team in 1997.

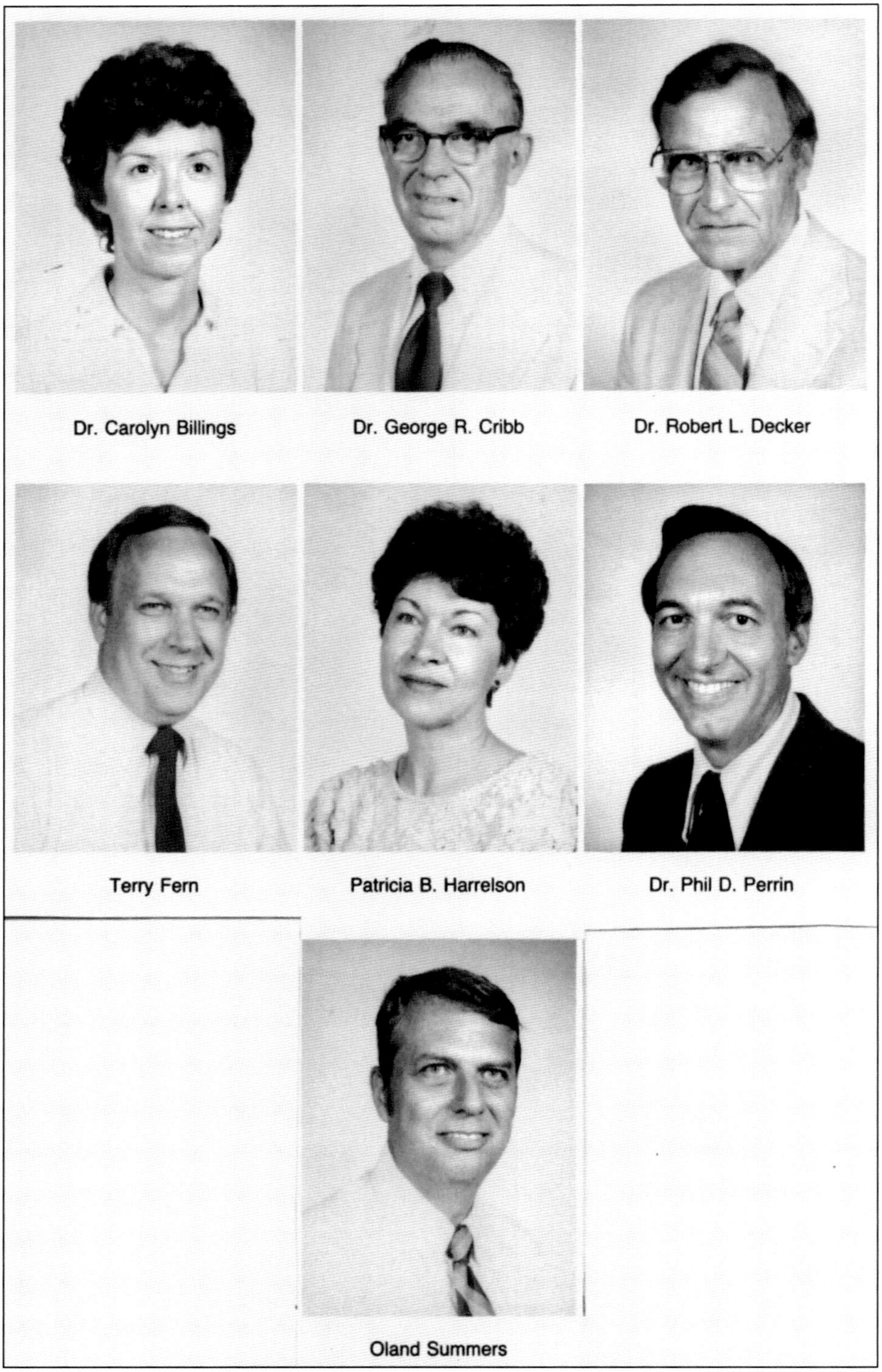

Gardner-Webb's music program is accredited by the National Association of Schools of Music (NASM). The professors pictured here have built a quality program for GWU's music program. Twenty years after this photo was made, four of these professors are still teaching. Drs. Cribb, Decker, and Perrin retired at Gardner-Webb.

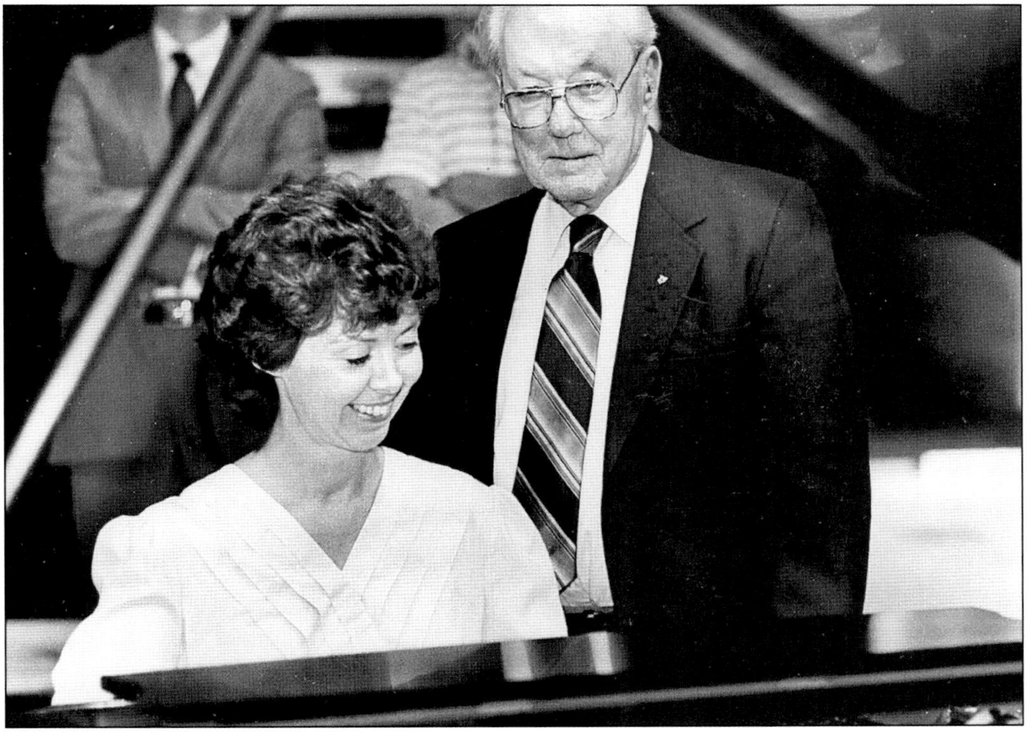

Charles I. Dover watches Dr. Carolyn Billings play the new grand piano. President Chris White looks on happily in the background.

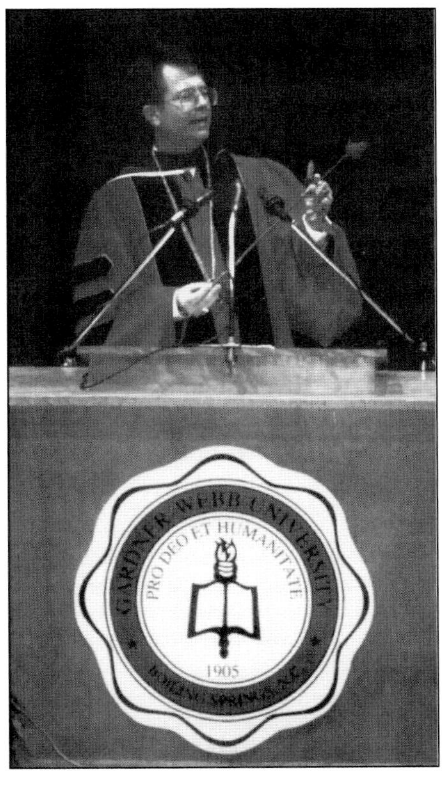

Dr. M. Christopher White is pictured in 1993 at the school's first commencement as a university. Dr. White realized the overall growth of GWC's academic programs. He felt it was proper to move to university status to better describe what the institution had become.

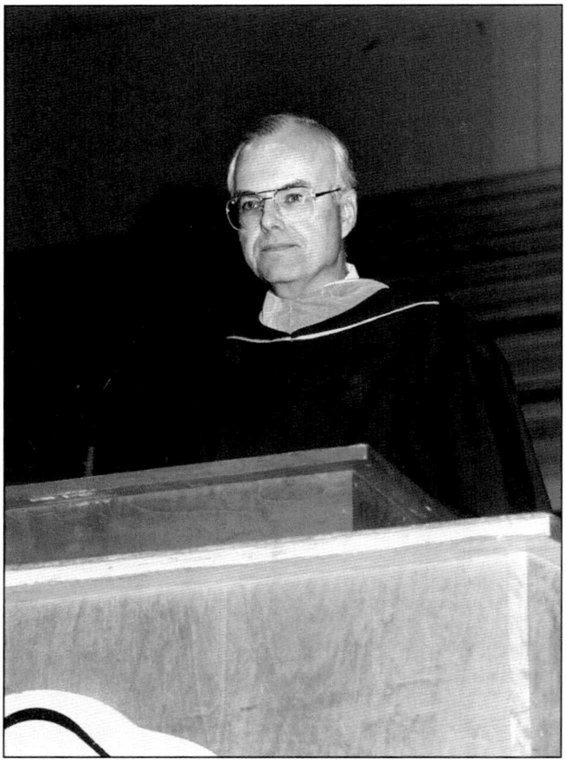

Ralph "Scoot" Dixon Jr. has been at Gardner-Webb twice in the last 20 years and has been vice-president of two areas. Scoot led a successful $30 million financial campaign in the 1990s.

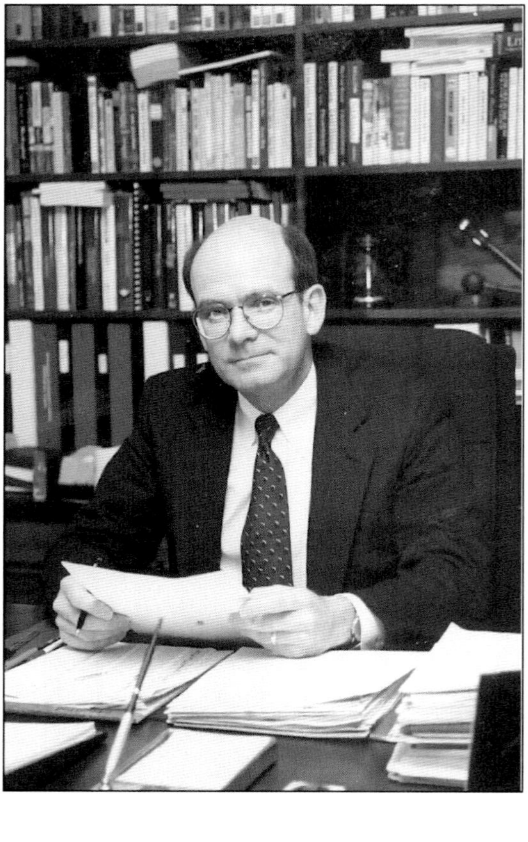

Dr. Frank Bonner has been at GWU for over 15 years. He came as academic dean and then moved up to provost, basically making him the number-two man on campus. Sometimes he gets drafted to teach his beloved English literature.

Vice president for business and finance, Donnie Clary is a capable and effective administrator. Clary has kept the school "in the black" since coming to GWC in 1987.

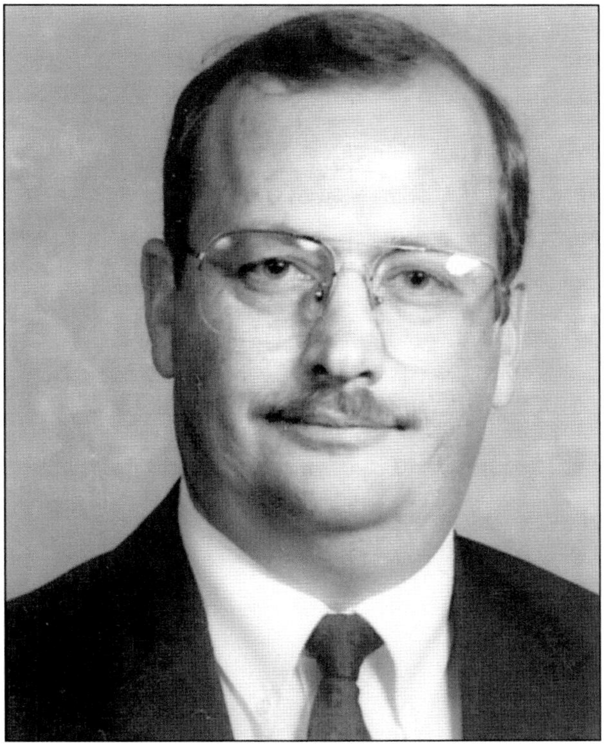

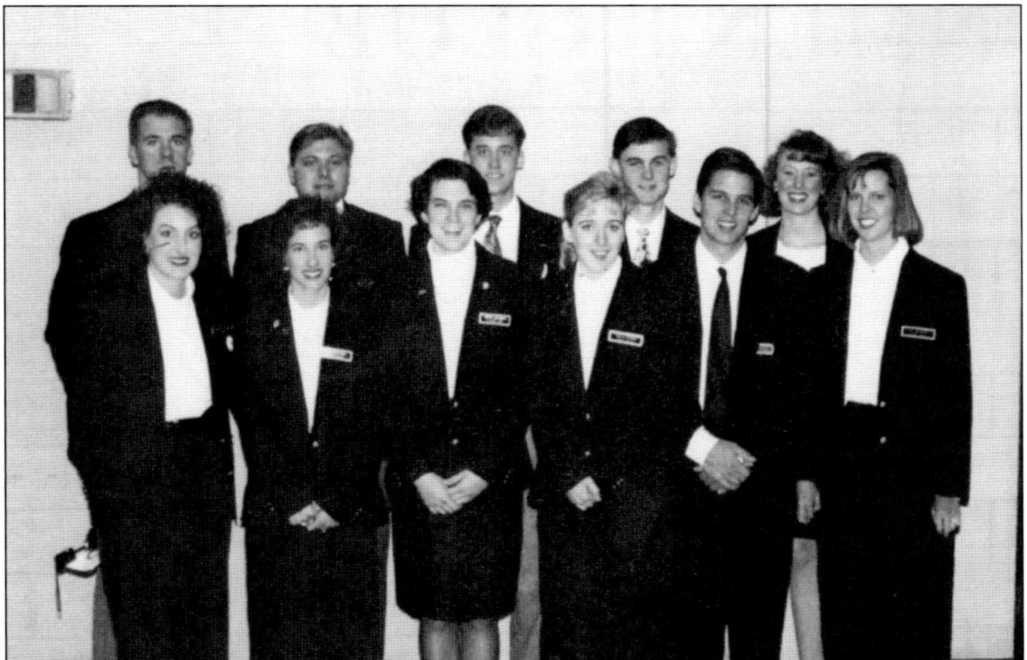

Outstanding young men and women students are chosen to be presidential associates. These students build their social and leadership skills while serving at university functions. This 1993 group includes Kelly Edwards, Melanie Haine, Andrea Dockery, Mike McCalley, Jill Galloway, Chad Harvey, Marty Elmore, Marty White, Jeff Price, and Nicole Nichols.

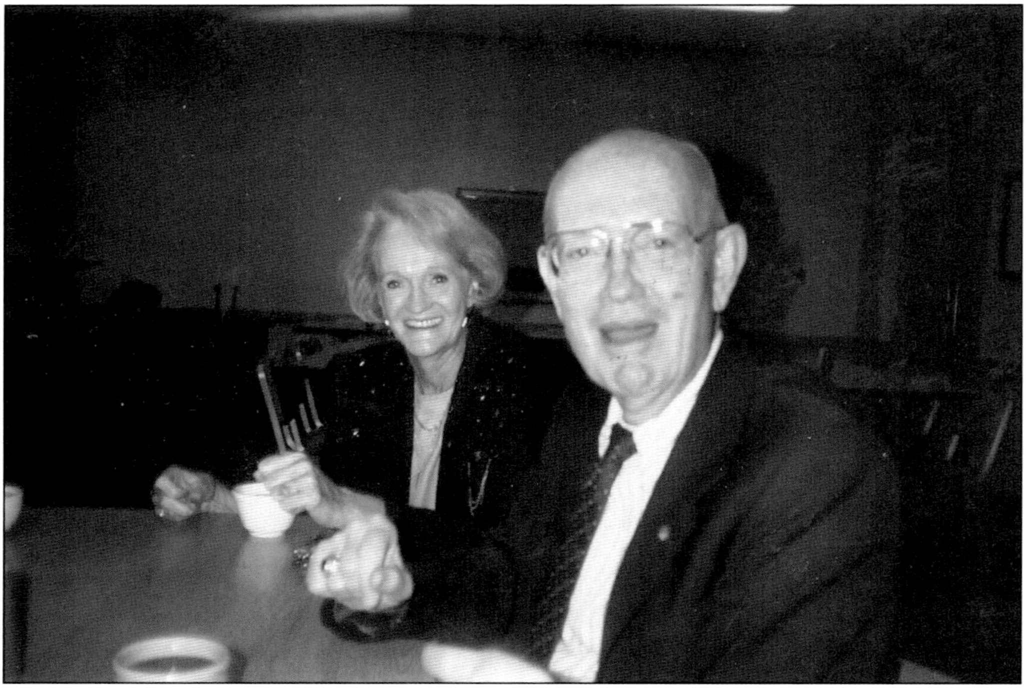

Dr. Jack Partain spent over 15 years as a missionary in East Africa before coming to Gardner-Webb. He was a missions professor in his actions. Dr. Doris Banner taught math in the 1970s and returned later as a professor of education.

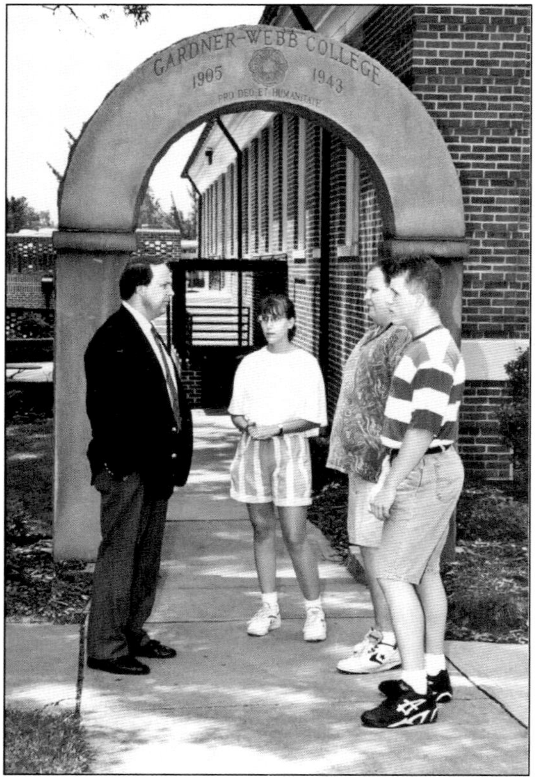

Vice President and Dean of Student Development Bruce Moore chats with students by the Huggins Memorial Arch.

Dr. Gil Blackburn was one of less than 10 people who had 36 years of service at Gardner-Webb. He started in 1968 as an assistant professor of history and served as graduate director, assistant academic dean, vice president, and academic dean. He regarded professor of history as his highest job. Today he is senior provost at the University of Virginia's College at Wise.

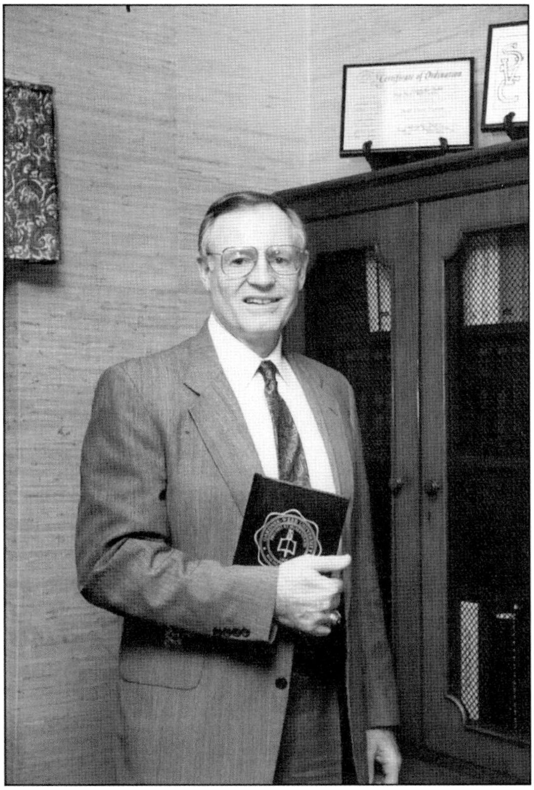

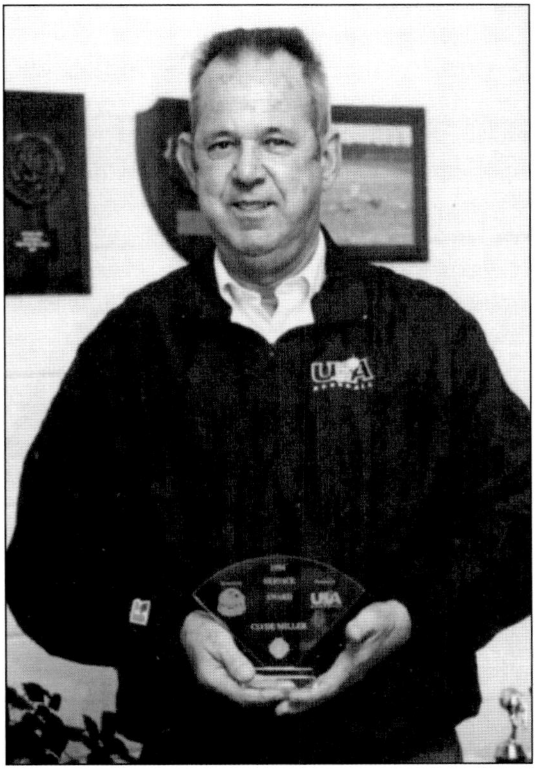

Clyde Miller is pictured in 1994 receiving USA Baseball's prestigious Service Award. Coach Miller surpassed 800 victories in his years as a head baseball coach. The university was saddened in March 2005, when Clyde died after a brief illness.

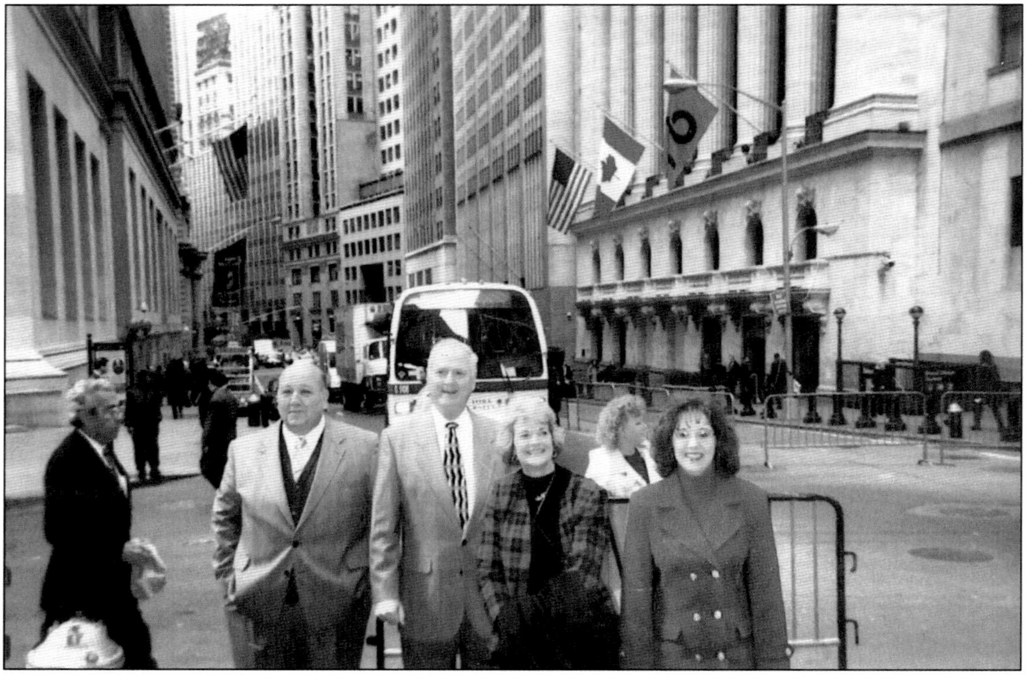

In the 1980s, world travel became popular at Gardner-Webb. Students and professors went to Europe, Latin America, Canada, Israel, Russia, Africa, and other places. "Campus New York" has, for over 20 years, allowed students to visit New York City. The tour leaders, from left to right are Barry Hambright, Keith Griggs, Carolyn Jackson, and Emily Foss. In 1997, the New York Stock Exchange (in the background) was not the guarded fortress that it is today.

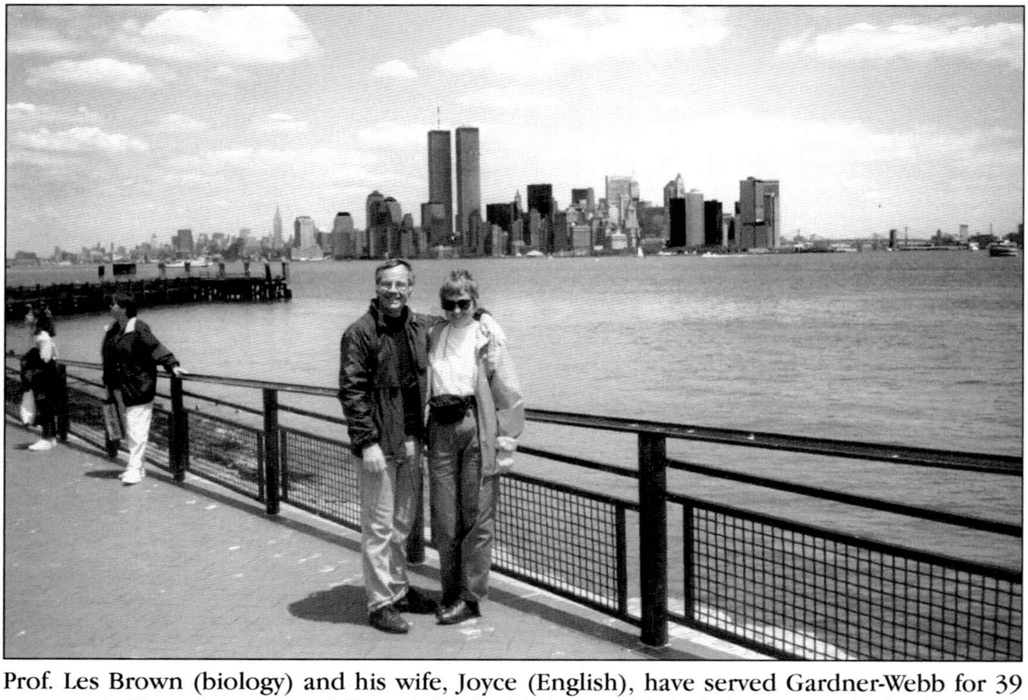

Prof. Les Brown (biology) and his wife, Joyce (English), have served Gardner-Webb for 39 years each. Here they pose at Liberty Island with the World Trade Towers in the background.

Darlene Gravett and her husband, Ray, enjoy a hike in the mountains. Dr. Gravett came to Gardner-Webb as an English professor, and then became the first female dean in an academic area. Today she is associate provost for schools. She also serves on the Boiling Springs town council.

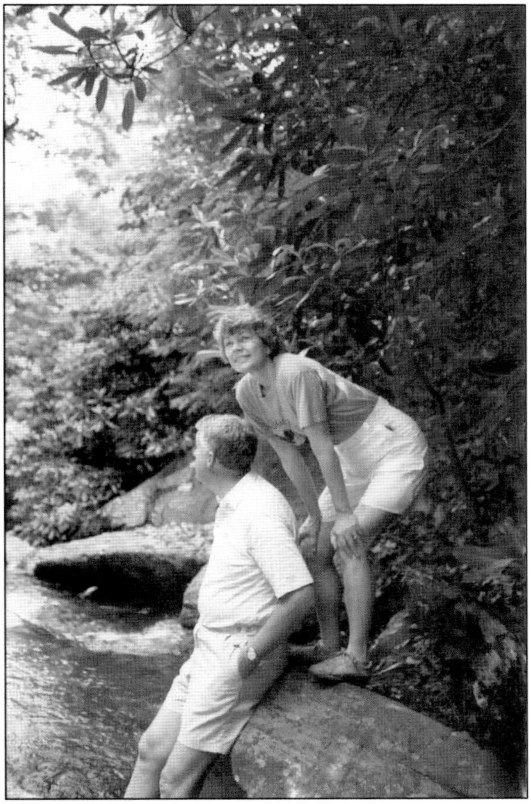

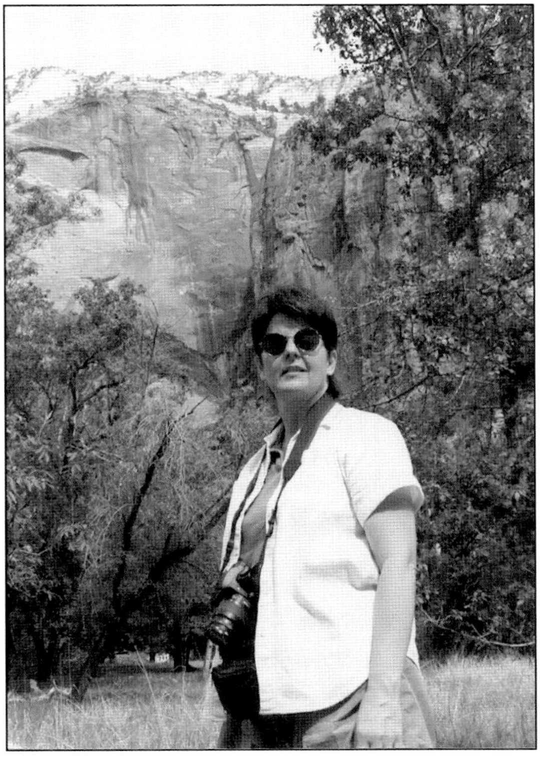

Dr. Tom Jones and Dr. Les Brown have taken groups of students on western tours. These are not for the weak and lazy. English department chair Dr. Janet Land survived one such tour.

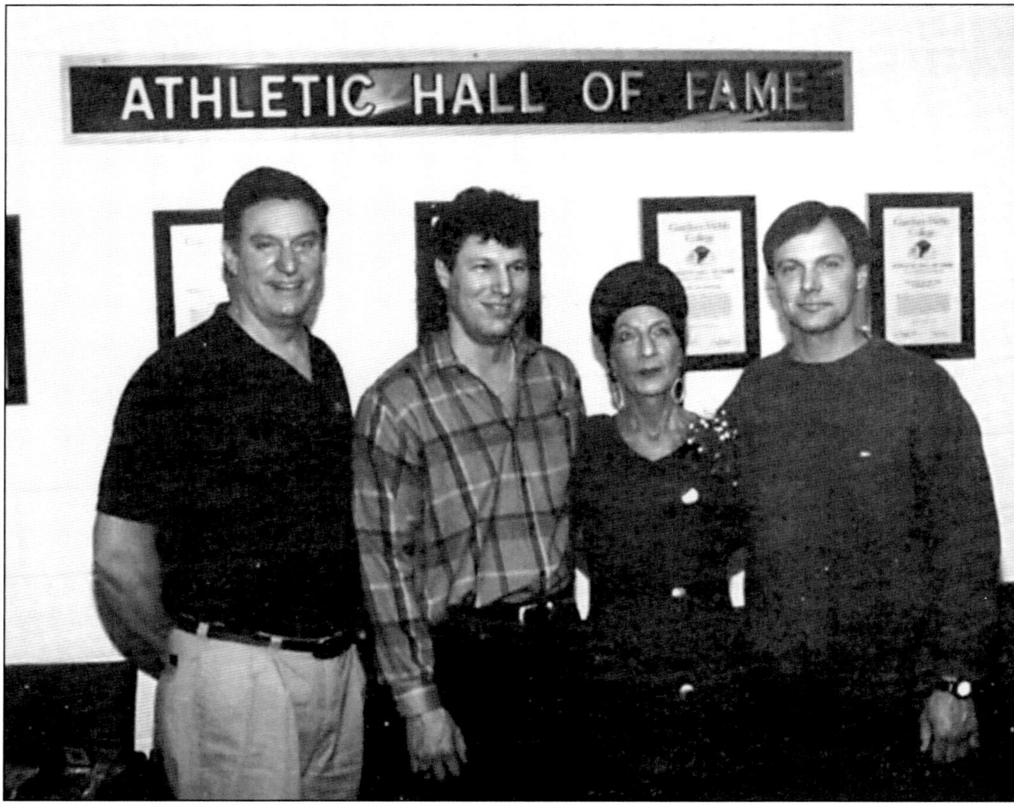

The Bulldog Suite in the Lutz-Yelton Convocation Center was renamed to honor the J.W. Abernethy Jr. family in January 1994.

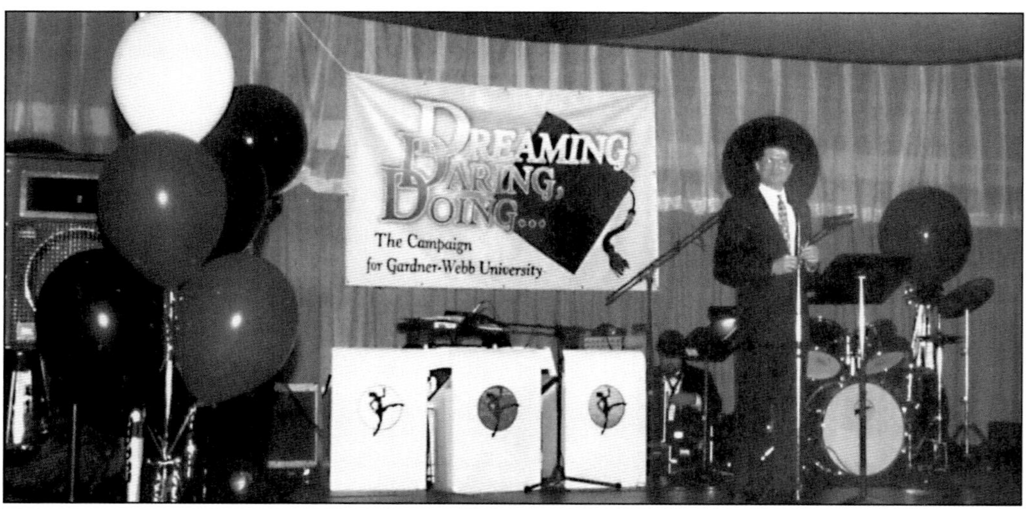

Gardner-Webb conducted a major capital campaign in the mid-1990s. Director of development for religious studies Bruce Rabon coined the phrase "dreaming, daring, doing" that become the campaign's slogan. Gerry Vaillancourt, Gardner-Webb graduate and WBT radio personality, served as master of ceremonies for the campaign celebration.

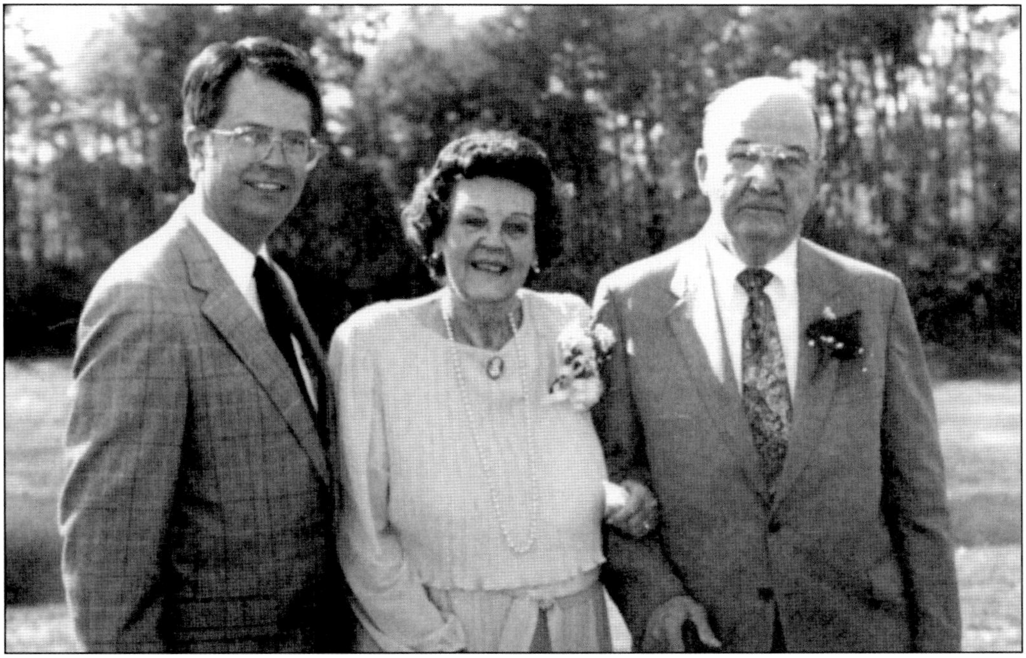

Dr. Chris White poses with benefactors Wyndolyn and Hughy Hollifield as they tour Lake Hollifield. The generosity of the Hollifields forever changed the face of the GWU campus.

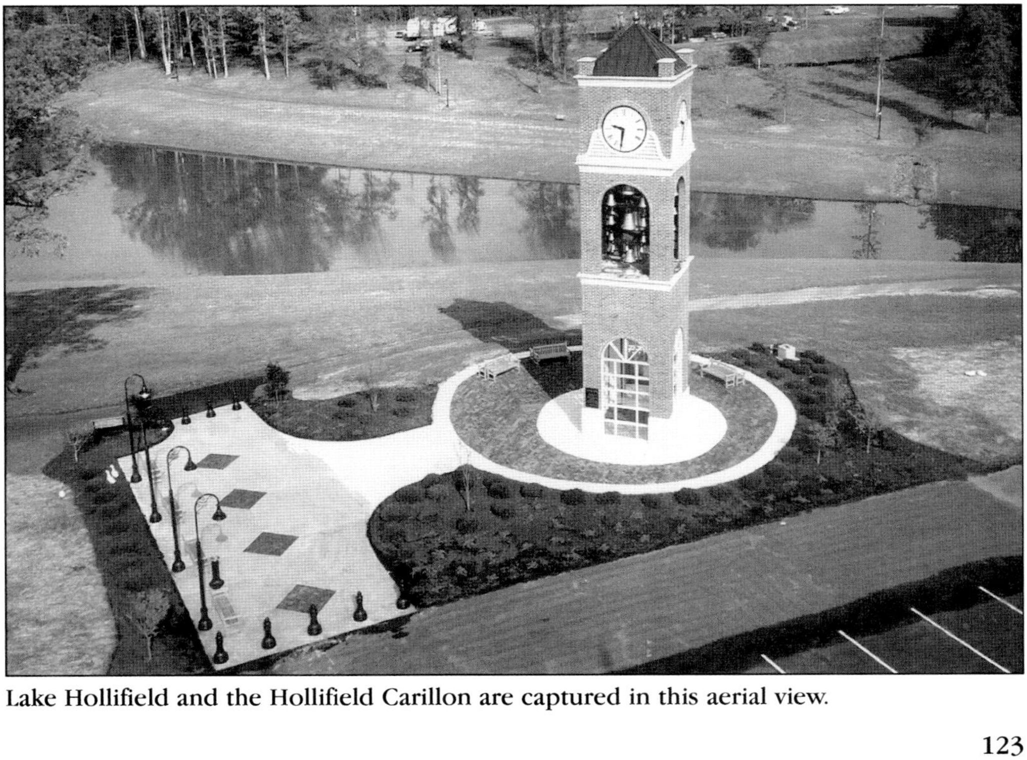

Lake Hollifield and the Hollifield Carillon are captured in this aerial view.

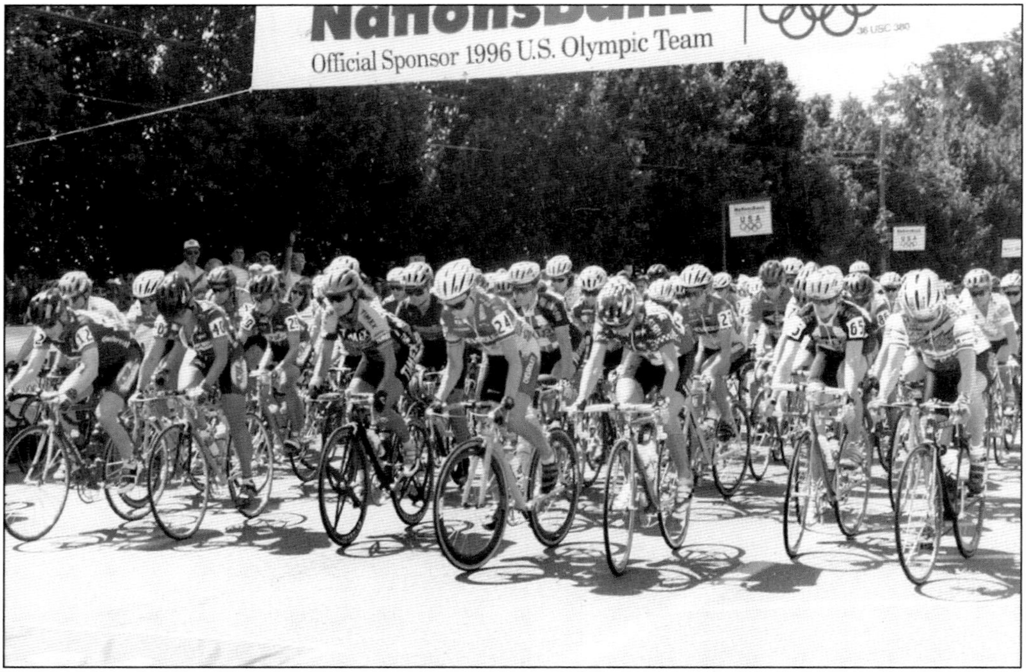

The road to the 1996 Olympics in Atlanta ran through the streets of Boiling Springs. On June 1, 1996, the town of Boiling Springs and GWU hosted the last trial for the United States Women's Cycling Team.

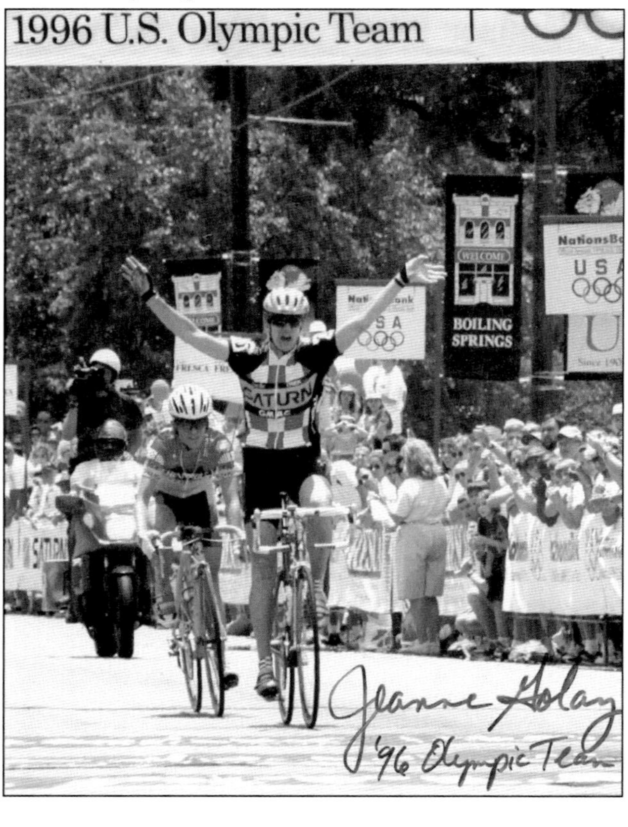

Jeanne Golay captured the win and the opportunity to represent the United States in the Olympics in Atlanta.

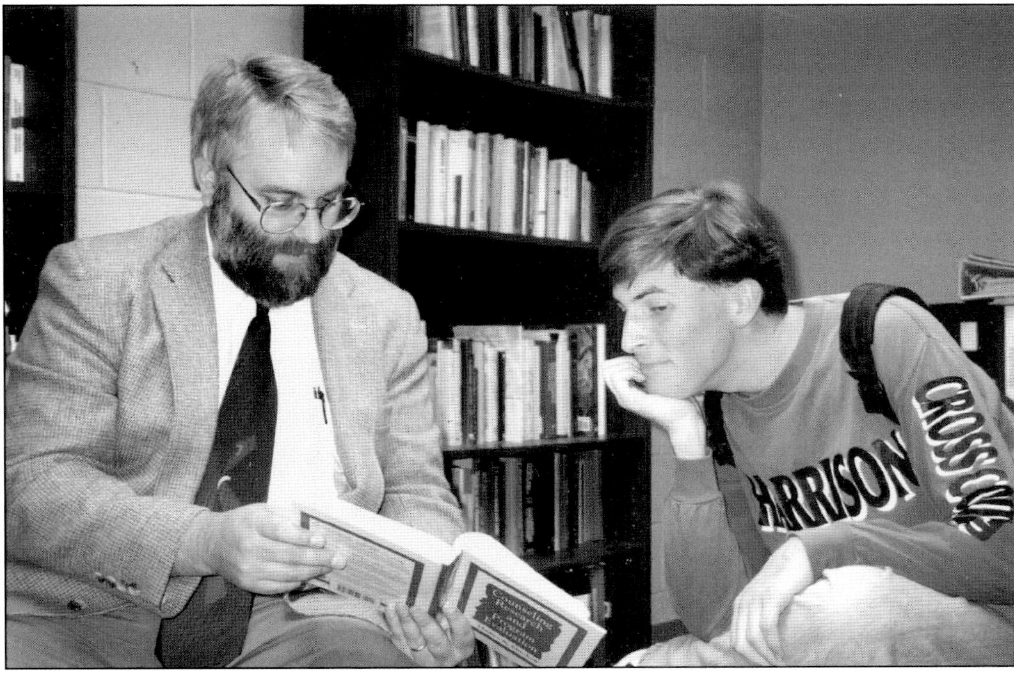

"People Who Care" is more than a slogan. Dr. David Carscadden, universally recognized as one of the nicest people on campus, always has time for students. His colleagues expect him to be late for lunch because he will never turn away a student.

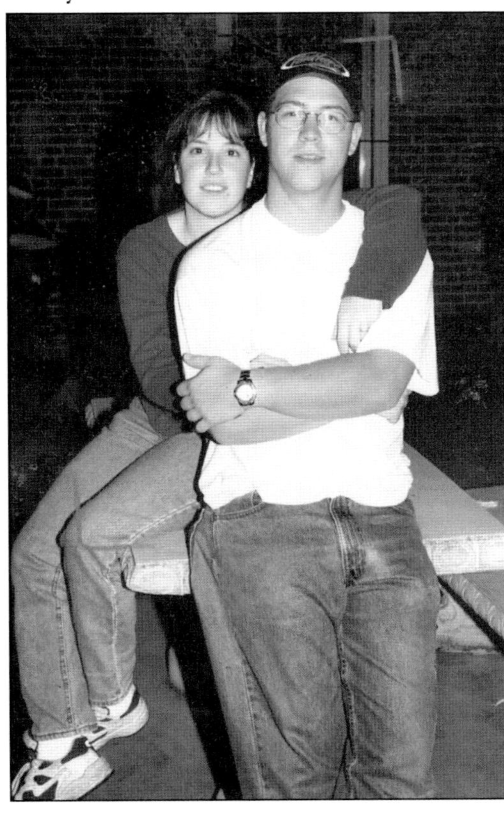

Here are two modern-day graduates who have more than one link with GWU. Matt Norman and Michelle Walters met at Gardner-Webb. Matt's parents are GWU graduates. Both Matt and Michelle came back and worked at the university after they were married. For two years, Matt and Michelle have been Cooperative Baptist Fellowship (CBF) missionaries to international students in Toronto, Canada.

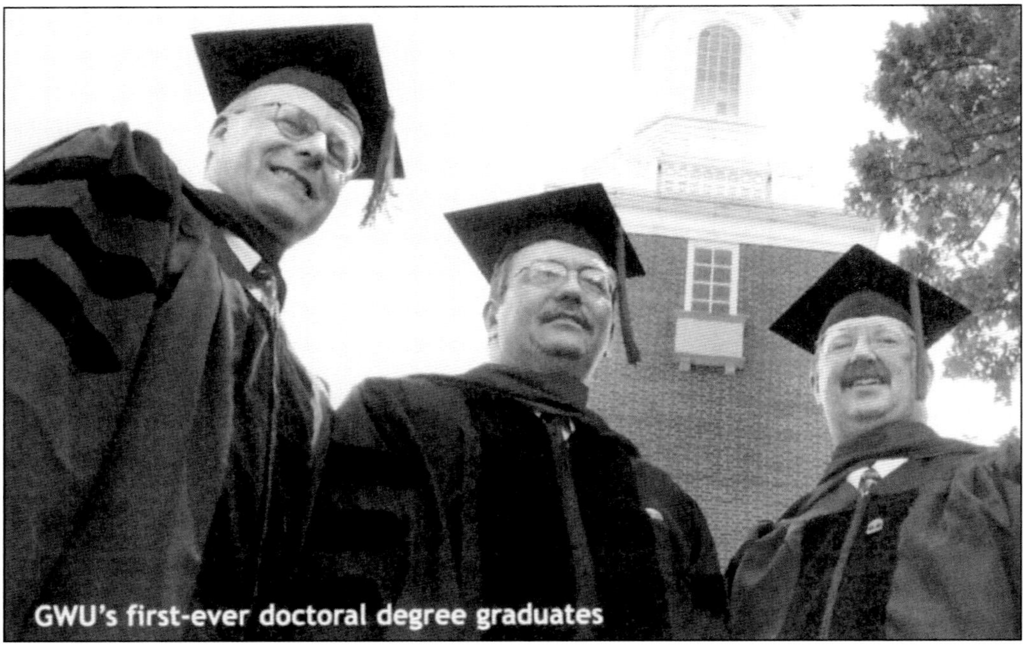

Graduation 2004 produced the university's first doctoral program graduates. Gerald Bontrager, Brian Johnson, and Mark Gaskins graduated from the doctor of ministry program, part of the GWU School of Divinity.

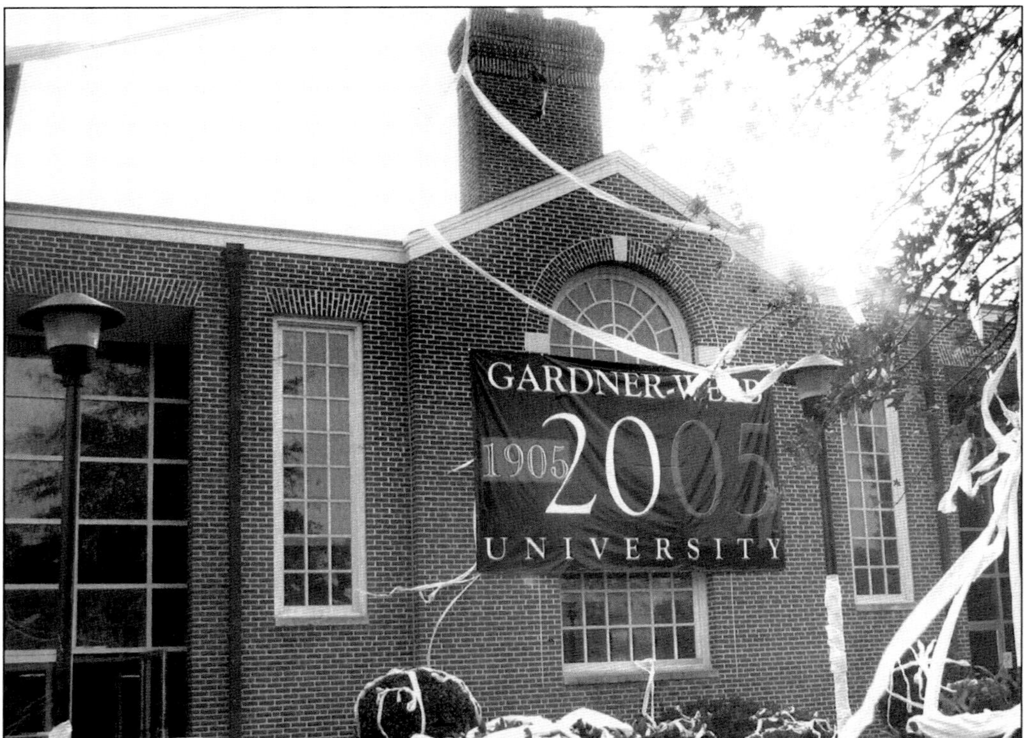

Homecoming 2004 initiated the 100-year anniversary at GWU. The toilet paper–draped banner denotes the anniversary celebration has begun.

Retired Averett University president Dr. Frank Campbell came to Gardner-Webb in 2002 to serve as interim president. Campbell has served admirably in a period of transition for the university.

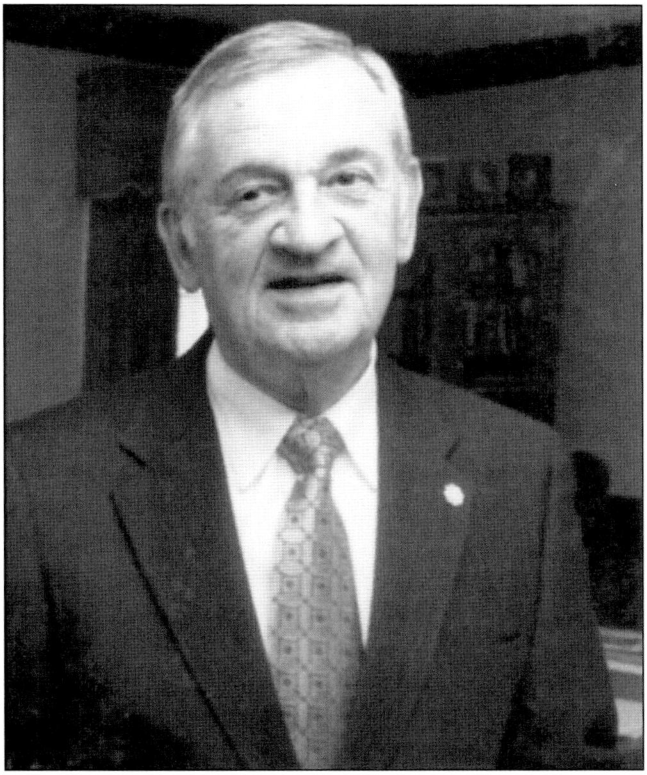

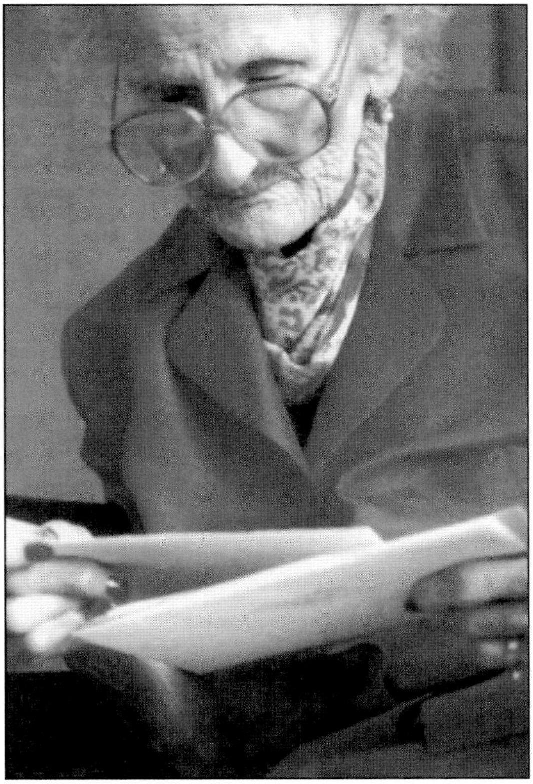

Ophelia "Cookie" Cooke Shepherd and Gardner-Webb both turn 100 in 2005. Mrs. Shepard graduated from Boiling Springs High School in 1928 and from the junior college in 1930.

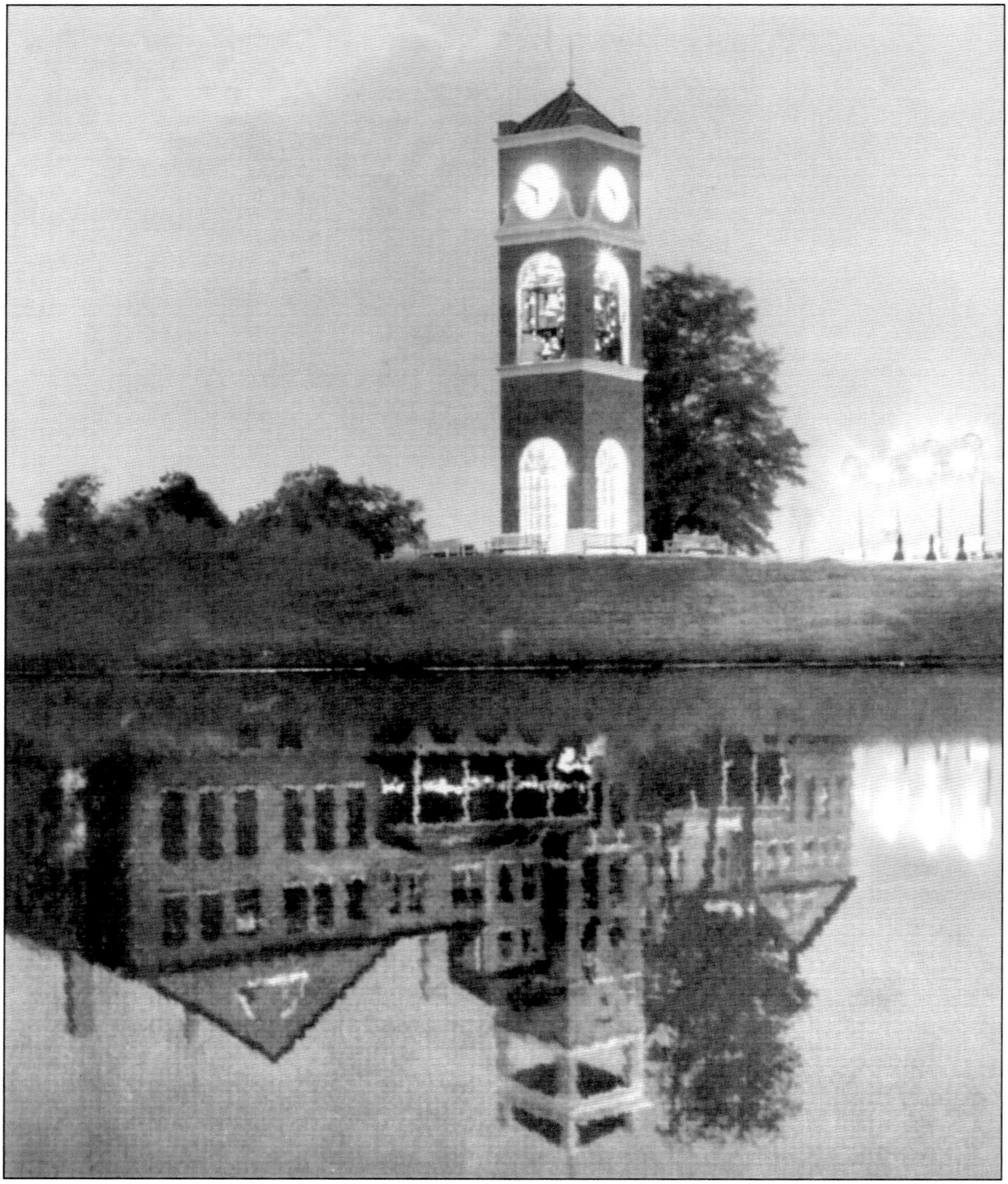

"May we always appreciate the rich heritage of our forebearers," said Lee B. Weathers, publisher of the *Shelby Daily Star* from 1911 to 1958.